SALT OF THE EARTH :
A SCOTTISH PEOPLES' HISTORY

Compiled by Howard Mitchell

Acknowledgements

The hundreds of individuals who have contributed a colossal amount of experience to this collection, and the tutors who worked with them are the people who are central to the successful part of the project.

However, acknowledgements are due to the members of staff of the WEA for the initial concept of Salt Of The Earth and the successful realisation of such an ambitious and far reaching project; especially to Alan Rca in Aberdeen who has been involved at many levels throughout, and whose irreverent sense of proportion has lowered my blood pressure at several crucial phases. Also to those whose design skills and transcription have been much appreciated, Fraser Stewart, Sarah Austin, Jenny Oswald and Paula Cuccurullo, and to those who have provided inspiration, criticism and sustenance at the right and wrong times, Chris Bowman, Elizabeth Bryan, Ross Murray and John McCaughie.

Thanks are also due to the many local organisations who helped us achieve the project's goals.

Howard Mitchell

ISBN 0 902303 46 5

The Workers' Educational Association (WEA) was founded in 1903. Throughout its history, the Association has aimed to promote equality of access to education and provide adults with opportunities to participate in organised learning based on democratic principles and with a social purpose. It is founded on the belief that access to learning throughout life, for all, is essential to the creation of a healthy, participative, democratic society.

People's history has always been a common theme in WEA community-based courses throughout Scotland. It was a natural choice for the WEA's first national project proposal to the newly-launched National Lottery Charities Board in 1997.

Our Tutor Organisers jointly developed the idea of a history project which would be unifying nationally, but diverse and responsive in its local dimensions. Cathy Moncrieff, Depute Scottish Secretary, distilled the ideas of the team and created the project which became known as The Salt of the Earth: A Scottish People's History Project. It embodied the values, and applied the methodology, of the WEA to an ambitious, multi-faceted and inclusive adult education project. Physical obstacles and barriers to participation were overcome by offering free classes, access to good equipment, providing creches and carer support where needed. The format and organisation of group activities were flexible and sensitive to local needs, and the WEA's well-established network of community contacts was important in encouraging new learners into the project. The enthusiasm and creativity of everyone involved in the project was outstanding.

In his letter of support for the project, Professor TC Smout noted that from his experience of the oral history work carried out by the WEA "... it has enormous value both to the recipient - ie posterity - and to the giver - ie the participants in the project".

Howard Mitchell, project co-ordinator, brought to the project an expertise in and enthusiasm for oral history, as well as a wealth of technical skills. This and the guidance of the project Advisory Group of social historians ensured that the project lived up to Chris Smout's expectations. Speaking at the handover of the project's collected oral archive to the Scottish Life Archive at the Royal Museum of Scotland, he told students, tutors and supporters of the project that "oral history is a good rich source, the texture of peoples lives. To conserve that you need the skills of the WEA, the enthusiasm of a Howard Mitchell, people in communities willing to share and the ability to preserve their histories, together with expert conservation offered by the museum".

The archive, this book, and the many other products created by participants, are a resource for communities to use and to enjoy now and in the future.

Joyce Connon
WEA Scottish Association Secretary

CONTENTS

This book comprises edited transcriptions, representing some of the hundreds of recordings from the WEA Salt of the Earth: A Scottish Peoples' History Project, plus descriptions of many of the individual elements from around the country.

The project, funded for a period of three years by the National Lottery Charities Board, was devised to collect oral history material through tutor led adult education initiatives and construct a picture of life in the 20th century from the perspectives of ordinary people. This has manifested itself in the form of a sound archive of all the recordings held in the Scottish Life Archive of the Royal Museum in Edinburgh, together with a number of publications and imaginative productions. The participants in the project have not only contributed their experiences towards a valuable national resource held for posterity, but have also been involved in a valuable educational process that has promoted the learning of new skills. Many have also had the stimulus and satisfaction of interpreting and presenting the oral history back to their communities in innovative and accessible forms, often utilising contemporary communication technologies.

While oral history has been a significant recent contributor to the historical record since the 1950's, this form of personal or community experience is the contemporary manifestation of the medium through which pre-literate societies communicated their histories for centuries. The value of current oral history in highlighting the experiences of individuals and groups who might otherwise have been 'hidden' from history, and complementing and even challenging documentary sources, is widely recognised today.

If, as the maxims suggest, history is rewritten by each generation in response to the needs of the present, and that history is less about the past but more a metaphorical view of the present, then this collection should be as informative about life in the year 2000 as it is about past years. As we hopefully move towards further appreciation of previously marginalised members of our society, and recognise and encourage the contributions of minority groups and alternative perspectives, a picture emerges that is influenced as much by current philosophies as past experience.

One challenge for the project has been to avoid looking back and merely reminiscing. We have attempted to chronicle disappearing ways of life in recent times, explore change and diversity, and address current issues in relation to the past. While many more active participants have learned recording and interviewing skills and ultimately become independent practitioners, others have contributed their own valuable and fascinating personal stories.

The book attempts to portray these various aspects in the choice of life history excerpts and to suggest the breadth of Salt Of The Earth in the descriptions and illustrations of individual projects. The variety of formats is also evident with group and individual interviews and discussions, audio and video recordings, written pieces and photography all represented.

Over 450 people have been involved in the project in 43 geographical locations, generating the archive and 16 different productions. I hope this book is both an interesting and enjoyable read in itself, and an appetiser for further investigation of these Salt Of The Earth outcomes.

Howard Mitchell.
Project Co-ordinator.

The Salt Of The Earth Project in this area combined with other WEA classes, in creative writing and photography, to achieve one of the most ambitious and successful productions. The cross fertilisation resulted in a book with accompanying audio Compact Disc (CD), and a photography and oral history exhibition with a launch and performance by the Creative Writing Group at the Scottish Mining Museum, where the Creative Writing Group were awarded Scottish Qualifications Authority certificates for their educational achievements.

Jane Durie's account illustrates rural life in Midlothian, so close to the city of Edinburgh, and her experience of emigration, a common one for many Scots.

Margaret Muir's upbringing presents us with some of the more negative aspects of life in a mining community.

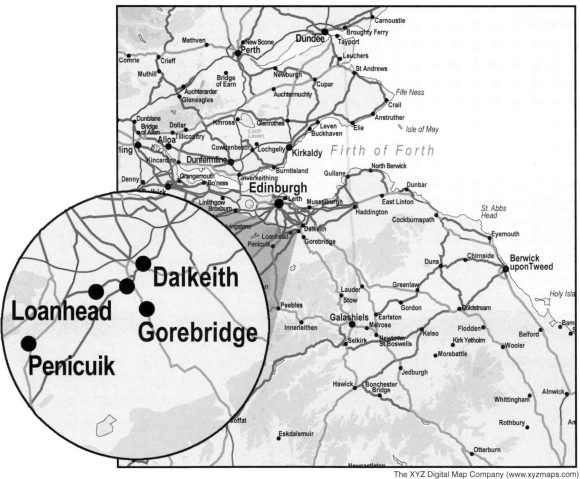

The XYZ Digital Map Company (www.xyzmaps.com)

Abe Black, portrait by Gorebridge Photography Group.

I was born on a farm outside Colinton, called Bonally. It's no longer there now, it's all built up.

Do you know when she [your grandmother] moved to the Lothians?
Well, he...my father.....moved himself, when he was five.

Can you mention again, as you did before, the "strange circumstances" involving this?
Well, in those days, the crofters were very poor, and they didn't have any work. They needed the money, so a lot of them came down into the Lowlands [from Skye] to look for work. And my...father's, my...my gran, it would be, yes... she must have come down....at that time to work, and got work on the farms in East Lothian. There she met my grandfather - I don't know an awful lot about this - and he worked on the farms in East Lothian. He was what they called the "gaffer" - you know, it's sort of like the manager but not... y'know, under the farmer, in charge of the other workers. And... then the baby arrived - there was two babies - twins. So they couldn't afford to keep two babies, so one went back to Skye, which was my dad. And he lived there until he was five, and then they brought him back to go to school. He didn't have any English at all, he could only speak Gaelic. Of course, he would be able to talk with his mother. But going to school and not having any English must have been very hard on a wee boy.

Who did he stay with when he lived in Skye?
His granny, my great-granny, uh-huh, who lived near Portree in Skye.

Was that in a croft?
In a croft, uh-huh. I've never been... well, I've been to Skye, but I don't know where the croft is. But my elder brothers have been and they have seen the croft, the old croft house and things. But I've never seen it.

As for your mother's side of the family, where is she from?
Well, my mother actually came from this area... I'm trying to remember the name. I think she went to school there, and her father was a gardener. And it was he, I believe, who laid out the big park at Newtongrange... But as far as we were led to believe, my grandfather laid... which was a beautiful park... he laid that out. At the same time, ... the gentleman he worked for had estates in Ireland, and when they were in Ireland they took the head gardener with them..., with the result my mother and an auntie were born in Ireland! It was County Antrim... although they had Scottish parents, they were born in Ireland. And then they came back to East Lothian when the people came back, who they worked for.

You would tend to think there was less movement in the past, though when you hear stories like yours that seems wrong.
Uh-huh... going where the work is.

What were your earliest memories of Bonaly?
I can't remember it at all, no. Although I was baptised there, and my parents... when my father stopped work, they went back there to live, so I was married there as well. I was baptised in Colinton, married in

Jane, seated, with brother and sisters.

Colinton, and I lived in Colinton for a while, but I can't remember... I mean, I was obviously just a baby.

Where did you move to, and go to school?
Well, my father was a farm worker, so he just worked... the first place I can remember was a wee farm called Redside. Do you know this area at all?

Slightly, not very well.
It's near Carrington, the village of Carrington. I went to Carrington School... and then he moved...

Can you remember much about the house you lived in then?
The house... well, I do know that it had, [a toilet] but it didn't have a bath, 'cos I can remember us all getting bathed in a tin bath in front o'the fire, starting from the wee-est up. And I was the second wee-est, so I wasn't too bad.

How many brothers and sisters?
Well, my parents had ten children - they had five boys and five girls. They had a gap... they had six, and then had a gap of about six years, I think, and then had another four, about two years between 'em all. So I was in what they used to call their "second family" - I was the second youngest. So when we were small, the four of us, the others were away - y'know, working, at war...

What was the spread in ages between the eldest and the youngest?
Well, in recent years we've lost quite a few of them. There's only two brothers left and two sisters, and myself. So there's half of them passed on. But... I was a wee girl at the school, and my brothers were away fighting in the war - y'know, there was that much of a gap, maybe twenty-odd years. There was quite a gap.

That first house you can remember, how many rooms would it have had?
I think they would have... they usually had two bedrooms, and a kitchen. But in these days there was a bed in the kitchen, which was for Mum and Dad. And then the boys would have one room, and the girls would have the other.

Did you sleep in the same bed?
As the sisters, aye.

Can you remember it as fun or awkward?
Quite fun, and quite cosy, because you were always cold. You know, you'd wake up in the morning, and there'd be half an inch of ice outside the window, y'know. So you could all cuddle up together and keep warm.

And that would be the thing that... the one in the middle used to get bribed to turn 'round onto your back and keep you warm, that sorta thing.

Was it a double bed you shared?
A double bed for three, aye. Mind you, one of them was quite wee - two years between us, maybe, y'know. And then... well, you left school at 14, so... and had a brother in between my older sister and me, so she would be 14, and I would only be 10, y'see, so... then the other one was eight by this time, so she would be a wean. There would just be the two of us.

Was your first primary school there?
Ehm... actually when I remember, it was at the time... it couldn't have been the Depression or whatever, but in the early Thirties, there was no work on the farms, and my father couldn't get a job. And he went into Edinburgh, I've been told, and worked in the brewery driving the brewery horses, 'cos he was a horseman, y'see. And we had a flat in the Tollcross area. And I have a vague recollection of that, but very vague. And then, of course, he didn't like that 'cos he was a country man, so as soon as he could get work in the country he was back in the country again. That's when I went to this farm near Carrington.

What was the primary school like?
Nice wee primary school - one teacher. And... can't remember her name, but she was quite nice. Uh-huh, in Carrington it was just one teacher. And then we moved to Temple and there was a two-teacher school there, in Temple.

Did your mother work as well?
No, she was just in the house. She would have enough to do, 'cos there was four children, and two sons and my father working on the farm. The only time I can remember her working was maybe at the time when the threshing machine would come in. Have you heard of the threshing machines? They used to travel round farms, they had steam engines... and the farmer might ask her if she could go out to 'fork to the mill' as they called it - y'know, 'forking the sheaves' up to the mill, or cutting the sheaves on the top o'the mill and feeding them in to the drum. And if she... if they were short, and they asked her if she would go out, she would obviously get paid for it. And then the farmer's wife would make the dinner and take it over to the house, y'know, so's that we could have something to eat at dinnertime. So that was how they seemed to do it.

As a child, did you ever do any work on the farm?
No... well, I say no, but as we got older they used to have what they called a "potato week". We got a week off of school in October to go and gather potatoes. And we used to get ten shovels a day for gathering potatoes... you'd take it home to your Mum and you'd get a threepenny back to

Jane at Temple
Farm, age 15.

spend. And that's the only thing that we did, more to get off school than to, y'know, to enjoy the work.

Did you stay at Temple for long?
Mmm... I was in a few primaries at Temple, and then we moved to another farm. The thing was that my brothers were getting older, y'know, and they needed work, and if there wasn't work for this one, we had to go to another farm so they *could* get work, y'know. So... we moved to another farm called... Hawkerston, which was near Middleton, and I had to go to Borthwick School, and that was a three-teacher school. You heard of Borthwick Castle? Well, it was a wee school... I presume it's still open, I think it is. And we went there. So they had the three teachers there - you went right through to qualify in that school.

Can you remember how you felt about moving so many times?
Oh yes. I remember... especially my brother... he always had a hard time. I don't think us girls had such a hard time, but my brother did because all the boys would fight him. You know, he had to fight with all the boys, and it must have been pretty hard for him. He was two years older than me, and at playtime the boys would all be lining up - they'd pick their toughest one, y'see, to fight my brother - and then he had to go down the line if he beat him, y'know. He would have to fight the... or maybe they didn't start with the toughest one, I don't know, but he always had a few fights in the course of getting accepted into the school.

Was there anything similar for you?
No, not really. They wouldn't let you play with them and that sort of thing because they didn't know you, y'know. You wouldn't be allowed to play with them or sorta join in the games. You would just have to stand back and watch them, and eventually you would get...

But you would always have a brother or sister to support you?
Uh-huh, uh-huh.

Did you ever feel, "I belong in this school," or, "I belong in this village"?
Well, ye didnae really get, y'know... when you're a child, you don't realise it but, y'know, you didn't have a permanent sort of place. You know, you always seemed to be sort of on the move, that sort of thing. But that seemed to be the way it was.

Were you quite happy as a child?
We were happy. I mean, we were well fed, our mother wasn't hard on us or anything... our father was hard on us, but... as long as you were in for your mealtimes and things, that was about it.

In what way was he hard on you?
The thing that I remember most was when the news came on [the radio] at 6 o'clock and you'd all be there having your tea... and the news would come on... Of course we were too wee... two brothers away fighting. And here's [my father] desperate to hear the news. And of course that was the time when the kids would start to giggle, and once you started to giggle you couldn't stop. And if you had four kids giggling around the table and you're trying to listen to the news, I mean... and the more he shouted at us and told us to be quiet, the more noisy we became, 'cos we couldn't control it [laughs], and it must have been awfully bad for him, y'know. But that's one of the things we used to get into trouble for. And I think it got to the stage where we knew it was going to happen, so every time the news was announced, then it would start. You can understand it now, but at the time we couldn't understand, y'know, why it was. So that was the main thing we got into trouble for.

Would you get a smack, or some other punishment?
Shouted at... probably told to get outside if we couldn't be quiet, y'know. And that would be it. He didn't really smack us a lot, but he got very cross. He must have mellowed, because he used to smack the older ones a lot, I believe, but not with us younger ones.

Did you then move to a secondary school?
That was a junior secondary, at Gorebridge, uh-huh. We were never encouraged to do anything - you know, academically or anything. It was just, as soon as you're 14, you leave the school and get a job and that's it.

Was it also expected that you'd do something surrounding agricultural work?
Yeah, you never got a choice. I mean, I was 15... I was 14 in the November and I left the school at Christmas, on the Friday, and my mother had already decided that I was going to work on this farm - not the one they

were on, but the neighbouring one. And on the Friday morning, I was despatched down the road, carrying my case, to start work at 8 o'clock in this farmhouse. I was only 14!

Was that at the end of the war?
That would be '45, aye, uh-huh. So you didn't get any choice.

Do you remember how you felt about that?
Well, pretty homesick. Pretty homesick.

Were you told about this long in advance?
I don't think so. I think it were just, sort of... you were at school today and you were told, "Well, you leave the school today - you're going there tomorrow," that sort of thing. And that was it.

How far away was your new farm from your family?
It wasn't very far, it was the neighbouring farm.

Did you stay there?
You had to stay in, uh-huh.

What sort of work did you do there?
Well, you had to learn to milk the cows. Well, you were taught how to milk the cows and feed the calves, and the hens, and feed the pet lambs, and all this sort of thing. And help with work in the farmhouse as well, and that was it, uh-huh. You didn't have to work out on the farm... you didn't have to go and work in the fields or anything, but you had to do these things that were associated sort of with the farmhouse, which was the hens and the lambs and the cows and things, and milking - that sort of thing.

Did you feel like a farm servant, or part of the household?
No, you weren't part of the family. You were separated.

Did you eat with the family?
No, you didn't even get to eat with the family. You were eating on your own.

Were there other women in the same position?
No, no, just me. A wee 14 year old, can you imagine?

Would the family eat at a different time?
No, they ate at the same time, but they ate in the parlour, and you ate in the kitchen, y'see?

Sounds terrible - did you enjoy it?
Doesn't it. I don't think... I think I enjoyed... well, I know I enjoyed being

outside, and working with the cows and the wee calves - the baby calves, and the baby lambs and that, chickens and things. But I hated in the house, hated it.

Was there any time for entertainment?
Well, I used to get a half-day off a week and every other Sunday sort of thing. But you didn't get away till your work was done, and that could be 4 o'clock in the afternoon, y'know. And that was your half-day! You got a pound, a pound a week.

What would you do in your spare time?
Well, I used to go to the Women's Rural a lot - you can see a wee 14-year-old... I was wee 'cos I didn't mature till, God, I was about 17 or something. And I used to go to the Women's Rural... and you went to the church twice on a Sunday. You went to the church, and then you had to go to the Bible class at night. So we always had to do this when we were small. We were sent to the Sunday School in the morning, which was before the church. And then we'd be walking on our way home, and we'd meet our Mum and Dad going to the church, so you'd have to turn back and go to the church with them! So it was sort of a thing you did - you went twice to church on the Sunday. And if there was any whists, you went to the whists. You went to the dancing on the Friday night if there was a dance in the village... And that was it.

How long did you work on that farm?
Believe it or not, nearly five years. And I couldn't get away! Every time I tried to give my notice in... because my parents moved away, they went away to East Lothian so I was there on my own... and every time I tried to leave, they wouldn't... they wouldn't accept, they wouldn't let me leave!

Was there any formal contract or just an understanding?
No, no, no... they just wouldn't let you leave, and that was it. And you didn't have a lot o' education - you didn't know your rights and things. Maybe some women did, but I didn't.

What would they say to you - "No, we need you here"?
Yeah, yeah - "Well, you can't leave, you have to stay here, you work here," that sort of thing. So what I did was got all the papers, got my dad to sign them, and emigrated to Australia. That was the only way that I got away. Emigrated to Australia... I tried to go when I was 18, but they wouldn't take me till I was 19 'cos I was going on my own.

So were you able to discuss this situation with your parents?
Yeah, but... well, where would you go? I mean, you've got a job, you'd better stay where you are, you've got a job...

Was that their attitude?

Uh-huh, uh-huh. So when I said I wanted to go to Australia, my Dad said, "Well, if you want to go there, fine," and signed the papers.

How did you know about Australia, and want to go there?

Just reading about it in the papers, listening about it on the radio... that was about it. And since I didn't have any money, and my parents had not a lot of money - 'cos, I mean, they had worked hard all their lives and brought up a large family and things. But you could get to Australia for ten pounds. Saved up, got my ten pounds - I think I had about twenty-five pounds as well to take with me, which was a lot of money. So I got to Australia. In fact, I said to my Mum and Dad that I was only going for two years, and I intended to come back in two years. Because you could

The ship Jane sailed on to Australia, the R.M.S. Orontes.

go for two years on the £10 - you could go off for £10, but you must stay for two years. If you didn't stay two years, you had to pay them back the money they paid to get you out there. If you stayed two years, you could come back if you like. Those two years were taken up saving up enough money to come back again.

Did you know anyone else who had gone?

No, no.

Would that have been about 1949 or so?

1950, uh-huh. The beginning of 1950, I think it was.

Where did you sail from?

We sailed from Tilbury Docks... in London. And... went to Freemantle in Western Australia.

ORIENT LINE

S.S. "ORONTES"

ENGLAND – AUSTRALIA

26th MAY to 2nd JULY, 1951

What were your feelings about going away?

Oh, just excited. That was it... but, upsct about... well, my Dad didn't come to the train because he wasn't very well. But my mother came to the train... but I was upset about going away. But that soon passed 'cos it was so exciting.

Did you organise a job or accommodation in advance?

No, no... accommodation, yes - there was a hostel which they had for the immigrants. And on the boat, a big boat... but it was all immigrants that was on it, all tourist class. And it was lovely - I mean, it was heaven. Four weeks on the boat, lots of young people on their own. I made quite a lot of friends - you know, young people from Ireland as well as from Scotland...

Were a lot of the people from Scotland?

Uh-huh. But... a lot of Irish... and they were nice, I made a lot of nice friends. A lot of Catholics as well - which I wasn't, I was Church of Scotland, but it didn't make any difference. We were just all... and when we got off the boat at Freemantle, we were taken to this hostel which was nice, and the food was very good... quite bare, but it was clean. It was nice, and you could stay there for two weeks without paying anything. But if you didn't get a job within the two weeks, then you had to pay, I believe. But when I got off the boat at Freemantle, I had my kilt

on. And there was this Scottish couple, and they must have noticed me, and they came up and spoke to me. One thing led to another, and they said they knew somebody who would have a job. So we went... and they lived 70 miles north of Perth. And eventually they had phoned through to the hostel, and there was this Scottish... these... people, Mackenzie their name was, who had a station in Western Australia, a sheep station... they were Scottish.

So... it was all arranged, and they were interviewed, and one thing or another. And it was discovered that they were suitable people and I went up there. And they had three little children, and I just helped look after their children. And I was there for ten months, and that was live as family, you know, you're just one of the family, looking after a baby and two wee kiddies. I went on holidays with them and everything, you know, in the hotels... and it was lovely. Then I was there for ten months

The Committee
of the
Wagga Wagga
Amateur Picnic Race Club
request the pleasure of the company of

Miss J. Goodall

at the

Club's Annual Race Meeting

to be held on the

M.T.C. Racecourse, Wagga

on

Thursday and Friday
21st and 22nd May, 1953

This Invitation is sent at the request of

J. L. Stewart

W. H. Stillman,
Secretary.   R.S.V.P.

and... I had known of people... the farmer in the neighbouring place where we were [in Scotland]. They had relatives in New South Wales, and they had a big sheep station. And the lady wrote to me, and asked me if I'd like to go there and work for them. So eventually it was arranged, and they paid my fare by train - first class from Perth to Sydney, which was a week on the train. And that was a lovely experience as well.

What was the town like?
Just like you would see in a Western - you know, the verandas and the wooden poles holding the buildings up and... that was then, y'know, they've all changed now. And no...

roads as such, just all corrugated... red gravel roads. I mean, you couldn't pass a car in front of you, 'cos you couldn't see through the dust.

Were there any immigrants there?
There was a lot of... European immigrants... that went and lived in the farms - well, on the stations. They would have cottages and that... was it Ukrainians?... I think there was a couple there - you know, that they might have been prisoners of war, or people that came out of Europe during the... and they worked there. 'Cos they had the "white Australian" policy - they would take white immigrants, but they wouldn't take any "coloured", as they called them then. I mean, now they're black or Asian, aren't they? But then they were termed "blacks" or "coloured".

How long did you spend there?
15 months. That gave me... took me up to my two years, when I could come back home again.

Were you desperate to return home?
I... wanted to go back home.

You always followed that plan?
Yes.

Did you ever have thoughts about settling down in Australia?
Well, I could have got married in Western Australia, to a young Scottish immigrant lad, but... I wasn't interested.

Was that the only way for you to settle there, rather than settling as a single woman?
No, I wouldn't, 'cos I was missing my family too much, y'know. 'Cos when you're part of a big family, you do miss them a lot, uh-huh. But it was nice, and I managed to... well, if my employers went on holiday, like if they went to Sydney to the show - the agriculture show there - they would take me with them, to live in the hotel.

They used to breed race horses, and they used to go to Wagga Wagga to the racing... and, I mean, it was all what they called "picnic races". They all took picnics with them, they all sat with their picnic hampers and had picnics at the races. It was all good fun. And I had a holiday up in Queensland as well. I managed to afford to see a wee bit, and still keep over money to pay... 'cos I remember the fare was £107 or something to come back home from Sydney to Southampton, which was quite a lot of money I suppose in these days.

Were your parents still in the same place?
No, my Dad had retired by then, and they lived in Colinton.

Did you go back to live with your parents?
Well, I did, but I got a job pretty quick. I went to work at the children's village in Humbie - have you heard of that? I worked there as a housemother... well, an assistant housemother, there was an older woman. And I quite enjoyed that as well. Aye... and I got married about a couple of years after that, because I had known my husband before I had gone out, but hadn't wanted to get married then, 'cos I'd never been anywhere or seen anything.

What did he do?
He was a blacksmith.

Where did he work?
In East Lothian, in a village called East Saltoun. He was the third generation in East Saltoun to be a blacksmith, but his grandparents had been down in East Linton and Thorntonloch y'know. They'd always been blacksmiths.

Did you leave work when you married?
Aye... until the children got school age or a little older. Then I went and did nurse training, and trained to be a nurse and worked there...

Jane, back row third from right.

How many children did you have?
Ahhh... I can't remember... in Humbie?

No, yourself.
Oh, myself! You must be wondering why I can't remember. I had two, a boy and a girl, uh-huh.

Was your house attached to the shop?
No, it wasn't attached, but there... in the olden days it would have been. But it was used as a store, y'know, for the iron and things. We had another house. Then he had bad health, and we had to give up the blacksmith's shop, sell it and whatnot. And we moved to the Western Isles, and lived up there. We moved to the Western Isles, to the Inner Hebrides... a small island off Mull. Two islands off Mull, actually, called Gometra. They looked over to Staffa and Iona. It was lovely. There was only five adults lived on the island - including our two selves, five adults.

What made you move there?
Well, my husband wasn't able to do the blacksmithing anymore, or the horseshoeing, 'cos he wasn't well. So he went as a manager for the Shetland Pony Stud, as he was very knowledgeable about horses and everything. He got that job.

Did you work there?
No, I didn't work there.

You'd always been part of very small communities, but how did you feel being part of such a small group of people?
We thoroughly enjoyed it. It was lovely... uh-huh, it was lovely. A different life altogether. My husband used to say, when you got up in the morning and opened the curtains, that was him working. If it was a good day, he went out, and if it was a bad day, he just got his books out and did some reading - that was fine.

How long did you live there?
Fifteen years. The children went to school... in Oban, and then they went to... my daughter went to university at Glasgow and my son went to college in Ayr. But when they went to school, I mean, they only got home every three weeks, y'know, they couldn't get home every... which they didn't like very much at first, but they got used to it. They liked living... they liked the idea of living where we lived, but they didn't like the idea of not being able to get home every night. They got used to it though, accepted it, and that was fine.

Why did you leave there and come back to this area?
Because again my husband wasn't well - he'd had a heart attack, a bad

heart attack, and he had other illnesses It was too remote. So we came back down to Dalkeith, where we could get medical care. That was the only reason we came back.

Jane at home, 1999.

Do you still live in Dalkeith now?
Aye, uh-huh. And that was it.

Why did you choose Dalkeith?
Well, the reason we chose Dalkeith is because we didn't have anywhere to come back to. The family home in East Saltoun had been sold, and things like that, and... we just wanted to come somewhere so we could look around and see where we wanted to live.

What year was that?
'83. And... they were opening a new sheltered housing in Dalkeith at the time. I got the job as... there was two wardens there, and I got the job as one of the wardens, with accommodation. So the idea was, you know, to see how it went and look around... 'cos my husband kept racing pigeons and it was very difficult to get his loft established, y'know. You had to have somewhere where you could have a racing pigeon loft and what have you. However, we stayed there for five years and... then he

23

wasn't well. He had several heart attacks and cardiac surgery, and one thing or another. And eventually I was left on my own, so...

Are you still in Dalkeith?
In Dalkeith, aye, but not working.

Have you retired now?
Aye, retired.

What do you think of Dalkeith now?
I like it. It's a nice wee town. People are very friendly. And being in the sheltered housing, I made a lot of friends - you know, people coming in to see their parents and things like that, so... I made quite a lot of friends. Now I go to the bowling... the bowling club, indoors and outdoors. I go to the Women's Rural Institute... go to church... amuse yourself... come to the writing class here, see if I can learn anything.

Do you feel this is home now?
This is home, this district, now, uh-huh. My children, they don't live here - my son still lives on Mull, and my daughter lives in South Ayrshire, but I have a car and I can go whenever I like. You know, I can go to Mull and stay any time - I can go to South Ayrshire and stay any time. They've got a nice place... my daughter's got a lovely big house with grounds and ponies and... all the rest of it. My son's got his own place on Mull - he's got his own fishing boat, y'know, employs men. They've got their own house and a wee holiday complex attached to it, y'know - caravan and flat and what have you. It's nice - they've done well. I'm quite happy. I've got six grandchildren - four from my son, two from my daughter [and two step-grandsons]. Quite happy, uh-huh.

I love that glorious island,
Where we spent happy years.
Sometimes as I remember,
My eyes just fill with tears.

Each day is filled with gladness,
So many things to do.
Or walking through the heather
In the early morning dew.

The lonely hills foreboding,
The dark sea's sultry sigh,
The soft cry of the curlew,
As the clouds go rolling by.

'Tis winter on the island,
The day is fading fast.
The lights of home are twinkling,
The wind a surly blast.

'Tis difficult to walk,
Against the winter's gale.
Straight off the Atlantic,
The wind-the snow-the hail.

Summer twighlight on Iona,
Or moonlight on her sands.
Across the turbulent water,
That lone and hallowed land.

The throbbing of the hoof beats,
As the ponies thunder home,
Reaching for the fodder,
That is for them, alone.

Now, safely in the shieling,
The dusk that fades and dies,
The fire-light on the ceiling,
Only the barn owl cries.

A feeling of contentment,
Within the room is sweet,
The lamp light on the windows,
Dogs curling at your feet.

Jane Durie 2000

**Jane on
Gometra**

I'll be 53 this year. My mother met my father in Antwerp - she lived over there, and he was stationed over there. He came from Blackhall - Stonehouse, to the west. My mother came fae a middle class family - her grandfather was a director of the docks in Antwerp.

I never ever met my grandfather, because my mother, at that time... they were staunch, staunch Catholics - very, very strict upbringing, tutors in the house. And, of course, my mother at 16 or 17, met this man who she fell in love with, and got pregnant. And that was a disgrace, especially there. So they put her in a convent - they would not allow her to marry him. She was eight months pregnant when finally her father relented to let her marry. He never went to the wedding, and disowned my mother since then. She never ever saw her father again, which was tragic. But her mother kept in touch - she came over here when I was born, and ten days later went back to stay with relatives. My grandfather died when I was 13, and I always remember my mother sitting on her bed in the early hours of the morning, sobbing her heart out because she'd got this letter early on in the day that her father had died. And I often look back and think of the pain that she suffered and... how could someone, how could her father disown her for that? And he didn't... he forbid the mother and sister and brother to keep in touch with her. But they did, and my grandfather died through an accident at work, and my grandmother came over here. So my mother saw her mother... I was 17 that first time.

She ended up coming here to stay... I cannae remember what date it was, I'm gonna say the seventies, and she died here, which I always found comforting, because my grandfather's buried there and her mother is here. She had a hard, hard life, my mother. My Dad was a drinker, and coming from the life that she had to this... She was, unconditionally, an excellent mother, but I never, ever got on with my father. Never. And of course, then my father was a drinker, and I would be termed now as a battered child. So being brought up in that environment at home, and then school with the dictators, it really... I just was that quiet, terrified. I ended up, I wanted to be a nun, because that's really all I knew. I was forced into religion... and then again at 13, the Pope changed the law, you could eat meat on a Friday, that was in April I remember. And that's when I started to look into other religion

What was your father's occupation?
He was a miner, in Easthouses pit. A clever man - a clever, clever man - but the drink again... He was a bit of a dictator himself, but he was... honest. Black or white, there wisnae in between with him. Excellent at his work, well liked, but different at home.

Had he been in the pits before the war?
Now, I cannae... I really don't know about that. I don't think so, 'cos he was young when he went to war, when he went to the Army. And in the

Army he was a boxer, and he done everything there - gunner, and he got a few medals. I'd say he was quite a brave man. He did what he had to do for his country, I suppose.

My mother couldnae speak English at all when she came here. And when she came here at 17 with a baby, and she couldn't speak a word of English, and she came to stay in Stonehouse with my father's mother... and people there were so ignorant........ they made fun of her because she couldn't speak English and they taught her to say bad words. Money... she didn't know her money, and people would steal... there would maybe be a five pound note and a silver half-crown, so she'd get a bundle of these .... You know, she was done to, a lot of things - they really were awful to her. My grandmother wisnae good to my mother, as I've heard, and yet I loved... my grandmother, to me, was my mother. 'Cos when my father came back from the war, there was jobs through here, so he came through here, got a house and work, and my mother came with him and left me with my grandmother till they got settled, and my grandmother brought me up until I started school. And she was absolutely... I found her wonderful. I cannae remember a lot of seeing my mum and dad. No, I must have. But the security was with this woman, and the love. There wisnae any shouting, and I never saw my mother getting hit and things like that, so I had to blank off an awful lot of my childhood. I cannae remember. The only things I remember is being with my grandmother for those years - I cannae remember any good times at home. It was fear again, so I must have switched off all that.

I have brothers and sisters, and they were brought up the same as me, more or less. And we arenae close, any of us, and it's through... I got stability and security and love from my grandmother. My sisters and brothers never got any. My mother tried her best, but fear again... she was torn between my father and us, and the fear with my father. I mean, she did protect us. I was the lucky one, that I got stability at home, whereas the others havnae 'cos they've just been in trouble, really, fae when they were young. Which is a shame.

My brother was a clever laddie - clever, excellent musician, very clever. But he would come home and my father... when we had our homework, that was... we'd just sit at the table. It was his tone - you couldn't even think of the question, because you knew you were gonna get a hammering. They wet the bed, things like that. And [my brother] just rebelled. He took somebody's motorbike, run it round Edinburgh, 'cos my father had promised to get him one. He always broke his promises, and he ended up taking it. From then it was just for years, petty crime, petty crime, right up into his forties. Then he met a Swedish girl who wrote to him while he was in prison, and he ended up marrying and moved over to Sweden 10 years ago. And he's been a different lad - three kids, brilliant father, hard, hard worker. So, my sister... I don't think there's any hope for my sister, at all.........And I would say that the thing is that my sister was the one that wisnae a bad child. She was the opposite. She seemed to be... my Dad never hit her. He used to take her out on walks and things. He was different when she was born - why, I don't know. If anybody was to... I would have thought, if anybody was to get into trouble, it woulda been the ones who never got the love. We certainly werenae close.

I went to St. David's School at... where's that again? Is that Whitehill?
Yes, Whitehill. You know, first of all I was at Dalkeith St. David's Primary School, and the teachers there... I tell a lie, I was up the St. David's Church, was our primary school, and Miss .... was our headmistress. And I'm sure she's in hell at the moment, 'cos she was a bad, bad woman.

Yes, she did terrorise the kids. You know, when it's snowing and you're at school and you're freezing cold... we didnae have shoes, we had rubbers with a hole in them and a bit of cardboard. When it happened to rain or snow, and your feet are soaking, and... she kept you outside. And you couldnae pick up your pencil. Now, I was five or six, and I always remember in the classroom you could smell the plasticine and the fear, and we had to write something, and my hands were so cold that I couldnae pick the pencil up and hold it. And she lifted rules... rulers... that's why I said rules, 'cos I called them a ruler... and we used to get our fingers broken, 'cos she would say, "the ruler is the queen". You know, one o thae women. And pick up the rules, and click five, and if you werenae writing properly, she'd whack you over the hands.

Do you think everybody felt the same way about her and the school?
She had her favourites, the ones that were clever and... they were, it was like you were talking about the "lits" and the "domestics". Because when I was in school, there wisnae "O" grades or highers, it was just all... everybody was the same, except one class was what they called the "literary". That's you took French or whatever. And they were the special breed. So they were concentrated on, and the biggest majority werenae concentrated on. There was some teachers were quite good - your science teacher, the cookery teacher - but, like, Mr. .... and them, they were terrible teachers. They were awful. And that was just in Dalkeith. I mean, I'm no saying all the other schools were the same, but our schools, they... I'd say 85% of the teachers were dictators, or they had a problem, definitely. 'Cos they certainly didn't... I learnt more after I left school, y'know. That school... I would not go back to school if they paid me a thousand pounds a week.

Were all the teachers from the local area?
No, Edinburgh, a lot were from Edinburgh. The majority o'them were from Edinburgh and Eskbank, yeah.

Were they from a different kind of social class?
Oh aye. Definitely, definitely, aye. They were all middle and upper or would be... they'd all forget where they came from.

Now talking about the High School in Croft Street, Dalkeith. Did you get the belt?
Got belted regular. If you went over the line - you know, your paper had lines, and on a Friday it was pen and ink day and if you went over the line with your pen or blotted it, you got belted. And that could have been, well, until you finished your composition or whatever. You could have five blots, and that'd be four, you'd be given double handers for that. And the arithmetic teacher, as we called him then, he was the same.

What did double handers mean?
Like that [gestures], and you'd have welts up here [gestures]. And when it was really bad, you were put outside the door and belted. Far too much religion. Far, far too much. When we went in in the morning, it was half an hour's prayer before you even started work. Then you'd get an hour's religious instructions, and then it was milk break. So you'd ten minutes' prayer before you went out for the milk, and ten minutes when you came back in from milk. Then you had maybe an hour and a half of a subject - history or whatever... I mean, I was in my third or fourth year of school and I was still getting fractions and pence. You know. I didn't go any higher than that, because the religion took over the teaching, the catechism.

What age were you when you left school?
I was 15.

What was the first job you held?
I looked after the house, because my mother worked at the fields, and...

What kind of fields?
In the potatoes. Everything, she did everything. She was a hard, hard working woman, because my father worked at the pits, but he drank his money at the weekends. So my mother had to go out and work.

So you looked after the house...
I looked after the house at 15. I cooked the dinners and did the fire, and things like that.

What about the rest of the kids?
When they came in, everything would be ready. I didnae... I really quite enjoyed that... except there was a... I cannae remember what day it was- my father would be drunk, and he was a type of man. If you woke him up, even if he wisnae drunk, oh God. You had to go about whispering. And this day my brother came in fae school and asked, ... the dinner

29

wisnae ready. And he threw his schoolbag at me, and I ducked. It went right through the living room windows. Well, that noise woke my father, so I went down the stairs - I still had my school pinny on, y'know, that green checked pinny that we made, and I went down the stairs to pick up the glass from the neighbours' window, 'cos they didnae get on. I thought, "Oh God!" So I picked up, and came up the stairs, and my dad, I remember, was standing at the other end of the lobby, raging with the burnt tatties in his hand. And I got some tanking. He was awful - he was terrible. He was an awful man. My mother... I felt so sorry for my mother, 'cos she did love us and she showed it, but she really couldnae... she protected us as best she could. Whereas nowadays, we wouldnae put up with that - we would leave. But at that time my mother, she was 16, came here, couldn't speak English, there wisnae Social Security, there wisnae any Women's Aid... it was just a way of life to her, and [she] hoped that we would forgive or understand.

So did you move out of the house?
I left when I was 17 to go back to my grandmother's. And when I left school I could have went to art college - I was good at art, and my art teacher had come up to see my dad about getting me into art college, and of course my dad didnae want that. He wanted me out working to hand in money, and that really... I was devastated with that, 'cos I wanted to do that. I ended up working... I started work when I was maybe about 16 or 17, so really a year looking after the house, then I went to work as a window dresser. I went through the West and worked in a lot of shops. But my mother, she wanted me back home and I felt I had to go back home to protect her, y'know, so I did that. And I was a window dresser till I got married and had my kids. But the abuse was always there, even when I was 20, right through...

How many children do you have?
Did I have? I had two boys.

Did you work when you were bringing them up?
No, I was lucky enough... I had a good husband, and I didnae work when I had my kids.

What did your husband do?
He was a painter and decorator.

Is he local?
He's from Gilmerton....... these days.

Where did you meet him?
I met him at the Lothian Arms. It was a pub, and I didnae drink then. And he was my first boyfriend... no, that's not true, he was my second boyfriend. I was 22... 21 when I met him. I never had boyfriends, 'cos of

my... I was too frightened my dad wouldnae let me out anyway, even... y'know, a lot o'the young ones go to the discos and the... I wisnae allowed out. 'Cos at my work, I did a lot of fashion shows and things - 'cos I was younger and slimmer then - and I did a lot of modelling for them. So it was makeup girls were coming in, and if I had lipstick on, that was it. And he was the type o'man, he said nothing during the week. He waited till the weekend. So I had to wash my face before I came home. And it wisnae caked in makeup. But he just had this... he thought all women were tarts, he had no respect for women at all. But he would make me go into the Coal Queen. He forced me into that for years, which I hated.

What was that?

He worked in the pits and it was the Coal Queen... Queen of the Mines thing... once a year, it's like a beauty competition thing. And he forced me into that every year - I won it every year for about eight years, and he forced me into it. And I hated it, because I hated the thought of thae people thinking, "Who does she think she is?" I hated that. If I didnae go in, I got battered. I literally got hammered for that... so I went in for it. I used to pray to God there was somebody they'd pick, that I'd maybe get second. And then one year there was a girl, fae Dalkeith... because you make a lot of enemies when you do things like that. People... judge you, they think you're... because I had a hard life for years, even that way. Because you were pretty or whatever, you were penalised for that as well. So I had a hard time with that. 'Cos I didnae think of myself at that time... I didnae think I was bonny, I was just me. But he made me go into that - that I didnae like, and I hated him for that.

What age are your boys now?

My boys are 26 and 23. I divorced my husband after six years, I think. 'Cos I'm a black and white person as well, the majority of the times. So I divorced him then, which was awful. It was tragic, 'cos he was a good husband, and my children took it harder than a lot of kids that are in an abusive relationship. But I have no regrets about that, none. And the kids... I asked the boys, 'cos you never know if you're a good mother or how it's affected them, but it hasnae, because we spoke about two years ago about it. We sat down... they think I did the right thing. They still see their Dad, obviously. But then again, it depends how you handle that as well. I never ever said a bad word to them about their Dad. So I was on my own - I brought them up. It was hard - I had three jobs then. But I was still lucky when they were young because I got jobs while they were at school, so I was always in for them after school. They were never latch-door-key-kids, because I tried... because of the way I was brought up, I'll never put my kids through that. And I was always there for them, and... this is gonna sound awful, but I've never ever had to hit my children, never. Because they've never... were never cheeky - I think it was just my tone of voice, and I've been awfy lucky with my kids.

31

What are you looking for, for yourself, in the future?

Me... Nothing, really, I'm really quite happy with my lot though it sounds awful. But I had... ten years ago... there's hereditary heart disease in the family, and I had it, which I didnae know, but my father had it. So, as I say, I worked for the social work department after being a window dresser, with elderly people. And I loved it, and then started taking wee heart attacks and things. Then, ten years ago, I had a triple heart bypass. So I class myself as being awful lucky to be here, so I'm really quite happy. I'm no saying I would... I think the government should give us that wee bit extra money to live on. I would like no to have the worry. But I'm really quite happy. I just take each day as it comes. I think if I get my holiday each year, I'm ecstatic. So I dinnae really want anything. I like people and I like... I like to help the elderly and I enjoy people. But I really dinnae want to go back to work - I dinnae want any more pressures on me. I feel I've burnt myself out at 53, 'cos I've worked hard. But I'm quite happy with my lot, mostly because my sons are settled and they're up and I know they're okay. But other than that, I'm quite happy with my life.

Alness was the location of one of Salt Of The Earth's pilot groups, and the participants have been closely involved with the project from beginning to completion. Their recordings are part of the Highland area's multi- media archive production on the COMMA software package, along with the groups from Avoch, Ardersier and the Highland Women series of interviews.

The Alness group enjoyed an exciting video conferencing link up with the Thornliebank Salt Of The Earth group to discuss common work and interests. On a weekly basis they met to contribute their experiences of, and opinions on, a range of subjects. The following piece traces extracts of Farquhar Ewan's contributions, augmented by some of his written work.

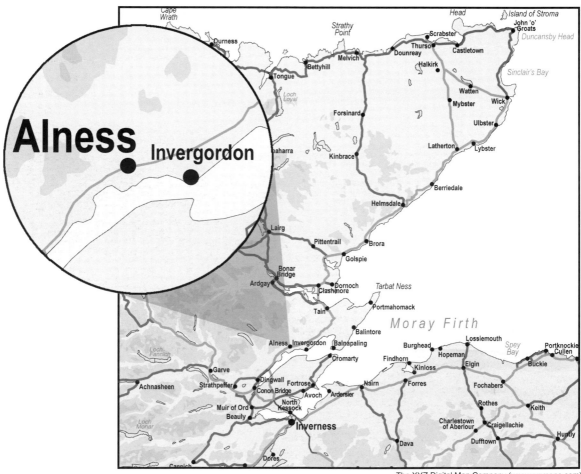

The XYZ Digital Map Company (www.xyzmaps.com)

Video Conferencing with the Alness group

View of Alness Main Street in the 19th Century

Do you remember your grandparents?

I remember one lot of grandparents. My mother's father and mother who lived here in Alness most of their lives. They were of farming stock people. My grandfather was a cattle man and my grandmother was of course at home, a housewife, and she had 12 of a family of whom five survived. She had three sets of twins who died shortly after birth and one daughter died at the age of seven. My mother was third oldest of the family and they lived as I say in Alness and around Alness on the farms. My other grandfather and grandmother lived in Perthshire. I never knew that grandmother because she died in childbirth and my grandfather I met twice and I hardly knew him either. He was a forester. Not only that but my grandmother was 29 when she married and she had 12 of a family after the age of 29 and her people lived in the Black Isle on Alness Ferry. They were Makays and the fourth generation is in that farm at the present day.

Maternal grandparents

My father as I say was born in the Haugh of Ballechan in Perthshire in Logierait. I don't know if anybody knows that place. A place called Logierait. Well this was a big estate and it was called the Haugh of Ballechan and he was born there so he had two brothers and two sisters and he lost his mother after the childbirth of the youngest of the family, about a year after, she took pneumonia and died and my grandfather was left with 5 children. My father was 11 and he was the one that had to look after the younger ones and through time they got housekeepers, different housekeepers you know. Some you could depend on, some you couldn't depend on, but my grandfather was working and couldn't keep an eye on things until he would find out how things were going when he got back home and of course it was very difficult for him. He had a very hard life with five children but they survived. So when my father was 17 there was no work, he worked in the forest as a wood feller and he came back north to Alness. And the most peculiar thing was, when he came to Alness he had to look for somewhere to stay and he landed with my grandmother as his landlady and of course that's where he met my mother. My mother was a housemaid in the Ben Wyvis hotel in Strathpeffer and when she would have her day off in the month, of course she met my father. And one thing led to another and they got married in 1911. My father was 21 and my mother was 18 and from then on he did all wood felling all round here and Invernesshire. He was

Farquhar's mother, father and three sons. 1915

37

what we call a contractor feller and he used to get contracts. He was never at home. He was away all week and he only appeared home on Saturday afternoon and went away on Sunday morning and I hardly ever knew my father.

How did you have so many brothers and sisters?
There was no television. There were nine of us. There were seven boys and two daughters. First daughter died at birth and the rest of us survived. It was a hard life.

Was it a happy life?
Happy for that day because we were one of the fortunate families, because my father was always in work and we were sort of relatively well off as far as home wealth was concerned. There was such an awful lot of people out of work and such a lot of poor people. Well we used to help one another an awful lot in that time. If you saw a poor person you'd give them a diet of potatoes or a diet of bacon, you know, to help and you'd be very surprised at how appreciative these neighbours were from my mother giving that because it was life savers.

What do you mean by a diet of potatoes?
A basin full. Maybe several meals but we just called it a diet and then in that time of course we all had our own gardens and we cultivated all our own vegetables, potatoes, everything most of the year. My mother dug the garden, planted the garden, as well as look after the family and my father was never there. When my brothers started getting up a bit they used to help her.

So you'd say your mother had a hard life.
Oh she had a harder life really than my father because she had to bring us all up and reprimand us, dress us, get all our complaints. Everything.

And yet she lived to a good age.
Six months to 100. 99$^{1/2}$ when she died. She used to sew and heel our boots and do all the knitting and washing. It was all hand washed and water, water to be carried in, there was no water in the house. No lamps and all that, scrub the floors. No carpets in that day.

Well I was listening to Lena there talking about the times that she had in the outskirts of Alness, three miles out whereas I was living in the village of Alness. The part that was known in my day as Bridgend of Alness, not Alness. The other side of the river bridge was known as Alness because it's in the parish of Alness. The end that I lived in was in the parish of Rosskeen which was known as Bridgend. All our birth certificates said born in Bridgend, not Alness. Now we're all Alness which I think is wrong because they're taking that away from the people's birth certificates in our day at the present moment.

We had our school at 9 o'clock, Bridgend school. My older brothers went with Mr Makay but when I went it was a Mr Macdonald who we had a byname of as Gaelic Mac because he came from the West Coast and he spoke the Gaelic and he got the name of Gaelic Mac and we had five teachers. We had Miss MacCulloch. She had infants, lower and higher infants. She was a very hard teacher. And then we went from there to Miss Ramsey who was the most fearful teacher that was ever in it, but a teacher that if she wouldn't put anything into you she would knock it out of you one way or another and she had two classes.

If you didn't get your lessons you got the strap and I can tell you she delivered it with venom when she'd give you the strap. She was far worse than the headmaster giving the strap and she lived in Dingwall and she used to go back and forward to school on her motorbike. She had a motorbike, and it was an old Riley and she used to have a leather coat and a leather helmet and her goggles.

In my day she had a motorbike and she would travel back and forth on the motorbike and she was one of 12 of a family. Miss Ramsey and everyone of her family died of cancer.

We looked up to our teachers and we looked up to our ministers and we all showed respect to all those professional people. Today the children show no respect. We had to salute our teacher no matter where we met her.

As I say Alness was quite a thriving little village. There were farms all round and farming was the main work round the area and we had a distillery at each end of Alness and still have to this day, and they were fishing at that time from Belleport. They had fishing boats come in there and we had a lot of coal boats coming in with coal and, in fact a lot of groceries and that came by boat, didn't they Gordon, before they came by road by Invergordon, but there was very little transport.

The first bus came to Alness was brought up by a man from Glasgow, and he lived in Invergordon and he had the first bus in the north and his name was Stevie. And he drove that bus himself and then, when the Highland Bus Company started up in Inverness, he was driving this bus from Dingwall to Invergordon. I don't know whether it passed Invergordon but it was more like this area that ran the bus, and then through time the Highland Bus approached him and took over his bus, and he had a driver's job for the remainder of his life with a big pension. They more or less took over his run.

There were no radio, no television. I remember when we got the first radio I'd be a boy of about eight and it was run by batteries, the radio, wet batteries and a dry battery. You had a dry battery then you had a wet battery which you got charged down in the garage, and one did a week. You'd get one in, one out, you see, and that was the first radios we had.

The winding gramophone. The first ones were the ones that sat on the table with a horn, but then after that there became ones that you could carry in a case, but these were the ones after the ones that sat on the table, and the music that we had.....There were John McCormack, Count, well he became Count John McCormack, Al Jolson and there were the McCullochs, but I've got a lot of these old records still in the house. One of these old famous records that I have. I don't know if they still have the same records, and it's by Sir Hugh Robertson of the Glasgow Choir.

The rented house that we rented..........had no light, we had no water, we had no toilet facilities, nothing and we had to take all our water in. In fact, it's just a matter of 36 years exactly since I left that house and there was still no water, no light, nothing. That's not so long ago, 36 years. That's until I went into the present house I live in now. Of course the house that I'm in is my own house but in that day we rented houses, always, because we couldn't afford to buy houses. There were no wages and no houses to buy except to people that had one or two, the wealthy people. And then they maybe had one or two that they could let and then people pay a rent. And the rent that we paid for that house if you'd like to know Doraine, we paid £10 a year, £5 every six months, May term and November term, and not only that the landlord that we had they were that poor, as often as not they'd come down to the tenants and said "give us some of your rent to tide us over in advance." That's the rent that we paid for our house, and all that we had in that house was a little room, room about 8 by 10 which we called the kitchen and then we had a big, what we called the front room that did as the best room and there was still a bed in that because it was a big family. And then we had two rooms upstairs and that had to do for 10 of us. A father and mother and eight of us.

By living in the village we could walk to the shops and get our messages but for the people in the country they couldn't do that. They would get maybe the van once a week . They supplied themselves up and cycled down during the week if they had a bicycle, if they could afford one, through the week to get one or two other messages, you know, light stuff.

Another thing that was always instilled in my family at home, I don't know about anyone else's family, was that we were never allowed to take any money from anybody. If we did a message for a neighbour or that and, you know, they'd give you a ha'penny for doing it. My mother used to send us back. "You give that back. They can't afford to give you that." You do it with the kindness of your heart or not at all, and my mother taught us never to take no money from neighbours because they could ill afford to give it.

We used to get the big pandrops and my mother used to break it so we would get four, and we'd get a bit each. We would go to church and we would get a wee section each. These big pandrops, they were about this size, and she would take a poker and hit them and they'd come into about four pieces or so, and you'd get a bit each. I can mind that perfectly well. I can mind that. There were plenty of things that we got.

I remember when my mother used to get the bowl of oatmeal and we used to have a kist for this bowl of oatmeal. And it was such a lovely 'kist', as they were called. But the one that we had was exactly the same as a chest of drawers and, if you looked at it, it was a lovely chest, a mahogany chest of drawers, and it was six drawers but it wasn't a chest of drawers at all. You lifted the top and the top came off in a hinge and then you lifted the two top drawers down and you emptied a bowl of oatmeal into it and then put up the front and that was a chest of drawers. And I never ever seen one like it anywhere.

I heard my grandmother talk about that they used to make the porridge and leave it in a drawer for over the weekend to settle. That was our main diet in the morning. Porridge and milk and a cup of tea, and maybe a wee bit toast.

My grandmother used to make it all. She used to make black puddings and white puddings and she used to get the blood from the butchers to make the black pud. My grandmother was great at all this, home made.

It was a case of that you had to go by your parents' rules. You wouldn't dare miss a Sunday in church. We all used to go to church, Sunday School and then carry on for the rest of the service in the church and then home.

Is that the same now today?
Not really, I mean those children that go to Sunday School, they don't have to go to the church. They are not forced to go to church, I think we were forced in our day.

Was that a good thing?
In one way because I think it gave us a better and a clear priority in life for the future.

You don't think that it gave you standards?
Yes, I think so yes, forms of standards. I mean even to this day I keep the Sabbath. I am not a member of any Church, but I am a regular member of going to a church, but I still keep the Sabbath, I never break the Sabbath, and I think that was instilled in me. Whether that was good or whether that was bad, it just depends on the person.

I am quite sure in your day your mother started preparing for the Sabbath on the Saturday night.
Everything for the main meal was prepared on the Saturday and all the dishes that were collected on the Sunday were washed on the Monday morning.

Well, my mother wasn't that strict, she did prepare everything but we had to wash the dishes.

There were different religions. My mother was of the Free Church and my father was of the Church of Scotland you see, so she was brought up in the free aspect of religion and that was their way of doing things.

I like the way you say the 'free aspect of religion' as attached to the Free Church, but they were much more liberal actually than the Church of Scotland.
In many ways, but that was their way of being brought up through generations you know, and it is still there.

I believe they still 'put out the line' with the Precentor. Describe what putting out the line was?
Well, they started the first two lines of the version of the psalms via one of the Elders at the door, called the Precentor.

Because there was no music in the Free Church?
There's no music still to this day, and still the same today.

Did it not really come from the times when people couldn't read and the Precentor put out the line and then the people sang the line?
From the Gaelic Churches really and then it came into the English.

Well I'm still waiting to get old. I have always had a bright and young outlook and I think if you've got that that you never get old.

Why do you think that?
My disposition is so good.

It's because you never got married.
Being a single man I had no petticoat government over me and that is a great boon, you know, because you have your own thoughts and your own ways. You've got to do things and get out and about, whereas a married man hasn't got the same freedom when he has to put up with a wife and vice versa. I'm not being one sided so, you see, I'm speaking from the point of view of being single all my life and the only petticoat government I had was my mother and I think she was 10 times worse than ever a wife would have been. But it didn't take any effect and I

think I'm enjoying my life very much since I retired, because my life and my work was just my life. Because I started work at seven in the morning and I didn't finish until seven at night, and I didn't have much free time except going to a dance at nights, so since I retired I've got the whole day and the whole night now. Who said I would ever want someone to nurse me into my old age, because by the time I get to that age I hope there'll be a pellet in it that I can take and go wheech and not bother anybody.

There's nothing depressing about life. You take every day and every hour as it comes. Some people are very lonely, they won't go out.

Well I said when I was left alone that I would never feel lonely. I would get out and about and do something. And if the day would come that I wasn't fit, well that I would be reconciled to, and I think that if you have that state of mind it's a great boon and you can live by it. But if they can't live by it I feel sorry for them.

I think there's a lack of education for the old people, for all the changes that is happening. They forget that we're in existence. The people that are introducing all these changes, they're not helping old people to convert to the changes. We've got to learn by trying to pick it up from the younger generation gradually. Especially people with no families to pick it up from. Where are they going to learn it? We're not educated and they're not helping to educate us.

I know all about counting. We had no machines for counting. Everything had to be counted by brain or jotted up there and then and very, very seldom did we make a mistake. I've seen a lot of mistakes done by your computers and they blame the computer, not the person.

When I went to the doctors surgery here lately, and I went in with a prescription and there were three items on this prescription for this elderly lady. And I myself had wrote down what she required, handed it in, and I went back there at the proper time to collect it and, of course, just collected it and went down to the chemist and handed it in, and I presumed it was correct and this was it. Went to collect it from the chemist. One item. I thought the chemist had made a mistake so I went straight back to the chemist. "Oh no Mr Ewan it's just the one item." What? So I had to go back to the surgery, so I went back to the surgery and said look, I came in for this prescription three quarters of an hour ago and you've only got one item on here. "That's all you put on" and I said "No it's not" I said "It was me personally put it on and it was three items." "Well that's the computer." I said "You have a special computer here do you?" "What do you mean Mr Ewan?" "It works itself does it?" I got no answer.

There's no permanent real work, really work now, for a person to be working permanent. In my time my work was a trade but now it's not. It's all pre-packed. When we started work we started as an apprentice too because I was working as a grocer and when I went into the grocery shop first we weren't allowed to go near the counter. We were allowed just to stay in the store and we had the job of making up all the goods for the shop sort of all pre-packed now such as sugar, butter, oatmeal, flour, all that had to be made up into quantities. It came in bulk in big bags and we had to carry that in, which a young boy like me at 14, having to carry that in was a great heavy job. A lot of people thought that being in a shop was a very light job but if the half of them had come into the shop and tried it they'd have been dashed glad to get out of it. Because many a time I felt like I'd like to go somewhere else and do something else but there was nothing else to do around where I lived here in Alness. Nothing. Just the distillery work and that was all fully employed by permit workers, as you were already talking about. Farm work was the same. It was permit workers. There were no openings so you were glad to get an opening in anything when I was a boy of 18 here. You just worked in the store and did all the menial work in the shop. Everything and then gradually you got into the shop and started filling the shelves and then pricing the goods and then serving the people, and then we had to take our share then of doing everything.

When I went in there I had to be taught to tie those bags because there was a certain way of tying them and of course that was a part of the trade. And then we had to do all the hams, bone all the hams and then roll them and tie them. Today they're all pre-packed. We had to slice all ours, bone it and roll it ready for the ham machine. That was a job in itself too. That was part of our trade.

Did you have a test of arithmetic?
None whatever. They presumed we were well-versed. Mind you, that was one of my favourite subjects in school, so I don't suppose I'd have failed in a test anyway. I was very good at 'maths', as they call it nowadays. Then it was arithmetic.

There's all changes from work, from what we had, and today you see, as I said, they're all taught by computers for the new type of works, most of the people are, aren't they, and that's a different world again. Maybe in 30 years time they'll maybe just press a button and a computer will do it. Not need a computer at all, a robot will do it all.

Unfortunately I only got two years of my apprenticeship when I got my call-up papers for the Army, for when you reached the age of eighteen, which I did, you got called up to do your two years conscription. This was introduced by the government just after the war was over, and all young men of eighteen had to do it. I was called up on the 6th June 1946 and had to report to Fort George for 10 weeks training. This entailed how to do all rifle drill, marching drill, how to dismantle a rifle and how to clean it, also a bren-gun, and to learn how to throw a hand grenade.

The following is part of Farquhar's written account of his experiences.

We lived in the Fort itself in one of the barrack rooms which held thirty soldiers and consisted of 15 double bunk beds, one floor locker and one wall locker. It was a very strict way of life. We had to get up at 5.30am and do all our ablutions and have our bed made up and looking immaculate as they were inspected every morning after ablutions. We had to go out on PT parade dressed in singlet, shorts and plimsolls and got half an hour of physical instruction, then in for a shower and then get ready to be marched to breakfast.

After breakfast it was marching drill, rifle drill and when we were not doing that we were given lectures on just about everything. Of course when you were in your training you were not attached to any regiment until you passed all your tests. Then they would consider what would be the most suitable trade to place you in nearest to your civilian occupation. I was placed with the Royal Army Ordnance Corps as a Stores Clerk, but I had to go on a ten week course, to Portsmouth, to learn all about store work army way and all the paper work concerning what to do with stores that require to be transferred, and all the documents for receiving and delivering and for filing. It entailed an awful lot of learning but I managed it and passed as Stores Clerk Third Class so that meant I was to be posted to my first proper camp which was to Thornliebank, Glasgow. The barracks were nissan huts and there were about twelve soldiers to each hut, and this was at the start of the winter and they were very cold, they only had one little stove heater in the middle of the hut which burned wood, so if your bed was not near the middle it was very cold as we only had three blankets for our bed: one to put under you and two for above, so we used to put all our uniform and greatcoats on the top as well. I thought we would all die of pneumonia. Not only that, where we had to go to work or have a shower was about a hundred yards away. We nearly froze coming to and fro.

Then I got posted abroad to Egypt which was to the biggest Army camp in the world. There were eight different camps in one and the whole size in acreage was as big as the town of Inverness.

We travelled to Egypt by the troop ship SS Franconia. There were two thousand troops on her going to all different parts of the Middle East. We left Liverpool docks on 10th May 1947 and it took us ten days to travel to Port Said. The weather was fairly good but my goodness what a lot of the soldiers were sea sick. I was one of the lucky ones by not being under the weather. I was the only soldier that was taking food during the whole journey on our mess, out of sixty. I enjoyed the journey as we had nothing to do.

It was like a holiday cruise only not the comfort.

We arrived at 3.00am in the morning, so we disembarked and were taken to a transit camp for the night and next day we travelled from the transit camp to our main camp which was Tel El Kibore where we were to remain the whole time I was in Egypt.

We were put into camp E which was huge. The first day was used up by being allocated our bedding and what row our tent was in. You see we were billeted under canvas - four soldiers to a tent so there were no wardrobe lockers, just the metal box type which was kept beside your bed and locked all the time, and all your other belongings were kept in your kit bag and also locked, as there was a lot of stealing going on in the camp. It took some getting used to as all the rows of tents looked the same until you got to know them. We were kept there until we were posted to our respective jobs.

I think we were kept about six weeks and then I was posted to 109 Warehouse, away out in the desert, away from the main camp. This warehouse was like an aircraft hanger in size and was built of corrugated iron and consisted of two large sections for stores of all kinds, and our living quarters, which consisted of one bedroom, one sitting room and one kitchen/dining room. There were three other soldiers, Taffy, Darkie and Dick and myself. A Scotsman, a Welshman and two Englishmen and we got on great together. I was senior soldier with my qualifications and got paid as a Corporal three star stores clerk. We had thirty Egyptians working for us every day. One of them was a foreman who was called a Ryce (an Egyptian word for foreman) and one of them was detailed to be our cleaner and dobie man for our living quarters. He had to keep them clean and do our washing and cleaned our brasses and our boots and make our tea for us. Our main meal of the day came by transport from the main camp cook house every day, so it was part of his work to serve this to us and then clean all the pans afterwards.

Now a lot of the transport driven in and around the camp were driven by German POW's, accompanied by an armed soldier. But of course they were quite willing to do this as it gave them a lot more freedom instead of being cooped up in the POW camp all day and every day. We also had to take our turn of escort duty, which entailed a truckload of stores been transferred from our camp to other camps throughout Egypt, such as Fanara. I was detailed to do this one to Palestine and as luck would have it we arrived at the beginning of the 1947 uprising, so we had to get our stores delivered and out quick, as there was shooting going on all the time. And as I had to go to the office headquarter to report, and get someone in charge to sign for the stores, I got shot in the leg by a stray bullet, so I had to be taken to sick bay and be treated and patched up. That kept the whole escort late in getting away. In fact they thought we were not getting away if it got any worse, but thank goodness there was a lull in the shooting and we got away under darkness. So they sedated me very heavily and I had to be taken to hospital when we arrived back in our own camp, and I can tell you that was a journey that I don't remember doing. So I was put off duty for four weeks. That was an experience I did not expect. We were supposed to be the peace time soldiers. My three brothers were all war time soldiers and none of them got wounded, and here was me the opposite. So after that incident I was never picked for escort again and life went on as normal as ever it could be in such heat. It was 120 degrees in the shade of course. We did not work after eleven in the day, as we started work at five in the morning because it got too hot to work, so we just lay on our beds with nothing on except a pair of shorts. That is all we could bear to wear until it got cooler by four in the afternoon, and it became dark very quick about six at night. There were no twilight, as we know it. At home, it was light one moment and dark the next. We got our midday meal at 12 noon and usually we passed the rest of the day writing letters home or reading, or playing cards, cribbage or dominoes, or too exhausted to do anything with the heat so we just lay on our beds. That was the way of our life while we were stationed in Egypt.

Of course we had our off-duty time as well. As there were four of us, two had to be on duty all the time. What I mean by that was that two had to be in the store and billets at all times in case of break-ins or attempted ones. The Egyptians were terrible thieves. We had to be very alert and keep our eyes on them all the time, as the 'wogs', as all the British Soldiers called them, were very poor and very poorly paid. But it was always money to help them and their families survive. Also being able to steal something out of our store huts was a big bonus for them to sell in the black market, even though they were all searched when their day's work was done, and this was done every day. There were plenty stores going missing and they were hardly ever caught. So that was our every day existence while in the army in Egypt. By the time we were there for several months we were longing for our demob number to come through on the camp notice board, my number being seventy seven. But when it did it was the best news we got, as it was getting us all down, that kind of life. We embarked on 21 July 1948, on the ship the Empress of Scotland. It was not such a large ship as the ship that took us there, nor as comfortable. It was very cramped, but we did not mind that as we were going home to dear old blighty.

When we arrived at Liverpool docks there was transport waiting for us to take us to the transit camp to await our turn for getting demobbed. That took two days. We had to get a medical and then we had to hand back all, well not all, the army clothes, except for two pairs of socks and your underwear, and you also got your plate and your mug which I still have to this day. Also a pair of boots, and then the army supplied us with a demob suit, shirt and tie and hat and we were allowed to buy our army greatcoat if we wanted to. I did not. We also got six weeks wages, which at that time was 12/6 per week, and our railway ticket paid to wherever we lived in the British Isles. And that was that part of my life over. It was an experience that I enjoyed and will never forget and I think it is an awful shame it was ever stopped because it certainly made men out of boys.

All soldiers who had jobs when they were called up, that firm or industry had to take their ex-employees back for a period of six months, as it was compulsory for them to do so by government law. And then the employers could do what they liked with you, as Lipton's tried to do to me when my period of time was up. They wanted to transfer me to one of their branches in the Outer Isles but I refused. I could not afford to pay for lodgings and keep myself in clothes or have any money for any leisure time or entertainment, as I had to go there on the same wage as I was getting in Dingwall. And that was hard enough to live on, and that was me living at home.

Work was very scarce in that day, so the bosses could get young boys and girls leaving school to do the work on the belief they had a three year's apprenticeship, and a contract was given to them for that period. In other words it was cheap labour because they would only have to pay them about half the wages a 21 year old man or woman would receive, and we as workers could do nothing about it as there were no Unions.

So the workers did not have a leg to stand on, and this happened throughout Britain. Worse in some places than others. So there was nothing for it but for me to hand in my notice, which in that day was for two weeks. But I was very lucky, for in the first week, there was a job advertised in our local paper for an assistant manager in a shop in Tain. So I phoned right away and got an appointment for an interview on my next early-closing day so I did not have to ask for time off. So by good luck the manager of the shop in Tain was a great friend of my brother, who had also trained as a grocer, and they had worked together during their training. So I got the job no bother, for I was the only one who applied with my references. So being a friend of my brother was a bonus, so I just stepped out of one job into my new one.

When I got to know the people of Tain a bit better through contact at work, I was invited to all sorts of entertainment, such as dances, tennis,

badminton and darts. I was a member of the country dancing club and the badminton club in Alness, and a member of the tennis club in Evanton. We occasionally went to the big balls that were held in such places as the Ben Wyvis Hotel and the Pavilion Ballroom, Strathpeffer, the Dingwall Town Hall, the Northern Meeting Rooms and the Palace Ballroom, Inverness. All the big bands from the south would be imported north for these big occasions. Bands such as the Ivy Benson All Ladies Band, Ted Heath and Orchestra, Joe Loss and his Orchestra and many others. So we had many terrific times. That was the way of life in that day and of course we had our lady friends. In fact it was at dances that I met nearly all my ladies, so I say it myself, I was a great flirt, though I did have a few steady relationships. In fact I was engaged three times in my lifetime, the last being what I thought Miss right. I was going with her when I was 26 and courted her for over three years, which was the normal done thing in that day.

We had met at drama in Alness - she was a Groomswoman, looking after six to eight beautiful horses, training them and schooling them for gym. All through Scotland she worked, for Salvesens of Teaninich House, a large privately owned house on the outskirts of Alness, and I and two others used to walk her home after our drama sessions, and that was how it all started. She was a lovely girl and very down to earth. She belonged to a place called Helensburgh in Dumbartonshire. We were very keen on one another. When we got engaged we told no one and when her mother heard about it she was furious, and from that day on she made it her business to spoil everything for us. Finally she succeeded, by playing on her daughter that she was ailing, and she made her daughter give up her work, which she loved doing, and then she broke her engagement to me. I was heart broken and I have never felt or looked at another women in that light again. That was the final straw. I would never let another woman get the chance to hurt me in that way again. But don't get me wrong, that did not put me off women. I have had a lot of relationships and friendships with ladies right up to the present day, but that is one lady I will never forgive for what she did to us. I have even heard as recently as six years ago, that my ex-girlfriend never married like myself, but the person told me she did not know where she was living, as you never know, I might have got in touch.

While most of the contributions in this book have been presented in the form of individual life-history pieces, the majority of the project has involved tutor led groupwork. The Ardersier Evergreens are an elderly group of participants, also included within the Highland multi-media archive and who enjoyed many cross-generational sessions, sharing their experiences with children in Ardersier primary school. The following transcription illustrates the skill of the tutor in gently taking the three women through aspects of their early lives, and then addressing related contemporary issues.

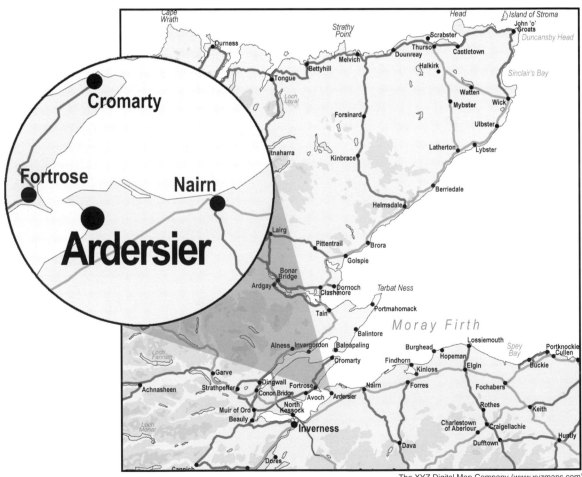

The XYZ Digital Map Company (www.xyzmaps.com)

What were your schooldays in Ardersier like?
Lovely, mostly. They were mostly good weren't they, the schooldays?
Yes.

You enjoyed them?
It was more like a reformatory.

Oh Meg!

You didn't like them?
I liked the school but, oh they were cruel. Many's a time they were cutting children's wrists with the strap. Of course, they're not allowed to do that now you see, maybe unfortunately, I don't know. Maybe that's how we were so good.

Miss Gray was lovely, the infant teacher.

She was a pet, beautiful.

So did you get the strap, Meg?
I got the strap for after school hours, yes I did.

What did you get it for?
Calling names at somebody likely.

So what happened? Did the teacher call you in?
Just there was nothing done about it. You didn't do anything about these things then, you just accepted it. Just had to really, there was nothing else for it was there? But oh, the school was more like a reformatory up there....with Speckie anyway and Miss Bain.

Were they very strict?
They were terrible, and Miss Stark the sewing teacher, remember her?

I got on fine with her.

She had a ring with a great big stone and you'd get it from her.

Did she knock you on the side of the face with it?
Yes. They just got away with all that then, you see. They don't get away with nothing now. The schooldays are great now.

How do you think that they've improved?
They get things that we never got. They get away with too much actually, I think.

54

Away on trips and what have you, you know, abroad and that. Of course, the parents have to pay for it.

What about you Mary what do you remember?
Oh aye, they were very happy days in school. I was very fortunate, we had an excellent Headmaster.

What school was it?
(Comure Easter?) Public School beyond Invergordon. That's where I went before I went to the Academy.

Was it a small school?
No, there were three classrooms and three teachers and they were all very good. The Headmaster was very firm. He would stand no nonsense but I was fortunate, I got on well with him, and he was our neighbour as well, which, of course, made a difference.

So you knew him quite well?
Knew him quite well.

So what would qualify as nonsense? What things would he be strict about?
Oh well, chatting and laughing in school and things like that, although he was a strict disciplinarian and there was no problem.

So you weren't allowed to talk and make a noise?
Oh no.

Was that the same here, you weren't allowed to talk or make a noise?
No, not really, you weren't, no.

I think most of the teachers were quite good apart from Speckie.

And if you could do your work you got on all right.

He was a brute, him.

Well he was. He was chased from Inverness. The women chased him with cabbages and turnips. Mrs Irvine chased him up the church one Sunday.

She chased him all the way.

Really? Was this the mothers?
The mothers.... He was in the Markinch School in Inverness. Well he was in that school.

What happened?

I don't know. Something must have happened with the children but the mothers all chased him. So he was chased out of Inverness. Where do you think he came.........Ardersier.

So you went to the Academy?

The Academy was such a difference. Oh it was different.

How was it different?

Oh gosh, you used to have the prayers in the morning, you know, the Rector used to have the prayers in the morning, and then you had your different classes, three quarters of an hour for each period. It was good.

You enjoyed it?

Yes.

How old were you when you went into the Academy?

We went into the Academy when I was thirteen. You had to sit a bursary.

An exam?

And you got a bursary. It was Green the minister, I remember, that had the papers.I left school at fourteen and straight into work, Menzie Buchanan's where the.....is now. It was offices that were in there. 7/6 a week.

So you were at school at .....?

Comure Easter till I was 11. 11 and 5 months and then I went to the Academy. I sat what is the 11-plus now but I was only 10 when I sat my 11-plus. It was qualifying then. That wouldn't be allowed now.

Did it feel very young?

No, no. I was in school at $4^{1/2}$, so I suppose that's why.

So what did you make of the academy when you went? Did you enjoy it?

Oh, I enjoyed the Academy, yes, lovely. It was quite different. We had to go by train quite a distance, to Invergordon, from Delny Station so it was quite a distance. We had to walk about two miles to the station first of all and then get the train. So the train would go up the couple of miles.

To Columnfield?

Yes, and catch the other one coming through and get on to that one, but we got the puggie home. It used to come into Inverness, at twenty past four it left, after school.

So it was Inverness?

No, no not Inverness, Invergordon, Invergordon Academy. He was a hard task master the Rector there as well and the boys were always tantalising him, and he wore a bowler hat and he went running after them one day and he fell and put a big hole in the top of the bowler hat.

We had a funny wee man, mind Herd.

He was nice though.

He was nice. He used to teach French and the boys used to make a fool of him. He was little, you know, and when he was giving any of them the strap he would jump up in the air.

He was small.

I liked Herdie.

Aye he was nice. We had a singing master and when he would say to the boys "Where is the doh" they would say "Standing on the floor" and when they put up their hands for the strap...he was a wee man.... they were taller and he couldn't get it above his head.

They were great for the strap. They don't use that now.

But the teachers have a hard life of it nowadays. They should really have some discipline cause my grandaughter, she's teaching, and the first day she was in the school there was a boy up on the top of a table dancing beside an open window, and she'd to go and get one of the male teachers to come and take him off. Just imagine what he was saying to her. So they have a pretty hard time of it.

Was he swearing at her?
Probably, yes.

So do you think that the strap was effective?
Oh. I think so. They were frightened of it.

If used properly, but you see, they used to take a spite at different pupils and then they got it all the time.

So, how was it actually administered? Can you describe what happened when you got the strap?
They just went out and held out their hand.

Not both hands?
No, just one.

And they got the leather strap across their hand?
Sometimes it would go round the wrist too, you know. Like Bill my brother-in-law, they asked him when the school was closed if there was anything he would like out of the school as a memento. He said "I would like the tawse", so he's got the tawse.

So did they discipline you in any other way apart from the strap?
Not really, we got extra homework or something maybe.

Did you get to write lines?
Lines, yes.

What sort of things did you have to write?
Don't remember that.

They were great with the writing then. They used to have the special writing books, copybooks. Up light and down heavy. Lovely writing. Now I don't think they've anything like that.

So were the words actually in the book and you copied them underneath. Is that what happened?
Not really. You used to get a line on the board to copy.

So it would be written on the blackboard to copy into your book?
Special lined copybooks weren't they? There were special lines in the copybooks.

What were the lines for?
Writing straight. And then you would write into them, you see.

So you'd form your letters going up in the lines?
Going up light and down heavy.

And the tail of the letter would go down to the bottom line?
Yes, yes.

What did you write with?
A pen with a nib with a wooden handle and a nib on it.

Two of three classes it was the slates, mind.

Slates and chalk?
You started with slates.

And an awful noise that they made on the thing.

Squeaky?
And there were the pens and the ink wells. Ink wells in the desks.

I had ringlets at the school and the boys behind put my ringlets into the ink well.

Dipped them in?
Dipped them in.

Did you have tiny little jars sitting on your desk?
Yes.

And that's where your ringlets ended up?
But it was a good school Ardersier.

But there was a lot went to the Academy when Speckie was there.

There was a lot of doctors and all came out of there, yes. It was a good school for education.

So do you think that the strictness helped?
It probably did because we were a bit afraid weren't we? We were afraid to get out of line.

But then I think the difference was that the children before they went to school were disciplined at home. I think that was the other thing. They knew what discipline was.

Yeah, but they're not disciplined now.

Course, then again they can't hit them, oh no.

So do you think smacking is something that helped?
Well, if they kept it in moderation.

A smack on the hand didn't do anyone any harm.

That's not where I got it.

On your bottom.

Plenty, yes, I was a monkey but my father only once did he ever smack me and I howled for days, because it was him.

So were you crying because it hurt or you were upset?
Oh no, I was insulted, that my father would dare. Mind you I deserved it.

Was there much bullying went on at school?
Well I was never bullied, were you?

There were the occasional ones that would bully.

But I don't think as much as they do it now. It seems to be bullying everywhere.

Denise used to get bullied a bit.

But they didn't think anything about it then. They never thought it was bullying and that sort of thing. They'd pick on her because she was quiet you see.

But that was the younger generation. In our time there was no bullying really, I don't think. I don't remember any bullying in school.

So did the teachers keep an eye on it or was it something the children didn't do?
I think on the whole children were better behaved then.

You think they were?
Yes I think so.

Just because they were disciplined at home.

Yet Lesley was telling me at the school she's teaching in down in the Borders, there's a boy and his father attacked one of the teachers, through the boy like. The father and the son both attacked the teacher. So he was expelled from the school and his sister with him. They weren't going to stand for the like of that. She said it was in the papers down there. I didn't see anything about it up here but that's what she was saying.

Remember anything like that happening when you went?
Gosh I don't know - Some of the soldiers used to come up.

Of course, the Fort children were in that school as well you see and they were always that bit behind with their education because they were travelling about so much.

Changing schools?
They were up in that school there and if anything went wrong the fathers would be up. We used to enjoy it you know. We enjoyed Speckie getting into trouble.

60

Getting his come-uppance.

So what did the fathers do? What did the soldier fathers do when they came to the school?

Threatened him I suppose. One of them had him pinned up against the wall off the ground.

Do you know why?
Must have been about one of his children probably. You wouldn't believe it unless you saw it. He would just go mad. Turks, he used to take, I think - brainstorms. Aye.

I remember one day Douglas MacKendrick... Dougie had glasses – you know, poor Douglas, and he was walloping away at Douglas and he knocked the glasses right off and they went down behind the radiator. So Douglas picked them up. "Are they all right?" When he saw that they were all right he started hammering him again.

With his hand, hitting him?
Yeah. Poor Douglas was one of the first boys in the village to be killed in the war, so he didn't get a long life. That's Mrs MacKendrick's brother-in-law.

That Jimmy Reid over there, he was telling me that Speckie threw that duster at him and he ducked and the girl behind him got it.

That was a wooden block? So could you imagine that happening nowadays?

No, never. He'd be in jail.

So it sounds like there was a very different atmosphere in school there? Was that the same for you Mary?
Yes.

Did you make the same things?
Lap bags, yes.

I think they made them in all schools. And we got cooking.

That's where I learned to make white sauce and I never forgot it.

I liked the cookery.

So you're good at the white sauce, are you!

So there was a lot of control over how you behaved and how you spoke?
Well I still reckon it was more like a reformatory school.

It was, yes, more like that than anything else, but now they've more happiness in their schools. I think so anyway. You never hear about the Ragged School reformatories now.

What's the Ragged School?
The reformatories. That's where they were put if they were naughty.

They were put away there, weren't they?

They used to say "If you don't behave, you'll go to the Ragged School".

Why was it called the Ragged School?
I don't know. I don't know if there's such a thing as it now. I shouldn't think so.

But they've got the special places too. They've got special schools.

So what did you have to do that was so naughty that you'd be taken out of your school and put to the Ragged School?
Something kind of wicked, I think, stealing, or maybe it was something wicked, wouldn't it?

I don't remember anybody going from Ardersier, do you?

No, but we used to hear plenty about the Ragged School.

I would imagine it would have to be something terrible.

What would be terrible, Sadie?
I don't know. I mean it would have to be something very bad before they were sent away, I would think.

I'm wondering what 'bad' would be? If it was bullying or damaging school property?
All we did was pinch apples, didn't we? - pinched apples. But that was nothing – everybody did it.

I mean, children didn't play truant then. Well they wouldn't play truant because they had what they called 'a whipper in'. And we had one – a Mr Curline that went round if you weren't in school to check round the homes to see why they weren't in school.

Went to the house, went to the door.

We'd sing: Old ....Curline, washed his face in paraffin, paraffin made shine, good ..... Curline.

Johnny Taylor's father was the one here.
Aye, Nippy Taylor.

But the parents are going to be fined now if they don't send their children to school.

Mind you it's difficult for them to know if they're going to school or not going.

They would have to follow them and see, I think.

It should be the school.

So they don't have a 'whipper in' now but they have fines instead?
I think they can be fined four thousand or something now.

The time that I got smacked by my father, I'll tell you what it was. My mother had done something to me and I said to her "The Cruelty to Children's in the parish and I'm going to report you". Well my father ....and then I started howling and I sat on the rug howling and howling and then she said "If you don't stop that crying you'll soon be like Alice in Wonderland, drowned in your own tears"

Did you stop?
I stopped then. A modern child that would have been nowadays. That's what they would say. Yes, they know the parents are not allowed to touch them but that was really bad. I deserved everything I got for that.

You think that's a bad thing to do?
Oh yes. I often think about it. Imagine saying that to your parents.

So do you think that schools have improved nowadays on the whole? I'm thinking maybe of the atmosphere inside the school.
Oh yes. They're taking a bigger interest in schools now. We were afraid to voice our opinion. Now they're not and maybe that's not a bad thing.

So it's good for children to be able to say what they think?
Just to say what they think. We wouldn't dare. We just accepted it and said nothing.

And how did that feel as a child, not to be able to speak up?
Well I suppose you didn't really think about it did you? You didn't think

about speaking up, not really.

But if you were to think back now to times when you were little when maybe you wanted to speak up, or you wanted to say how you felt and you didn't, do you think it did affect you at the time?
You wouldn't dare.
You probably would have done if you'd thought about it.

You wouldn't dare answer them back, would you?

Oh no.

It sounds like there's a lot of fear, a lot of discipline and respect as well.
My husband was in a class that he was in and Mrs Getty was in the class with him, you know, and whenever she sat down at her desk in the morning she started to vomit - fear.

Nerves?
Yes that was just nerves.

So it's bound to have bad effects on children.

Maybe they didn't learn as much, as easily as they might have done?
My Alec used to often talk about how she always used to start vomitting. She couldn't help it. Just pure nerves.

And what happened when she was sick?
That was just an every morning business when she went into school.

Did they do anything about it?
You couldn't do anything about anything like that then, I don't think, could you?

Well if she was sick, they'd have to do something about it. She maybe never told her folk, mind you. Her parents mightn't have known.

So the teacher wouldn't have told the parents?
I shouldn't think so, no.

That's what was the cause of it, just nerves.

Nobody tried to find out what was wrong with her, never tried to help her. She was just sick every morning.

We've had a wee bit of a break and we've been thinking of how times have changed since the old days in Ardersier and how people maybe are different now.
Well neighbours used to look after each other then.

Oh yes.

You know, if there was a neighbour ill all the neighbours were in looking after them, and you'd be sitting up at night and what have you. But now you see it's all carers. It's all completely changed.

I know you look after your neighbour Mary and she gets a lot of support from you. Do you think that's something that happens less and less nowadays?
Definitely, I would say so. Well my mother always, you know, looked after folk, neighbours, and I was brought up that way. So I suppose that's what it is. It never leaves you.

So did Mam. I've seen them coming to the house for her.

But then before, people looked after their old people. Nowadays they're shoved into homes.

That's right. I mean they looked after them like. I mean I had to stop at 55 to nurse my Mum, for example. I had her seven years, and Dr Farquharson used to come in and say "It's so nice to see someone being nursed in their own home instead of being pushed into a home or the person saying, I've got a sore back, I can't do it. I've got work to do, I can't do it". He said "There's somebody else I'd like to come in here in that bed, would you take them?" I said "No, one's enough".

And he felt that was quite unusual?
That was most unusual.

And did you feel it was your duty or was there a willingness to do it anyway?
I felt it was my duty. My father died very unexpectedly, and she fell and fractured her femur a fortnight after and I felt, well, I can't put her into hospital. Well she was in hospital, and they said if you don't take her home you can't have her because the two shocks are more than she can take. So I just said "Right, that's it", and I had no income, but dear me, God was good it all worked out. I had to pay my own stamp because I was only 55 and if I didn't pay my stamp I wouldn't get a full pension when I was 60. So it all worked out. My Mum used to cry because she knew that I was going to lose out over the heads of it but I said to her "Don't you feel that way about it, you were a good mother to me, so it's my duty to cope with

you now". That was it. And I don't regret having done it.
So she got the attention she deserved?
That's right.

It must have been satisfying being able to be with her?
Oh yes, it was a 24 hour service for the last six weeks. It wasn't just a day time.....it was day and night.

And did you cope with that yourself?
I coped with that.

So how do you feel now when you see other people?
Well if I see families that I know who could take them, I feel very bad about it. I mean there are some that couldn't. I don't feel angry just sad at this.

Sad for the old person?
Sad for the old person concerned.

So in what other ways do you think.........that social morals, if you like, have changed? Maybe in some kind of way it's about our moral duty. What other ways have the morals changed?

I think the young ones are a lot more open now. You know, we didn't discuss things like that when we were young, did we? Not really. We didn't talk about sex very much. I mean we just thought about it. But I think they are more open but they seem to think.....

Oh no they've gone over the score. They've gone overboard now. 12 year olds having babies. And they don't see anything wrong in that, that's the problem. That programme was terrible that was on the T.V. I didn't watch it.

George saw it. He said it was dreadful. There was two of a family both expecting about the same time.

Girls of 12 and they were getting money out of it.

Where was the money coming from?
Goodness knows.

From being on the T.V., for their story and that sort of thing, but they don't seem to say there's any wrong in it. I don't know.

Would that have been unheard of in your day Mary, as a midwife that babies were born to women so young?
Yes, we had a 12 year old and a 13 year old.

Did you Mary?
Oh yes.

How far back would that have been?
Well I've been away.........twenty five years ago.

There was an 11 year old, no 12 she was, from the Black Isle.
She kept her baby but to her it was just like a doll. Sad.

Do you think that it's sad that they have babies so young?
Yes it's sad.

They're not getting any life really, right from the very start.

I've seen a lot of them in that, I don't know if you ever watch that Ricki's programme from America, and young ones on there wanting to have babies, and maybe someone who'd had babies would come on and tell them about the life that she was having. It made no difference, they still wanted babies.

So these young women with their little babies that we were talking about. We were talking about attitudes nowadays being more open. Do you think it's important that such subjects are discussed openly? Do you think there's been an improvement there now?
Course they get a lot of sex education at school now, I think, which we didn't have.

Och, they're going over the score, I think. It's really terrible.

Pearl, when she was in the Academy, they got it, and Jean McGillvray from the garage down there and her, they had the class in an uproar with laughing. They were put out, the two of them. That's my eldest daughter. They laughed that much, the two of them.

I don't think it's necessary really.

I think maybe they start it too young.

What do you think would be a good age?
They wanted it to start with five and six year olds at one time.

You think that's too young?

Oh yes. Oh for goodness sake yes.

Let them have their childhood and play with the dollies and prams and stuff.

So what would be a good age?
Well, I suppose, when they come about 12. When they come to puberty then they would sort of assume it. Well I hadn't a clue what was going to happen. My mother never told me. I was 15¹ᐟ² before I started menstruating.

And you didn't know anything about it?
No, which is wrong.

So young people need to know about it. It's maybe making the decision when they're told and yet we were talking just now about girls of 12 having babies so at some point we need to..........

Maybe they didn't know. They must have known what they were doing wrong but maybe they didn't know what the consequences were.

So if they'd been educated sufficiently, they might have been pre-warned if that was the case? So we need to start earlier then?
But she must have matured quite young.

So what about all the other issues around sexuality like homosexuality. Was that ever discussed when you were little?
Don't think so, never heard of it.

Never heard of it at all? You wouldn't have known what it meant?
No.

Do you think it's important nowadays that it's talked about?
Well there's a lot of it now.

What do you think about that?
I don't know if it's right that they come out into the open. I'm not sure.

I think peoples' attitudes change towards them.

Do you think peoples' attitudes have changed and it's easier for them?
When they come out I think that peoples' attitudes might change towards them.

In what way, Sadie?
Well, they maybe won't like them the same, but I mean they're still the same as they were.

There was one when I was working at Croma Lodge. Well, I must just have been in my teens. The colonel lived in one of those houses on the common, you know, and his servant used to come in - a man - and I used to hear them talking about him, but I hadn't a clue what it meant. You know, Mickey McGuire and them used to be talking about him, so evidently he was one of them.

Were they gossiping?

Yeah, yeah, but I didn't know what they were talking about.

So you think it's better if they don't reveal their homosexuality because of what they'll get back?
It might be.

So did you think it's unfair what's being said about them?
Well they can't help it. It's not something they can help.

No, no it's something.....

Did you see that pair in the paper, was it last week or the week before. They'd been married for years and now the man has turned into a woman and they got married again. I thought that was stupid.

Och, well they don't know what their feelings are.

They're still staying together although he's a woman now.

Is that something you came across yourself Mary?
No, no. Well there were babies born that were neither one thing or the other but that's a different thing altogether.

And what did they do in that case Mary?
Well they leave the child to decide when they've come to an age what they want to be, what sex they wish to be. It's up to them to decide.

So I'm wondering if you think that the openness to things like that and the fact that attitudes have changed or are changing is a good thing?
Well, before they would hide it. They wouldn't speak about it.

Do you think that was better that way?
No I don't think so

It's just like couples that lived together long ago but it was never spoken about.

Same sex couples?

69

Just as they are now, and it was never spoken about.
Things are more open now, there's no doubt about that. I mean they're quite open about it now.

So you think it's a live and let live kind of a thing?
That's right. Well, it's their own lives anyway, they can do what they like.

So do you think that would be important to be part of a child's education, that these things are talked about openly to children as they grow up?
I think they probably are in school now.

There's so much of it in school now, the children – one-parent children in school nowadays.

Just before we finish – if you were talking with some of the school children, maybe ones along the road there nowadays, you know, and you were to say to them what you felt you had in school as part of your education that they don't have, that you feel is missing now, that maybe you think would have been useful for them to have, what might that be? What's gone?
They don't respect their elders. That's what's gone.

So some sort of training in how to be more respectful - you wish they had that.
That's right.

What would you like to see still there?
There have been a lot of changes.

Anything that you particularly regret?
Our generation before us, they were too strict. They went over the top the other way. You had to be in at a certain time and you'd to do this and do that. Now I think they get a wee bit more freedom.

Mam would be sitting up when we went to the dances during the war, mind. Dances were on to two o'clock in the morning, Mam would be waiting up. She'd be sitting up and I'd be sitting on the doorstep waiting for you.

So what do you wish for the children now, that you had in school, that's gone, that they might benefit from nowadays?
Children don't respect their parents in the way we did either.

They don't respect anybody Mary.

This thing about respect is very important to you?

And there's this thing about "If you hit me I'll report you to the police".
They're like the Nazis. That's just what it's like. They'd report their own
family. That's what it's coming to.

We were never allowed to call anyone by their first name, remember.
When I went down to Fife the ones next door used to call me Sadie. I
couldn't get over it, I mean, there was no respect at all.

So is that a sign of not being respectful?
Hmm, hmm.

Not to use your surname?
I remember I used to keep them for a wee while at night till their father
came home – their mother was working. Wee Scott had a chocolate
biscuit and George said to him "Go and get your hands washed Scott".
"No I will not". And yet the mother and father were very nice people.

*So what you'd really like for the children nowadays is a more
respectful climate for them to be growing up in?*
Things are so different really.

Well there's little Ross out there, Ross across there, Shirley's Ross. He
always says "Hello Mary", but I don't mind it at all. And the only reason
he knows is I got a lift home with his mum in the car one day and I was
down the church with them. So this is him. You'll hear him shouting far
away.

*So if you were doing that in reverse then. If you were to think of
what the children in school have today that you didn't have, what
would you have liked, especially liked, to have had in your
schooldays that they've got now?*
It's different, I think, altogether. It really is.

*So if you look at those differences and just pick one "I wish I'd
had that one".*
Possibly a bit more freedom to speak and voice your opinion, which we
wouldn't dare do.

And I would think they could discuss things with their teachers now.

And even children with their parents. They can discuss things with their
parents that before we wouldn't dare.

Part of the project involved a series of video interviews with Black and Asian Scots exploring issues of identity. The first person interviewed has asked to remain anonymous, and for most of the section relating to her experiences in an orphanage to be excluded. Scotland's self-portrayal as a nation tolerant of minority ethnic groups was certainly challenged by many of the contributors.

Where did your Mum and Dad meet?

In Leeds. Well, they met because the landlady at the time, two landladies, they both said that they had black tenants and they wanted to introduce them thinking that they were from the same country or the same origin, so they were introduced by their landlord, so that's how they met.

Do you know much about the previous generations of your Mum and Dad's families?

I don't really know. Well, I just know snippets. I know that my Dad's father he owned a timber business, a huge business, so he was quite wealthy and he was quite a, I'd better not say this on tape, what was he, he was a man about town, and he went around Europe and he spent a lot of money wherever he went, and he was more European than most Europeans, because he thought that was the best way to be, so he wore suits and hats and he made my dad wear a tie and collar and umbrella to school in the heat.

When did he come to Britain?

I don't exactly know but I know that Dad, he ran away partly because of his father's way of living and he wanted to spread his wings so he actually stowed away in a ship and was caught and then had to work his passage, but because he was such a young boy, he was only 16 or 17, they let him away with it so he landed in Britain without having any experience whatsoever, and he spoke English and French but he learnt his English, but some of his English is very strange and we used to laugh at him because he pronounced words like character as 'cheracter' and canary as cenary. So he ran away and ended up in Leeds and my Mum was dancing in Germany. I don't know if it was when the war broke out but they were thrown out. Her and her sister had quite a lot of gold and things and all their stuff, it was all taken off them, and they were just given 11 dollars and she arrived here as well and then she ended up working in a munitions factory.

Do you know about her family?

Her family, well they're quite interesting in some ways. Her Dad worked for a chemical company. I think he was the manager of it but I think when the British partition of India in 47, I think that he, they sacked all the people with Indian sounding names that were in good jobs. He was an accountant and he lost his job so they never had any money for a couple of years, and then he actually changed their name to Park, English version of the name Parick, so he got a job similar back again, but a lot of his neighbours didn't so what he did was he used to buy bags of rice and share it. He gave it to his neighbours but he didn't actually tell them it was him but he shared it with them. I think that was pretty impressive but it must have been galling to have to change his name to Park the English. An Anglo Indian so he could get work. My Mum and her sisters, they still lived there, they still went to good schools. My aunt told me, she was the bully, she was the tough one, she played marbles and she beat all the boys and she was quite tough but my Mum was quite, had dysentery when she was little so she was quite frail so she was spoiled. She was the spoiled one. So she got looked after all the time and my aunt was being looked after and it continued all their lives actually.

How long did you stay in Edzel?
I think only a year.

So you've no memories of it.
I've no memories of it at all. I keep meaning to go back there. I heard the place was closing. I just wanted to see it. I was, when I was born there was a thing set up for mothers and babies, and it was the first in Dundee. In fact it was in the Dundee People's Story and it was the first acknowledgement that women were not natural mothers.

Where did the family move to?

That's the difficult bit. All the children moved to Aberdeen. My Dad stayed in Dundee and my Mum moved to London so the family broke up. They all went off to an orphanage..... Pretty grim.

There followed a graphic account of the woman's experiences of ten years in the orphanage that she asked to be excluded from this publication.

Was being Black an issue then?

Well it was and it wasn't. We never got called names but we knew we were Black because there was one other Black boy there, and people used to always say "Is that your brother, is that your brother?" And I would say "No, he's not my brother", you know, so it was an issue around that.

Nothing overt?

No nothing overt. No names. No that's quite surprising. We never got any. Not that I'd remember. I don't remember it. I remember feeling it but I don't remember hearing it.

From the other kids?

I don't remember. I do remember feeling, I remember feeling different. I don't remember ever being called names.

At school?

At that school. No. Not when we were at the convent. Probably too traumatised. Probably didn't hear it. Probably traumatised and didn't know it.

But I remember I got a black doll and I didn't like it. My Dad called it Congo Sue and I hated it. I hated the fact that he'd called it Congo Sue. Why couldn't it just be called Sue. I didn't know why. It was funny. I remember thinking to myself why I didn't like that, but I didn't. People used to ask me the name of it I would just go (mumbles) "Congo Sue", you know, so I didn't like it. But I actually liked the doll. I didn't like it. The fact that he'd attracted the blackness to it by calling it Congo Sue and I didn't like it. I remember feeling embarrassed by it and I didn't like it. I did like the doll and I did take it home with me.

To Cowdenbeath?

To Cowdenbeath yes. They were horrible to us at school then. I wrote a poem about it because I hadn't really realised I was black until I went to Fife and then I was walking along the road to school when everybody kept shouting these names at me and I was literally like this, looking over my shoulder going "who are you shouting at?" And it wasn't until the third or fourth day and I was like, "It's me" and I was like "What's this?" because I hadn't heard it before. And then I got a real shock being black and started feeling less because it was constant everywhere I went. It was constant. It was from the adults as well. It was constant. It was daily. There were always people talking about it. Always people staring. It was just like we couldn't go anywhere without comments being made and I hadn't had it. It was quite a shock and I knew that it was derogatory as well but I didn't understand it. I couldn't figure it out you know.

What would people say?

Blackie, wog and sparkie, nignog.

Just from the other side of the street?

Yeah. Just from the other side of the street. I'd just be walking past or they'd just point and laugh. They'd just go (snigger) like that whenever I appeared or somebody would come up and just push someone into me and run away laughing. It was something to take in because it was sprung on you.

Was it a council house?

It was a miner's cottage. Miner's cottage. It was called Miner's Road. Great big, huge. You see them in old 50s films. The staircase going right up. The outside staircase. There was five of us. There was only one bedroom so we all slept in the one bedroom, all the kids, and my Dad slept in the living room. There was a kitchen. There was no bathroom. There was just a toilet and a double sink. That was it but I thought it was fine, but when we got a bit older it was hellish. Well, I didn't notice at first but they were like, maybe I was about 11 and they must have been about 13, 14, 15, and we were still sharing the same bedrooms with each other, and we had two double beds and a single bed so me and my sister had one of them and my oldest brother he had the single one.

So it must have been strange not seeing terribly much of them for the previous 10 years or so and then...

Yes it was a bit strange. Well it was funny how fast we adapted, but we spent the next three years sitting around the table talking to each other because my Dad used to say "Have you not finished yet?" because we used to sit down at breakfast and still be there at teatime, still sitting there at teatime, talking talking talking talking talk. We did that for three years solid almost. We just talked and talked. We played cards and monopoly or something but we just sat and talked and talked and talked to each other, so it was almost like a ritual getting to know each other. That's how we did it. There was no happy social workers coming to and getting us used to no being in an institution then back in the family, or helping my Dad suddenly being a single parent, a single person and then suddenly having five very needy children all of a sudden. Nothing done to help us through that, but you know because I wasn't thinking about that, it wasn't there, so we just did it ourselves, we just kept chatting. I just decided "Well, fuck it". Missed the last 10 years so I thought I'm not going to miss the next five years, so I just joined every club I could think of so, you know, to try to fit all of my childhood into the next five or six years. It's the others. They tended to stay in the house. They just found it more difficult to cope with because they were older than me. I think I was luckier in some ways because I came home at $10^{1/2}$, so I had a year and a half at primary and I made quite good friends there, so you know, I had a bit of, I don't know, ordinary life, I suppose, so I grew up a wee bit with two years staying at that primary school which was just a wee one, an Mr Bryce was really nice and I had a wee gang and, you know, they were very tolerant of me because I was upside down and inside out because I didn't know what to do. It was a strange world, so I just kept running around and getting into trouble and just being really rebellious. I don't know. I didn't know what to do with myself because it was just too different and the headmaster was really nice. He kept taking me in for chats but he was really good, so I think my life would have been a lot more difficult if I hadn't spent it there, because the rest of them went straight to secondary school and they didn't get that kind, of support that I did and the people were already established, so friendships.....and we were much younger than our age. Do you know what I mean? My sister was 13 and my brother was 15. In reality, because we were institutionalised, we were about five years younger than we were. We were like, a lot younger. We didn't know things that our peers knew. So like babies, so it must have been really difficult for them but for me it was easier. I was with, I just managed to get into a good group, and they were quite excited to have me in their group especially, when they found out I was $10^{1/2}$ because they said "Oh great, you're in our group," and it was really nice because I was in that group til I left and it was just, I had space, a bit of space to grow up before sort of plunged into secondary school. It gave me time to adapt a bit to being normal living so I think I was a bit luckier than the rest of them or maybe just a different personality.

Were there any other Black families in the town?
No. We were it.

Were there any Chinese or anything?
No.

Any other kind of incomers even?
No. We were it. When we arrived they opened their windows and
opened their doors to look at us. They couldn't believe that these five
Black children were walking in. Cowdenbeath of all places. To take us
there. God, he could have taken us to a town, a big town or something,
but to take us to Cowdenbeath. It was ridiculous.

Did your Dad talk about being a Black man down the mines?
Well he did a bit. Well there was a Polish man there, Bobbie Lair, and
him and my Dad teamed up because they both got stick all the time and
got called names and got a hard time, so those two sort of banded
together, so he did talk about it a little bit but not that much. He just got
a hard time. He also talked about Bobbie's hard time because they would
lift up poles and say "look what can we see. We can see a pole", and
things like that so he used to come round to our house a lot. We didn't
really talk about it a lot. We were a bit pissed off with him because he
didn't really educate us about being African and he didn't educate us
about being Black and he didn't tell us how to survive it, or when we
came home from school he didn't really listen to what was being said to
us, and we kind of knew that there was no point in saying to him, so he
didn't prepare us for it and we were a bit pissed off about that later on.
He could at least have warned us that this was going to happen, you
know, and then what do we do with it because it's happening all the
time, and he didn't say much about it at all. And he used to say that we
were older, we were teenagers, and we were really pissed off. There
was a man down in Cowdenbeath that used to call him "Boy". He called
him boy for 20 years and we were like "Dad! Don't let him call you 'Boy'.
Say something to him." And finally he did. He told him off. He said
"Don't call me Boy. I'm a man the same as you." And I was like "Thank
God." It took him 20 years of being called boy. I can't remember if it
was the butchers. It was some shop that he used to go to regularly and
this man was saying "What do you want boy?" and my Dad used to like
dress up a bit like his granda in jacket and shirt and tie and he used to
doff his hat to everybody. "Dad! Stop it!" He was so polite to everybody.
He was very Nigerian but they took advantage of it. They didn't respect
him for it you know. They just thought he was a strange Black man, but
even though they called him boy and all these things, he'd still lift his hat
up and say good morning and it was like "Dad!" He'd just come from a
different generation and they thought this was the norm and everything
being wonderful and happy. He was more Victorian than the Victorians.
He had books of proverbs and we'd say "Tell us some African proverbs,"

and he can quote us any English proverb from anywhere, and he had all these books on proverbs and classic Penguin books. Oh my God. We couldn't have had a more British upbringing and we were like "Dad"! Because his father had been like that too. He wanted to be European because he thought it would have been good, so he didn't really, you know............

Did you have any trappings of Africa around the house?
No. The only really thing that he sort of...well funnily enough his music was, he had lots of records and lots of music was South American, but we didn't know until we were older that his granddad was Brazilian, you know, so Gomez African Brazilian. That's where his musical tastes come from. His mother had played that music, but he was into classical, like Tchaikovsky, Chopin, and he knew everything about everything. So he tried to be very European and very polite and very well mannered and his writing, oh God, it was real old fashion copperplate, but even more so, and it was beautiful, but he was just always trying to be something else.

So you moved to secondary school. That was very different, was it?
That was a nightmare. Went up to high school so there was a separation of different class, classes, but a lot of it was to do with me being Black definitely. I felt like an untouchable and I was treated like an untouchable. It was hell on earth.

Again, were you the only Black family there?
Yes and by the time I got up my brother was just there for another six months, so my older brother and sisters had already left, so it was just him and me and because it was Catholic schools and boys and girls weren't together, so there wasn't any sort of support from him, but then he left and it was just me, so it was pretty hard. It was hell.

What kinds of things did you experience?
It's too hard. Not one of the boys in my class would ever ever speak to me and they'd be quite open about it. They would never sit next to me, and even some of the girls. A lot of the time I would be sitting on my own and I felt very isolated and treated very badly, and even from the teachers. It was very hard. It was just a nightmare. I decided that being really rebellious and getting really into lots of trouble........That was my reaction to it because I thought "Oh fuck you. If you hate me then, well, fuck it, I'm not going to do anything that you want me to do," so I just became an absolute pain in the arse. That was my reaction. It was because I was really hurt and it's not nice to feel that all these people don't like you just because of the colour of your skin, so I became a pain in the arse. Got into lots of trouble. Some of it I enjoyed. I enjoyed being a pain in the arse. Other times it was quite lonely. It was quite hard, but

there was nothing I could do about it which was quite hard and I couldn't tell my Dad. Nobody was really acknowledging it. I couldn't really tell the teachers, so nobody was really that bothered and, of course, then they would say, "Oh it's her, troublemaker." Calling me all these names, "Brat," but if they'd just sat down and asked me why, I might have been able to tell them what was going on. They didn't bother us though. I didn't bother and they didn't bother so.

Did you fight?

Yes I did, physically, then I got fed up with that. It wasn't doing any good. I suppose my real fight when I look back was just being a pain in the arse, and pretending they didn't get to me because that was my way of coping.

How were you academically?

Shite. Well, I'm actually a very bright person but I was dyslexic at school and because I didn't know, they didn't know, so I was in the stupid class so I didn't do anything at school. It's funny enough. I don't know how I knew but I knew I was bright all the time. It didn't show in my work. The two things we concentrated on at school was maths and english and that's the two subjects dyslexia shows up the worst. With your grammar and your spelling and your numeracy. For me they were the areas that it showed up the most, so you were always being tested on those areas, so it always looked like I was stupid and I knew I wasn't, so my education was really abysmal. I educated myself.

Was your religion any bone of contention?

Yeah it was but my Blackness seemed to override it but it was more, we couldn't go through certain schools. There was a shortcut through Moss Side and we couldn't go through there because the Protestants would kill us, and you know, my friend used to walk down Stenners Street and she didn't tell us. We were mad at her when I was older because we were friends right up until our 20s and she didn't tell me that she'd get beaten up every day because she was Catholic, and she was the only person who went down that way because it was down to the High Street and most people would have gone the other way, so it was that kind of thing, so it was only group's situations. Sometimes they'd go "Get her because she's a Catholic" but then you don't have to run, but we were just as bad. I mean the two, the two schools. There was St Columbus and there was Beath High across the road and we'd all chuck bricks at each other and especially snowballs with stones in them and it would be, you know, just fun to go get the proddies. It was terrible but there was that kind of thing went on, but then I hadn't really understood the sectarianism until I was older, and then there was a lot going on about jobs, and different things like that, when I was older or just the way we were being treated, and we didn't realise it was because we were Catholics. We thought it was because we were Black but a lot of the time it was because we were Catholics and we didn't realise that.

Was your Dad a practising Catholic?
No. We weren't Catholics when we went into..... They baptised us without his permission so we weren't really supposed to be Catholics at all.

Did you feel at all religious yourself?
When I was growing up? It's a hard one because they force-fed it to us, so we were very religious in a certain sense because, you know, it was like being indoctrinated since I was one. I could read the Magnificat in full when I was three, well I knew it off by heart I was told. Things like that. We were very religious. My whole upbringing was religious so that's yes, I was religious.

Did you continue going to chapel when you went to Cowdenbeath?
Oh yeah, we thought we'd go to Hell if we didn't. We had to. My Dad even threatened to throw us out of the house. He threatened to throw us out of the house. Told us to pack our bags if we dared to go to church on the Sunday and we had a conference between us and decided that God would want us to go to church, so how's that for indoctrination? We really thought we'd go to Hell if we didn't go to church on Sunday, so we all went off. We left the suitcases outside the door and off we went to church. We thought we were being really good.

Why didn't he want you to go?
He wasn't a Catholic and he wanted us to be religious. He was changing his views about religion then so he didn't want us to go.

I thought he was kind of religious until that day and then I was really surprised that he did that, but then I was really surprised that we all went to church. We gave up our family to go to church because he was serious. We thought he was serious. We packed our suitcases. Off we went and I remember thinking how good we were. My brother and I often talk about it and he said that my sister, my older sister he says that she was amazing. She shouted at him and told him that he couldn't do that to them. If we wanted to go to church we should go to church because I don't remember that, but my brother says that my sister was really impressive and told him what was what.

I never got educated until I was 30. Well I never started my education until I was 30.

Did you continue to work in Fife?
Aye. I continued to work in Fife and I got married and I had children.

So what prompted you to go into education?
Well I was 29 and I thought "Bloody hell, I haven't done anything. I've

just been a housewife and in a factory, and I thought I haven't done anything." Well before that when I was 21 I decided to go to night school and got one O-level and I thought "Oh, I've got an O-level," and I was quite pleased with myself, and it was english actually.

Then I was pregnant..... and I decided to go back again, well I didn't know I was pregnant...... and I went back again to the night school and there were no O-levels and they said "Do you want to take a higher in history?" so I said "Ok, I'll try that," so I passed that and thought "I'm not stupid" and that was that and I gave up for a while, and then when I was 30 I thought "Oh fuck, I have to do something" so I tried the OU, Open University, and I thought I can do that with kids, so I thought "Right", and I got the first thing through and I was shocked I tell you. I owe my life to the Open University. The Open University changed my life completely. Completely opened the door and I can never thank it enough because up til that point I didn't have a didly of who I was, what I thought. I didn't even know what political right wing, left wing meant, I didn't even know what a legal party was. I didn't know anything. I was completely ignorant in that sense, in that kind of formal sense.

Yeah it did. It changed my life. God, if it wasn't for the Open University where would I be?

My life's just been one huge struggle so yes! I deserve a Twix at least for my life.

I was born in Cape Town South Africa. I was born when the VJ treaty was signed and my name was Vienna Jessica, and at school they called me Vienna sausages which is a really wee sausage, which is a red sausage, that's why my name is now Jessica, and I was called Jessica van Niekerk. I think the nurse must have told my mother to call me something with a v and they thought of Vienna because with VJ, the victory over Japan. I was born soon after that. That was August 1945 so this August I'll be 55 which has come very suddenly.

A lot of Boers, when I started work and I'd give my name would think I was white. And now I'm called Jessica MacEwen so now they think that I'm a wee Scottish lassie. But it's just one of those things. Part of life.

Jessica at school aged 7

My Mum was a housewife, she had 10 children and my Dad worked for the council. He was the driver on the steamroller that flattens the tar on the road and as a child I remember we would drive down to the beach and he would say "I made this road and I made that road," and he made every road in South Africa you know. And to try and supplement the income both my Mum and Dad worked as caterers. My mother always remembers the time when the two princesses came to South Africa. Princess Margaret and Princess Elizabeth. And it was her 21st birthday party and she had it in the city hall in Cape Town and my mum was the waitress there. And she says she remembers being in the room where the princess had her fur cape over the chair and the waitresses all had a little touch, they had a feel of the princess's cape, and my mum used to always tell us the story.

We always had food in the house but when she went out catering, whatever was left she would always bring it home, bits to eat and interesting food to eat. So that's how, they always were out and it was hard. And I remember as a child, Mondays was washday, no washing machines or anything like that. Monday was washday, clothes washing, and the next day was ironing and the next day was bedding: washing, sheets and so on, it would really kill me. It was hard I think, it was quite hard, and having 10 children. I think we were.......every two years we were born, every two years we had a child.

I think my Mum, I've not managed to find out much because when I went home they didn't talk too much about the background, but I think my ancestors must be from India. There was quite a large Indian population that came over to work on the sugar plantations in Durban and I think that they must have been the Tamales or people from Sri Lanka. But I'm never quite sure because we never got that history. So her ancestors must be Indian in origin because they look quite Indian. And my Dad his mother was white, hence the surname van Niekerk so he's from Boer origin. And that was..... Apartheid started soon after 1947, 1950, soon after Apartheid came into force. And before that people loved black, white, brown, yellow, all of them together. Some were married, some had children and when Apartheid came in these people had to be separated. Families were separated and whatever, so we were slotted in a group that the government called the Cape Coloured community because we were all of mixed race. My older brother who's dead now, sort of looked Indian but the rest of my sisters are obviously mixed race.

You weren't thought of as a person if you were Black, so you kind of kept yourself in the background. It wasn't a very happy time I must say

Jessica age 8 with her Mum and Dad and brothers, Keith and Tommy

and you didn't have a very high regard for yourself, because if you're Black you're nothing and I think I was the Blackest in the family so it wasn't very nice, which I thought at the time, growing up.

It's the usual in South Africa when a child is born, they want to know what colour the child is. I mean it's propaganda, it's brainwashing. And if you had a fight with your sisters the first thing they call you is Kaffir, this horrible word which is very.....quite an insult which you felt at the time. So yes, as a child I kind of didn't want to be noticed..... Very quiet, kept to myself. Because all the children in the Coloured community are different colours of people and I think I was just naturally a quiet person. It was ok. It wasn't too bad.

Where was your home?
In Claremont, which is sort of about seven miles from the city of Capetown. Very pretty area, and you had some parts of the suburbs white areas and some parts you had coloured areas. And the Africans were all mostly further along the coast in their area, in little sort of townships and because of Apartheid, and only the whites who could vote, you didn't get involved in any politics and you didn't say much even in the house, you just kept quiet. And when I started working and you didn't dare make any comments because your parents would tell you, "Just keep quiet."

I think I was quite quietly determined to get out. I was always the one who made a fuss about the government in Mozambique. I was told by my Mum to keep quiet and I was lucky to be alive and just as long as you got food in your mouth and a roof over your head you should be thankful. And I always felt that I'm not a second class person, I'm a human being and I deserve better, and I always felt that it was wrong what was happening to the Africans and the way people were being treated. I always felt that that was wrong.

Yes. Apartheid was the pits. I mean imagine walking into a public gardens and even the benches had .... you couldn't even sit on the benches and the buses. Black people had to go up to the top of the bus and you had heavy people African and coloured..... heavy with the shopping and the Africans always had lots of washing which they did for the white people and they had these huge bags on their heads and they had to get upstairs and downstairs would be empty because all the whites had cars and that kind of thing, you know.

What did it make you feel?
Just anger and that's why I had to get away. I planned it and saved up because there was no money in the house. So you worked and you saved up and you just didn't go out or do anything and you saved your money, enough money for the fare, to have this journey. And once I'd got enough of this money together I left.

I left school at.......must have been about 16,17, and I started getting really fed up when I was 21, 22 and when I started working and I was getting nowhere fast, so it must have been about four years I systematically started saving up with a view of leaving.

I left school and then I got a job as a clerk and then I went to evening classes to learn shorthand and book keeping and that was for four years while working during the day and earning a measly sum. And then I got a job as a secretary, I remember, in a big furniture company and I did all the correspondence and was always called in to my boss to take down dictation. And he said to me

Jessica age 17.

he can't be bothered with the Boer girl who was earning twice, if not three times as much as me because she couldn't read back her shorthand. And that kind of unfairness was going on all the time. Because you were coloured you did a job but you were never paid a decent wage and you were exploited left right and centre, and I just got fed up with the whole system and I just left because at that time, that was 1971. In the '60s a lot of people left or were deported. A lot of my friends went to Australia. I decided to come to Britain because I felt that I had the shorthand, the secretarial skills, and I could probably start and I knew that it would be better for me to try and get a job in Britain, and I had an aunt who worked for a very rich lady who spent six months of the year, in Britain during the summer and then she'd go to South Africa six months of the year and my aunt worked for her all her life. She didn't really have a life. So I came over and stayed with her for the first two weeks when I came to Britain and I found my way and then never looked back.

What were your first impressions of Britain?

I always remember first arriving. We came on the ship. We got off in Trieste in Italy and travelled through Paris and it was pouring with rain and we came to Earls Court where all the South Africans and Australians usually come to. It's still like that and we stopped in this hotel which we had for a week, and put down our luggage and freshened up. It must have been, what we thought, about five o'clock in the afternoon and we went outside and went for a little walk around and then my friend said "What's the time?" and we looked at our watches and it was half past nine and we said "What's happening here, it's so light?" and usually in

South Africa, seven o'clock come summer or winter it's dark, and we couldn't believe it was so light and then we went down to Piccadilly Circus and saw Black and white people walking together hand in hand and we couldn't believe it, you know it was amazing. 1970 was still quite serious Apartheid, terrible Apartheid. Things were getting worse, so it was really amazing and the policemen, because at one time we were lost, we went to visit someone, we'd been given an address and we were lost and we asked a policeman and they were really friendly and really nice and friendly and spoke to you in a civilised way and it was mind boggling. London was great, full of life and friendliness. It was good.

Why are some people racist? Is it fear? What is it that makes them think that they are superior. Where does it come from? Why does man behave that way, and even now when you think of slavery and what people do to their own human fellow, it's amazing, and a lot of the whites stayed there and

London, 1972

enjoyed the fruits of the country and exploited the African servants by saying to themselves, "Well, they prefer us putting the food out at the back door like dogs, a plate of food there, you eat, they prefer that and that's how you must speak to them in a different manner. That's the way to treat them because they're not real", and in the bible, the Afrikana bible, the African people, the blacks were put on this road to be treated like dogs and they're not really human. Well, what are they? And people actually believe that so where does it come from?

It's still very difficult for me to see a white South African and feel...I need to speak to that person for a while to get the vibes because you soon get the vibes. There are some good South Africans but few and far between.

How did that relate to marrying your white husband?
When I was in London, before I met my husband, it was quite cagey. Everyone I met I would suss them out and feel the vibes. And I slowly started trusting people because I had a really really nice German friend

and she was sincere...... and realised that not all people think the way the Boers do, and the white British who went to South Africa and became even more racist. And I started trusting white people. And when I met my husband it was at a party and my husband was working for the Race Relations Board and I went with a friend who was at the time working with the Community Relations Council or something. I think they've probably changed now but the two councils had joined together there for a Christmas party and that's where I met him. And he was funny, and because he was working for the Race Relations Board I felt that he

Jessica and husband after their wedding in 1974.

wouldn't be working there if he was racist or anything. And he was a lawyer ...and he became a legal advisor at the Race Relations Board, so I thought he was a good white, which he is.

That was '72 I met him and we went out for a couple of years. He's from Scotland. He lived in Scotland, and in August '74 we got married and we came to Scotland and I've been here ever since.

He had a flat in Gardeners Crescent, top floor flat, and we moved in to this flat when we came to Scotland. It was September so the weather wasn't too bad but we'd come and go and you'd hardly see anyone and I thought, you know, "Where are all the people?" And I'm always very aware that I am Black and people don't like me because I'm Black and I always thought maybe people are avoiding me because I'm Black and not knowing what to expect. But people just kept themselves to themselves because at home people was always walking past you, you're always talking to someone and someone is always coming in to the house but I soon found out here that you have to make appointments before you go and see people. You just can't go and see people and maybe after six months I met the family that lived opposite on the same landing as us. Elderly couple and they had a daughter. Lovely girl and I remember onc day going to the supermarket and I met the mother in the shop and I said "How's your daughter? I can't remember the name." And she said, "Oh she's fine. She's got a really nice boyfriend and as a rule I don't believe in mixed marriages" she said to me so I immediately thought "Oh goodness, Martin and me, Black and white." But what she was referring to was Catholic and Protestant........and I thought to myself, "My God, you're all the same colour, how do you know the difference?" But anyway, that was my first intro to the Catholic and Protestant. Because in South Africa that kind of news was not broadcast or on the radio or on the television, because of course the people of South Africa, all the whites stuck together and it was only the Black and white issue in South Africa. Whereas in the rest of the world it was all kinds of other bigoted racism.

Are you starting to feel Scottish?
Yes, I've got loads of friends in Scotland and I'm really settled in Scotland and having experienced just two incidents of someone coming up to me and saying "Go home", I've always felt really safe and happy in Scotland, and the theatres and studying and doing things and there's always somewhere to go and I feel quite safe in Scotland. I just wish the weather was a bit better.

You haven't had much experience of racism in Scotland then?
No, not personally. There's been undertones and I just put it down. I've lived with it all my life and I'm always prepared for it and sometimes I'll say something and other times I'll think , "You're really not worth it".

But only twice people have been...the one time when a person came up to me, she was a bitter old person, female, and she just said to me "Go home!" and this really upset me, but then I thought she's such a twisted old person, I'm not going to waste my time with her. And I try and avoid situations where I think it could turn nasty. People could turn nasty. And I try and avoid racists. I mean, I don't go out at night unless I go with my husband in the car, but not on my own. I won't go on my own anywhere.

Is this fear of racist attacks?
Yes, I've always been apprehensive...... you had to be careful in South Africa. So I've just as a rule...I don't feel happy going off on my own, walking about in the streets on my own.

Have you ever got involved in Black politics in Scotland?
Not a lot while my Mum was still alive. Because I wanted to join the Anti-Apartheid movement at the time and I wrote to her and I said I was going to do that and she said just remember that all your family was still living in Cape Town. And she said to remember that you will put us in danger, which was true so I never did. And I've been to maybe a couple of marches, but really low key because my family were there and I didn't think it would be fair on them. I mean the BOSS, the undercover police in South Africa were quite ruthless. You just didn't take any chances.

They were called the BOSS?
They were called BOSS, yeah. I'm not sure. Maybe it was a nickname. The special service.

What about in your job?
I've always worked for ethnic minority communities in the work place. When I first came to Scotland I worked for the Royal National Lifeboat Institute and it was ok. I mean I did go for jobs and I just didn't get work. Maybe it was racist, I don't know, but I just didn't want to work there if I didn't get the job because that's the feeling. You get that feeling, you feel numb, I don't need this. I don't need hang-ups like this, so I've always worked in places where I've felt good vibes. I've quite enjoyed my work.

I've got two daughters. I took them to visit my family in South Africa and within two days she started questioning, why she couldn't go on that swing, why she couldn't go and play on that beach and I kept saying, "We can't, it's for whites only." "Why is it for whites only?" We were there for two months and it was very difficult because she questioned all the time. Unfortunately, because when she came back, with a realisation that if you are black you are inferior and it was quite damaging for her coming back and having to cope living in a white society, because that's maybe, late 1970s, and I think it was hard for her so she hated South Africa, she hated my family, she never wanted to go back to South

Africa. So when she graduated, and I was very pleased that she did sociology and she did a paper on the Chinese, a paper on the Blacks in America and a dissertation on being a Black Scot. And when she graduated she said to me, "I'd like to go and meet your family in South Africa". And I was really pleased. So we all went to South Africa in '98 and my husband and I were there for about a month and they came and joined us and we took them round the peninsula and she kept saying "Mum, look at all these Black people. It's wonderful". Because she was so used to seeing white people here. And she said "Why did you leave?" Because it was the new South Africa and Capetown was really bustling. It was a wonderful feeling because it was November and I really wanted to stay on and the thought of coming back to Scotland in November, in winter, didn't appeal to me at all but we left them there with my sisters. My sisters were delighted to have them and they stayed there four months, so they loved it, and they decided they would go on to Australia and they're still not back so I'm hoping that, well, I think that they'll be back end of June, so they're still travelling, but she loved it. She feels, she said to me that she wouldn't mind doing her PhD in Cape Town University so I'll see how she feels when she comes back.

How do they cope with their white Dad?
They love their Dad so much. Their Dad is a very quiet person and very Scottish, doesn't like showing love and affection, but they smother him with love and affection. So its been quite good for him and its been a good balance, and one's got his humour. Very dry humour. He still makes me laugh. It's a very nice relationship. A very happy relationship.

So what percentage of Scottish would you say you are now?
I've been here longer than I've lived in South Africa, about four years longer. I think I'm more Scottish only because I've lived here most of the time, because when I did go home in, '97, the country had changed that much that I felt like a foreigner. I mean, I did recognise some places and, because the violence had increased, my sisters wouldn't let me travel alone. So I felt a bit unfamiliar with the place and my Afrikaans had gone to pot, and every time I tried to speak it they would laugh at me. So I didn't feel South African and I was under the impression that even though I was walking in the centre thinking that I was just another South African, I think that people took me for not being from South Africa. I think it was something my sister said, she said, "Watch your back and watch this and be careful. You stick out like a sore thumb." Because I did try and speak Afrikaans but it didn't sound right. Even to me it didn't sound right.

What do you think would make Scotland an easier place to live for Black or mixed race people?
When people say that they have been attacked and it's a racist attack it's good that they are recognising now that it is a racist attack and it will

Jessica on her 50th birthday.

not be tolerated. Maybe a stronger, not severe, but sentences to say that "Look this is not on." People should be allowed to live without fear. I think it's really an awful way to live your life when you are afraid to go out. But people should introduce laws. It all remains for the government to introduce laws. If not it could get worse. I mean, at the moment, with all this refugee crisis and what Hague is on about, it just takes a little thing to start something escalating. The world is getting more violent so you need laws to say it's not on. But I have lived with wonderful Scottish people. I find a lot of the Scottish people genuine, friendly and there's a lot of good people out there and Scotland is a lovely place, friendly. Especially in Leith. You stand at the bus stop in Leith, and my daughters laugh at me. Within a bus journey I will get a little old lady telling me her whole life history..... and this one lady I always meet at the bus stop and I said to her "My daughter's going to Australia" and she immediately said "I must give you my daughter's address." And then we sent them an e-mail and Martin said "Your mum's met a lady and she's given you her daughter's address." And she wrote back and said "I know the people that mum meets at the bus stop."

Ethnic minorities have got a lot to offer and there's a richness out there and it could be good and I think Scotland's a beautiful country.

91

Glasgow hosted three Salt Of The Earth groups. One was based in the Gorbals area, where the participants explored aspects of Scots-Irish identity and traditions. Another was in conjunction with the West of Scotland Society for the Blind, where experiences of disability and life in general were shared and recorded. The third was based in Maryhill Library and the group followed a weekly topic format. A book similar to the successful Midlothian format was produced, incorporating contributions from all three.

One of the participants from the Maryhill group has cerebral palsy and while he contributed each week in the recorded sessions, his speech difficulties did not allow his full story to be heard there. However, he has written down his experiences and has allowed us to present an extract here.

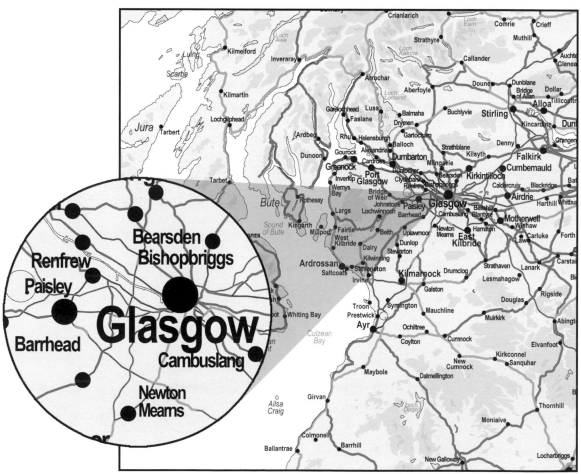

The XYZ Digital Map Company (www.xyzmaps.com)

Gorbals group

Maryhill group

My earliest memories are from the time I was five years old. I realised I was different from other children. I couldn't do anything for myself. My Mum Mary, my two sisters Cathy and Jean, and myself lived with my parents in 40 Mair Street, Govan. We stayed in a groundfloor flat. There was not a lot of room for all of us. We had a room and a kitchen with a tiny scullery off it. The toilet was inside.

My Mum worked hard. She was an engineering worker who went out early in the morning to Galloways in Middlesex Street.

Edward, his mum and sister

I was looked after a lot of the time by my Granny. She would put me outside on a decent day. I had a great pal, his name was Andy Brennan, he would come over and speak to me when I was outside. One of the other boy's, a guy called Jimmy, was cheeky and he used to hit me if he saw me.

At this time I couldn't go anywhere in my chair. It had three wheels but didn't work well. It was a wooden framed one covered in wicker.

I slept in a wooden bed chair till I was six, and the only way my mum could take me to the doctor or the dentist was to carry me wrapped up in a shawl.

I hated the dentist. He used to bribe me with a penny if I would sit still. I don't think I got too many pennies. Every time I passed the door of the dentists I would try to kick it.

Although my sisters attended the local school, Our Lady and Saint Margaret, I never got the chance of an education. This is something I regret to this day.

My mum used to go to the 'steamie' a lot. It was in Mair Street. She would get all the dirty washing and bundle it in a shawl and walk there. I always remember this. I suppose a lot of the washing was mine. I was always needing my clothes changed.

Edward's Granny and Grandad

My Grandad worked for Scottish Farmers. He was a driver of the milk lorry. He used to go out very early in the morning. Sometimes he would bring me home bottle tops to play with.

On a Sunday night we used to play dominoes. Grandad would put a penny on the fireguard and the winner got a hot penny. This was great fun.

My Mum's brother Robert was in the Royal Marines – the Commandos, and he used to come to stay when he got leave. I enjoyed playing with his hat and the other army gear he brought home.

Some Sunday nights Mum used to send out to the café for ice-cream. We had a large black jug and it was filled up.

As I got bigger it was more difficult for my Mum to look after me. She asked the doctor for some help and the result was that one day when I was about 13 years old, the 'Green Lady' came. We were not expecting her my Mum was still out at work. This person said that she had come to take me away.

It was wintertime. I had nothing ready. She took me down to a car. Granny put some clothes in a case and I was off. I was upset I did not get the chance to say cheerio to my Mum. My Granny was in tears. I was really worried and afraid. No one had told me where I was going.

I was taken to Caldwell House outside the village of Uplawmoor.

Caldwell House

We got to Caldwell House and it was dark. The place looked terrible. It was a big house. I soon found out that boys and girls were kept well separated. We lived and slept in our own houses.

Meals were brought round by van. It was just like a jail sentence. I think

Edward and his mum and dad on the right with some friends

now about the prisoners in Barlinnie. The staff were kind but the meals were terrible.

Our daily routine was so boring. We got up at 7am were washed and dressed and had breakfast at 9am. We then got board games to play for the rest of the morning. Sometimes it was jigsaws. It was the same everyday and I was so bored. I had great difficulty trying to use my hands anyway.

Lunch was at 12 noon and sometimes we got to sit outside if the weather was good.

In the summer we sometimes got on a bus run to Saltcoats or Ayr or Largs. If the weather was rotten we got more board games to fill in the afternoon.

Tea was at 5pm and after that we got ready for bed and we were in bed for 7pm.

With mum and dad.

The other really annoying thing was that my name had to be sewn on to all my clothes. Mind you, everyone else had the same treatment.

Some of the boys I first met at Caldwell are still my friends today and include Martin O'Connor and Brian McMaster. They are at Hillington now with me.

During my time at Caldwell my Mum remarried. My step Dad was called John Sharp. He was a really nice man and we got on well. John was a crane driver down at Govan Docks. He stayed next door to my Gran.

Every Saturday John and my Mum would come and visit me. They would get a bus from St Enoch Square and we would have two hours together. They always brought me something to eat and a bottle of ginger.

In the summer months when I got out to sit in the garden I'd get a stick and dig a hole in the ground. I was always keen to do some gardening but this was the only way I could try it.

The other thing I'd try at that time was getting around with my wheelchair. I'd get out of my chair and grab hold of my Mum's arm and try to walk a bit. Sometimes I would sit on the ground and shuffle around. I also practiced rolling to a hut which was in the grounds. It felt really good when I got there. The hut was empty but the hill down it was quite steep so it was a dangerous thing to do really. All these things helped me to cope with the boredom.

I got home twice a year from Caldwell. I got two weeks at summer and a week at Xmas. My Mum had to write to the doctor to get permission to take me away.

There was only public transport for me to get home. Mum used to wheel me to the bus and then she would carry me on. My chair had to get folded and then lifted onto the bus.

At St Enoch Square I got carried off and my mum would take us in a taxi.

By this time the family had moved to Parnie Street. This flat was three fights up. It had a room and a kitchen, which we called a scullery. We lived most of the time in the room as my wheelchair could not get into the kitchen, it was so small. I wanted to get around the house, I used to get one of the family to put me on my back and 'slide' about using my feet. My speech was really bad. It made me angry when people did not understand me. I used to get embarrassed. I could have done with a lot of speech therapy.

My mum used to have to carry me up and down stairs, this was not easy for her and on at least two occasions she ended up in plaster with a slipped disc.

For one week every summer we all went to Ardrossan. We caught a stream train from Central Station and stayed in a rented house. My folks did a lot of walking with me. One favourite walk was from Ardrossan to Saltcoats and back.

Sometimes we went to the 'shows'. I remember dad took me in the bumper cars. One day I said I wanted to go on the Big Wheel. Once we started up I got really 'feart' and was screaming my head off. They had to stop the whole thing and take me off.

Some days we sat on the beach. We all collected shells and filled our pockets with them to take home.

I also enjoyed building sandcastles. I would decorate them with shells and put a bit of gorse for the flag at the top.

Once I went to a home in Perth to try it but did not like it. It was for people with mental handicaps and there was no one for me to talk to. I suppose there was not the same amount of provision for people like me in those days. It was a case of trying out what there was to see if it was right for me.

During my Christmas holiday I often went out with my Dad if the weather was reasonable. We would walk through the Glasgow Green or along the shops in Argyle Street or up into George Square to see the lights.

On Christmas Eve my mum and dad used to tell me to go to bed and they said I had to go to sleep before Santa came. I remember getting toy cars and buses as presents. There were also sweets and tangerines.

During my time at Caldwell I never got any education.

Lennox Castle Hospital

I was around seventeen when I was transferred to Lennox Castle. The ambulance arrived one day and I wondered what was going on. In those days no-one really came along and explained things as they do today. I was taken to Ward Five, which was full of boys, some of them like me in wheelchairs, others walking. Brian McMaster and Martin O'Connor were both there. Today they are at the Centre with me.

The ward was big and long with thirty or so beds. Each person had a bed, a wardrobe and a locker that was all. This time I did not feel so bad as I knew a couple of guys.

Our day started at 7am, we were woken up to get breakfast at 8am. If it was a reasonable day we got out to sit in the grounds. If the weather was bad we played ludo. Lunch was at 12 noon and we sat around till

**Wards at
Lennox Castle**

3pm when we had a cup of tea.

Dinner was at 5pm and we were in bed for 7pm. Even when I was in my late teens we were still in bed by 7pm.

Once a month I was taken to Killearn Hospital for physiotherapy. I wore callipers at this time and I hated them, however they were to help me to walk.

In my ward at Lennox Castle I used to ask for the radio to be put on. This was kept in the office with only speakers in the ward, so to get it on was quite a struggle. Among my favourite programmes were Come Dancing, Mrs Dale's Diary, The Archers and music programmes.

The best times for me were Saturdays. My family came to visit. They would take me for walks in the grounds. Usually they brought me sweets and ginger. There was also a little shop where we could have tea. At this time I used a canvas wheelchair with a big handle at the back.

I picked up a really bad habit at Lennox Castle. I started to smoke. Everyone else was doing it so I copied them. We got five packets a week of Woodbine. We had to pay the staff for this from our pocket money which was ten shillings a week (50p in today's money).

As time went by I started to like Lennox Castle. The nursing staff were kind. I saw a doctor once a week. Usually it was Doctor Campbell. I also got some physiotherapy in the hospital. They used to put me under an ultra violet light to relax my muscles. I also got my legs massaged.

My Dad died during the time I was in Lennox Castle. He took a heart attack, he was not old, only in his early 60's. This was a really sad time as my younger sister Jean also died on her 21st birthday just the year before my Dad. She had been going with a guy who was killed in a motorbike

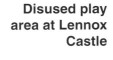

**Disused play
area at Lennox
Castle**

accident. My sister never recovered from his death and took an overdose some months later.

During my time in the hospital my older sister Cathy got married.

Around this period I lost my speech. It went away for no reason and it took around five months for it to return. This was really bad because I was not able to tell people what I wanted or needed. I was very frightened and frustrated.

One day in 1966 my Mum arrived at the hospital. She was very excited. She was a great worker in the local church, St Andrew's Cathedral. They were having a jumble sale and the proceeds were being used to send a disabled person and a carer to Lourdes. That night there was a raffle to draw a winner. My Mum's name came out of the hat. I was so happy. The next day I found out that every name in the hat had been my Mum's so it was a fix.

This trip to Lourdes in 1967 was the first time I had been in a plane. The group atmosphere was great. I loved every minute of the trip. The weather was awful. It rained every day, which did not bother me, but my Mum was staying in a hotel and I was in the hospital.

The programme went like this. Up at 7 am to have breakfast. Then down to the Grotto to have Mass at 10am. From there we went to the Baths. This was a most unusual experience. The water was freezing and when you were taken out of the stone tub you did not get a towel to dry yourself, yet when your clothes went on you didn't feel wet. After this we went back to the hospital for lunch. In the afternoon we went back to the Grotto for the Procession of the blessed Sacrament and the Blessing of the Sick.

After that it was back for dinner. In the evening my group would go to a local hotel and have a drink. Sometimes my Mum and I went off on our own.

The next time I visited Lourdes I went to a hotel and I really enjoyed it. I felt there was much more freedom this time. I could come and go as I pleased. I used to go with some of the group for meals in the evening before we made our way to the Grotto for the candlelit procession. Although I was on a pilgrimage it seemed like a holiday.

One Saturday my Mum and my sister came to visit me. By this time the family had moved to Eastwood. Mum said she had good news, she was taking me home for good. I asked whose idea it was and mum said it had been my sister's.

I was delighted but I had to wait for four weeks. Mum had to write to the doctor to get permission for my release. When it came through Mum came for her usual visit and said "That's you, you're free to go."

I'll never forget that day. My mum knew a guy who had a wee van and she had asked him to come for me. His name was Mr Gass. I went home to Fyvie Avenue.

Home Again

The house at Eastwood was all on the one level but there were only two rooms. We had a bed settee in one room for my Mum and my sister and I got a bed in the other room. The house was at 14 Fyvie Avenue and we stayed there for over 20 years.

For some time Mum had been trying to get me help so that I could do things during the day. An occupational therapist came one day and gave me work to do. I used to make baskets and then she would finish off the tops for me. People gave me orders and I sold a lot. I also did weaving. This kept me going till I got into the Scottish Council for Spastics place at Queen's Crescent.

A Social Work bus picked me up three days a week Monday, Wednesday and Friday. I met lots of people at the Centre but we didn't do too much. We talked a lot. Sometimes I took my basketwork with me. This was my Mum's idea, she thought it would keep me busy.

We got a lunch there and in the afternoon we played games like ludo and dominoes. I used to get back home at 3pm.

Some of the people I became friendly with there are with me at the Work Centre today: Margaret Cassidy, Ina Balsillie and Jean Campbell.

By this time I had managed to get a few home visiting teachers who came to the house to teach me to read and write. None of them stayed very long so I never had the chance to learn much. The people who came were attached to the volunteer centre. I watched the 'On the Move' series on TV and this helped me a lot.

I used to go swimming two or three times a week to Hillpark School. One of the teachers, Len Dallas, would pick me up. He was great. The school raised a lot of money to buy me an electric car to help me get around.

After three years at the Centre in Queens Crescent I decided to stop.

When my Mum died I took over tenancy of the house and I lived on my own for quite a while. I had a home help who came in three times a week. The rest of the time I managed on my own.

Hillington Resource Centre

Some time before I left Queens Crescent a Social Worker visited me. His name was John Leinster. He could not believe I had not had any formal education. He talked to me about the Centre in Hillington and I said I would give it a try.

It was a normal bus which came for me every morning. Molly Adams was the escort and she used to have a fit watching me crawl up the steps. The driver was John O'Neil. I left my own chair at home and got the use of one from the Centre.

The original centre was in Watt Road and there were about 30 of us. We worked at taking plastic off copper by melting plastic in a bath. We used to get loads of copper. The boys who worked with me were Eddy

McInally, John Gordon and Derek, Ian McGee and George Riddell. All the other people I knew from this time have all moved onto other places. One of my supervisors in Watt Road was a guy called Jack. We had no canteen facilities. The Centre van used to go to Scotscraig in Paisley, which was a residential home run by the Scottish Council for Spastics, and collect dinners in large containers. Other work done in the Centre at that time was putting clips on boards for venetian blinds, making stools, wedding stationary.

Every summer we had a day trip to Largs or St Andrews. This was always a great day. There were only about 40 of us, including support staff, on these outings.

We moved from Watt Road to Lorne Road across from the site of the present Day Centre. This is a much bigger place so more people were able to come into the Centre.

We also started to do different types of work. This included packing screws in bags and cleaning cones for putting thread onto. The printing section also started up. We used to do wedding invitations, name cards and printing for firms in the area. Honeywell gave us packing to do. We had an industrial sewing machine and we made up large bags for customers.

In early 1986 we moved to our present premises in Queen Elizabeth Avenue. This building was officially opened on Thursday 6th March by Councillor James Burns. This building had been an empty factory. When we moved in we had a lot of space but not much else. It was really drab and cheerless till we had it decorated. Many more people were able to come as there was so much space.

The factory was divided up into sections. I was based at the bit which worked on foil bottle tops. They were checked for defects then the good ones were packed and sent to the whisky bottling plant. I also worked at stool making. Isabel Gunn was my supervisor.

Today I am based with Catherine Friel. She is my D.C.D. I am keen to do some secretarial work. I have brought my electric typewriter from home. From 1992 onwards big changes have taken place in the Centre. We had to stop most of the work projects. The floor space was divided up into smaller units. In each unit a different activity takes place. We have a secretarial section, a games section, a gardening section, a book and TV section, a handcraft section, a work section, a keep fit section and the shop, which sells cards, gifts and wrapping paper.

The Centre takes part in many competitions, both national and international events. There have been great successes. Some of our teams go to the Special Olympics.

From the Centre I have been able to access education classes. When we moved to the present site our management asked Reid Kerr College to do outreach work. The first class to start up was for computing. Since then we have had literacy, numeracy, music and drama, catering, keyboarding, hygiene in the home, money management, independent travel and leisure-time activities classes running. I have been able to take part in some of these but more importantly I am now able to access the college.

I go two days a week and I have studied woodwork, cookery, social education, literacy, computing, safety in the home, support services in the community, communications and leisure time activities.

Holidays

Apart from my trips to Lourdes I have visited lots of other places. In 1983 I went to Fatima. This was not as organised as Lourdes. In my hotel a Danish football team were staying. They were great fun to be with. We did a lot of touring that week – all over Portugal. The weather was great and the month was June. We went to see the body of Saint Benedict. It is preserved in a glass case.

In 1982, and again in 1984, I went to Denmark with a group from Edinburgh and Glasgow. We went to a Sports meeting to represent Scotland. It was a good trip. We were away for six days and we stayed in a hostel. On our free day we went into town to do some shopping and sightseeing.

I went back to Portugal in 1985. This was the first year of the Special Olympics. From the Centre George Riddell, Tommy Steele, Elaine Leslie and David Duncan were competing. We went by bus. Joe Shields took the group. We drove down to the Channel and crossed over. We had some people from Edinburgh travelling with us.

I had a holiday in Ireland once. Joe took me and we travelled by car. It was a long journey. The boat sailed at 8am so we had to be up before 6am. We toured around and booked into bed and breakfast accommodation. We spent a day in Knock. Joe had been brought up over there so he knew his way around. We spent a night at Tommy's house. One night we could not get booked in so we had to stay in the car. It was terrible. I was so sore and stiff in the morning.In 1993 I had the holiday of a lifetime. With some of the other residents and care staff from Margaret Blackwood I went to Florida. We stayed in Orlando and visited all the attractions.

In 1995 I went back to Ireland. We toured and spent time in Donegal. A friend drove me all over the place.

Margaret Blackwood

I got on great living on my own in Eastwood. After a while some of my friends who stayed at the Westlands hostel started to move out to Margaret Blackwood housing. After a lot of thought I decided to apply for a place.

I was very happy when I was allocated my own flat there but also sad to leave my old neighbours. It was difficult to start afresh again. It took me some weeks to settle in and get to know people. I have now decided that this is my last move. I have the flat the way I want it. My one unfortunate experience was a couple of years ago. I was burgled. It happened on a Saturday afternoon. I was watching TV in the sitting room. The bedroom window was open and these two guys climbed through. They took my money belt and some other things lying around. I heard a noise and went to investigate but they made off. They were never caught.

The house is just off Argyle Street in Glasgow. I am really well placed for getting to places on my own. Every Christmas I go to a different hotel for my Christmas dinner. My local Church is St Patrick's which is just round the corner.

I recently went up in a helicopter. It was a great experience. The weather was bright and clear. I did not feel like I was going up in a plane it was more like a lift. We saw everything, Port Glasgow, East Kilbride, Cumbernauld, the City Chambers, The Burrell. We flew over Ibrox and Hampden. I talked to the Captain and the lady who goes up at night sometimes to do the traffic report.

It was a great experience and I will do it again someday.

Cathy's Story (Edward's sister)

Eddy was born when I was a year and a half old. I remember pushing him around in his wheelchair a lot. My Mum tried for years to get help for him. Our house was not big enough for all of us (we were still living in Mair Street with my grandparents). Eddy went to live in Caldwell House and we got a flat of our own in Parnie Street. I continued to travel back to Kinning Park to go to school.

When I left school I worked as an audio typist for D H Smith's, a Wholesale Chemist.

Edward in the year 2000

When I was 17 my mother had my brother John. She had remarried a widower John Sharp. He was really good to us. I was sorry that they only had twelve years together. It was wonderful having a baby in the family. My sister Jean who was four years younger than me, went to work in Templeton's carpet factory when she left school. When Eddy was at home he came everywhere with me. He knew all my friends and lots of people came to visit our house.

I frequently went to Caldwell house and Lennox Castle. I felt life was so unfair to Eddy. Mum tried to get help but every time she got nowhere. She was told by the family doctor Eddy was an imbecile and he should be put away. She later told me that she had been aware that Eddy had problems from the time he was about six months old. At his birth forceps were used and it damaged his head. He did not develop the way babies should.

My most outstanding memory of Eddy is the way he tries to learn. He has a great thirst for knowledge. It's as though he is trying to make up for all the years he got no education.

My saddest memory is of his grief when Mum died. If she were around today she would have been so proud of him. She would find it difficult to believe that he has a place of his own and leads a totally independent life. She always said he would never manage unaided. I visit Eddy every Wednesday and help him around the flat. We have some great Country and Western nights there. We both invite friends over.

My brother John is married with two children. He works in the Passport Office and Ann, his wife, works at Strathclyde University. I spend some time every week babysitting for them. We all get together with Eddy at Xmas and his birthday.

The Salt Of The Earth group was based in Kirkwall on the mainland of the islands. After initial discussions it was decided that meetings should primarily concentrate on interviewing skills and technical competence, and that the group would interview independently after initial training. As a focus they attempted to interview at least one person resident on each of the 17 inhabited islands. This involved quite a bit of travel, commitment and enthusiasm from the participants, and backup from the tutor. The resulting recordings - from a cross section of young and old Orcadians, incomers, and those whose families have stayed on one island for generations - have been edited and produced on an audio CD.

The transcription that follows, of part of an interview with David Towrie, illustrates many fascinating aspects of island life.

The XYZ Digital Map Company (www.xyzmaps.com)

**19th Century
South
Ronaldsay**

**The Standing
Stones of
Stenness**

I was born in this house Clackamain in Sanday, the 2nd of December 1922.

My father was a crofter and this was a croft of 25 acres, and he became the owner of this in 1919. So he was a small laird when I was born.

Did he make his living on the croft or did he do small jobs?
He made most of his living on the croft really because it provided the mainland milk and potatoes, things like that, and they went to make extra money on the kelp. He worked on the kelp all summer and they made a good bit of cash out of that you see.

Did he get cash from the kelp only or also from other things?
Well yes. He got cash for selling the animals, one or two cattle and some lambs, small number of lambs, and of course the kelp and he worked at the roadwork. Made something of breaking stones. Small hammers in that times. Breaking stones with the hammer and he got a lot, he made a good bit out of it.

And that's how he could buy the croft?
Yes. The croft was generally sold about the value selling price was estimated, and about 20 times the annual rental. The rent of a croft was £10 annually and it was £200 in price.

What did your mother do?
She was just doing the housework. All women worked out in them days. They worked on the turnips and worked on the kelp too. Helped in the kelp work too and, you see, they did knitting and churning the milk and making the butter and cheese. That was a great part in the life of the croft. And the hens. They kept poultry.......well, a small number. Self sufficient in eggs and things like that and made a....They sold the eggs. I think the numbers of hens and poultry increased because they would buy the whole messages from the vans or the shops out of eggs.

Did you help your parents? Did the children?
Back in the wartime when my father was here, but he died in the January of 1946 and we were home here in the wartime. My sister and me and my mother. We were sort of reserved. I was war age and we were reserved on the croft on the land to work. Well my brother he worked at a big farm down at Saville. A big house down there on the beach on the east side of Burness. He worked as a farm servant during the war. He also served in farm work there.

Do you have family of your own?
No, not married.

Never were?

No. I left school at 14. That was the age we left then in the mid '30s. Mid-1930. I was 14.

And came to work on your parents croft.

Yes.

How many of you lived in this house?

My grandfather had 10 children and his wife.

Was this your mother's or your father's?

Father's. Five sons and five daughters. My father was one of the 10. One of the five sons. That was like the end of the last century. Big families then.

Did they live in this house?

Yes. He put up this house in about 1890.

Do you remember him?

I don't remember him. He died in 1924. My grandmother died in 1929. Both in February.

What happened to all your uncles and aunts?

There was five remained in Sanday. I had an auntie down here. Another aunt, she was Barbara. Another Aunt, Mary, she was married to Thomas Muir. He was a joiner and he went to the lobster fishing and the kelp and another one was, she was Margaret of James Muir. They stayed at Mill o' Brackan and they just worked the croft the same way and worked kelp and my Uncle Walter had a croft over at Mire in the south end. He married a wife from that district and the other five, William, wir uncle, was killed in the first world war. 19th of July, 1918. He was in the Seaforth Highlanders and Thomas, my uncle, he was a tailor. He went to Glasgow and my uncle, he was in Glasgow, and Elizabeth was in Glasgow and Margaret, my auntie, was in Glasgow.

Did you visit them in Glasgow?

I've never been out of Orkney yet.

Have you been out of Sanday?

I went to Kirkwall. I didn't live on the mainland. I just visited.

You lived on Sanday all your life?

I lived on Sanday all my life. I've been from the north end to the south end of Orkney. I've been to North Ronaldsay too, with the shore there, where I was at the unveiling of the statue to the lifeboat men whose lives were lost.

And I've been to Stromness. I've been all over the mainland. I've been in all the North Isles except Shapinsay.

When you left, who was looking after your work at home?
It was usually when the work was done in August, but now, since we've been retired from farming we've been finding off any time we think to go. It's not very often. We pick a time of the year and we take a look to Kirkwall and get around there, but the Sunday trips here takes us round the islands on a Sunday. We've done the Sunday trip. We've been in Papa Westray, we've been in North Ronaldsay, we've been in Eday, I've never been in Stronsay but I've been in the football.

Inter-island football. How long ago was that?
That would be away in the 1950s. That was every year.

Did you always go to Stromsay to play football or did they come here?
We were away and at home. We usually went there and they came here and that happened all the time with the inter-island games. They're still happening now.

Do you still go now?
There's a cup thing there that's maybe not been finished. It's still there but I don't know whether they play the games yet. I think it's maybe doubtful if they've played them in the last year but it's still there to do. There's a parish cup they're entered in now. Sanday came to the final there in 1988 but they lost it to St Ola.

Do you go and support them?
I haven't been at that now for a year or two. When they visit Sanday I go have a look and see what they're doing.

How often per year could you afford to leave work and go to the visiting islands?
Usually made it once in the year at some time. It was usually in August when the work was finished. It doesn't depend on that now. Usually I make a trip once a year to Kirkwall. I had some business things to do. It's better to do, more satisfactory than writing and phoning and things.

How long did you stay when you went to Kirkwall?
Maybe at the most one night.

Have there been many boats to go backward and forwards?
It's become more popular now with the shorter travel there from the new pier at Loth five or six miles, I think nine and a half miles from here. It's about ten from Scar here. It's away fifteen from Sanday to Kirkwall. From Loth to Kirkwall it was called twenty-four.

What was it like before they had the ferry service?
Sanday pier was tidal and the boat just had to operate at the tides. About half tide over the high water, but there was enough water which you could come in and get off. She did lie at times at the old Sanday pier but it was just on the bottom and it was a great disadvantage. It would have been a difficult decision whether to put the terminal there or shift it. It's a massive job shifting it there you see. It required two miles of new road. They built a new pier and that makes it easier to go like a scheduled boat. It just goes like a bus service or a train service here. You can guarantee the minute that it's there.

Did you do any other jobs?
We did a small lot of fishing not very much, and we worked on the roads and we worked on tinnels that came in after the war. We worked on the tinnels that came in off the beach, drying them. It was different from the kelp. We didn't burn it. It was just tied in bundles and shipped dried.

How much money could you make in a year?
Just when it started, I think it started in about 1948 and it went on until it came into the management of industries, and I think it started about four pound or something a ton at first.

How long does it take to collect a ton of kelp?
It depends on the quantity that's landed, and we say this to that, way out there, you can put most of it up in a week easily given that if you were full time. We worked just about a couple of hours but if it was full time you'd put up two people, a man and a wife. Mr and Mistress Muir of Midbreckan would all put up to 70 tonnes on that beach.

In a week?
The whole year.

You got four pounds per ton?
Yes but it increased slowly all the time. It's the cost of living I suppose you would call it was rising. I think it ended up, we were up to 150 pound a tonne. It's finished now and there's no chance of it ever appearing again and that is an awful pity because it was right on your doorstep and it would cost nothing to put up, but there's something happened there that it's maybe difficult to restart. It was going up til 1996 anyway and you're getting up to 150 pounds a time.

Why did it stop?
I think they get the kelp from somewhere else. I'm no sure. We go to Harris, whether the product, they were making a lot of chemical stuff out of that. I hear no word of a restart or any effort to see what's gone wrong. I think it's being turned into a fertiliser that can be bought for

the gardens and it was processed for gardens. It's really very, it had salt and minerals you see and it's really a very healthy, it's organic and whereas in the old days they carted away, that's maybe all the loose stuff you're seeing on the beach, and put it in the land. I don't remember me doing that but it was done just up til when the horse and carts was working and before modern farming came in. It played a great part in the land. Where Sanday was poor it was a great help for growing potatoes.

Do you remember how it was done?
It was just carted up on a cart and we had a pointed like fork and you pulled it off the back in small heaps on the ground and they would pass on, just like the dung used to be, and taken off the cart and spread on the ground. It was ploughed in.

What did you grow on the fields?
Oats and potatoes and turnips.

Did you use the oats for yourself?
It was the oats were used in the days when they were milling at the meal mills and the grinding mills. It was milled into meal there. It was some of that would have thrashed in the barn with the miln, and fed to hens, maybe pigs and brose, and fed to horses and cattle and things like that.

Did people eat it too?
Yes very much. You were growing your own porridge. I think they should go back to that again.

What was the mill like?
Well in Sanday it was mostly horse mills. Up to two horses and sometimes there were maybe four horses or something in the big farms mills. Two levers and they pulled around a wheel in the middle and that was on a shaft in the barn. That was geared up to speed up a drum. About 800 revs. The drum of the horse mill and it could, it was too big a pull for the horses.

Did you have to pay the owner of the mill to grind your oats?
Oh yes. He charged the rate.

Could you pay in kind?
I'm not sure. I think the miller was entitled to some part of the grinding or something that was paid in there. Mulcher was a part.
The Sanday mills ceased I think, maybe just about the end of the war.

Have there been many mills on Sanday?
There's been many mills. There's an old mill standing down there. A water mill. It could be transferred when the water dried up I think. The windmill by that time of year, the wind had been getting less. Other

places had windmills. Just small windmills that drove the mill and the water mill. Grinding-mills at the time were driven by water, then they were fitted with engine.

When you took over the croft did you take your oats to the mill too?

Yes. It was a steam engine then. That they always turned to oil engines later.

Could the miller make a full time living out of the mill?

Yes, in winter I think, but then in summer it was no milling. It just was an annual thing. Milling was done in winter and then the grain, well it was all finished off before the grain stocks and the straw was eaten by the livestock in winter. Of course they had the meal that would last a whole year, but that was done in the wintertime and it was packed by in gurnels.

Did you have a gurnel?

Yes. They were actually having a years supply of meal.

Did you store anything else in the gurnel?

I don't mind us doing it but the dried cheese, and we stored the dry cheese up in the gurnel and it kept the cheese. Yes they made cheese. I mind the cheese cog things and there was no press, it was just stone that pressed the.......it was put in a cloth and then pressed the stone down in the cheese.

How long did it last?

Well usually I think it was finished up in a year's time. All eaten up.

Did you make your own bread?

Well they baked bannocks. Bere bannocks and hot bannocks. We grew bere as well. Corn they called it here.

Who did all the housework?

It was usually the wife that did the inside work and baking bannocks, they would bake maybe a dozen bannocks maybe on a Saturday afternoon and that would last the whole week after.

Did you do it yourself?

I never baked much.

Where did you get your bannocks from?

I think that came to an end. My sister did the baking but I think after that we just bought it. Everything was changing. We did put grain to Stromsay and Westray for some years into the 1960s, I think, to the Stromsay mill and the Westray mill. There was more farmers that did in Sanday.

And you're living in a modern house now.
It's just the same house done up.

What was it like inside the old house?
That was an old-type grate on the old house. And it changed their stove. There was that enchantress stove and then it changed to another one, what do you call it, Tarwood Dover, and it's all gone onto the gas and electric now you see. That just heats the house. It doesn't heat the water. That's the immersion heater.

When did it change to gas supply?
Just after it was improved in 1992.

Before that how did you heat and cook in the house?
We just heated water on that stove. The Tarwood Dover thing was always there and we washed with old, in the old days we washed in a tub. In the kitchen, and then we had a hand-washer turn on the tap.

Did you do your own washing?
Yes, and now it's an electric washer now. Powered washer.

What animals did you keep?
I think we had mostly up to 16 beef cattle, cows also. We had four cows and their followers, that was four, 16 or something like that really and two horses.

Did you work with the horses?
Yes. Worked with the horses.

How long did you work with the horses?
We put away, it was possibly the last working horse in October of 1972, and he was aged 27 and he was a very good horse on the legs still. He was a very grand horse to watch walking out and a very quiet horse. We just couldn't hardly put him up from the house.

Did you have outbuildings?
Yes there was, just like any other croft. A byre, a stable, a barn, outhouses and pig styes too.

You kept pigs?
I never minded but they kept pigs before. My father and that, they had a pig or two but usually for killing. I think they didn't make a job of selling pigs or raising pigs for market. A lot kept a pig and they boiled tatties and maybe neeps and they fed the pig and it really was for killing for the winter.

Did you have a tractor?

I think we had, we bought a secondhand tractor. An Allis Chalmers model B in 1955 and we didn't have it very long. We sold that and bought a Ferguson. Bought a petrol paraffin Ferguson in 1961. It was all Ferguson then.

What colour was it?

Grey. The grey Fergie. The dear old grey Fergie did a lot of work in Orkney.

I heard they were quite reliable.

Very reliable, yes. The Ferguson system and they had all the implements. They had the plough and mower. They had all the implements.

What happened when the tractor broke down?

It was very reliable. We never had just actually struck down at a garage. There were one or two batteries, needing a new battery, but it didn't do a big lot of work here. Just a few acres scarcely went. We didn't have a trailer and we keep it very tidy as we go and it went away lovely no bother. Oh they were very good but I tell you one great thing with the tractor. It was the diesel. When the diesel came in it shot up in power. That Ferguson we had it would never have been of use in silage. It was too little power. The diesel was the power. It can go up to 120, maybe 140. Massive tractors, and of course the first silage starting, I don't think possibly that a smaller one, but I couldn't say if it was a Ferguson. I think maybe when the diesel came in the Ferguson 35 a small diesel. I think it's been known to be in some silage with the......It cut in and lifted and put it in the cart like what they've got with the mower now. A great big harvester. I think it was maybe known to have done that but when Forage Harvester came in it could do it with sufficient power.

When did you start to do silage?

I think it maybe did start in the end of the sixties.

And before that what was the winter fodder?

There was a lot of hay then. The balers came in, I think it was maybe about 1960. They were doing the small square bales and that was, they were a great push ahead with doing a lot of hay work and making hay. Just before that they just put it in coles and it was all hand work pitching it up on trailers or carts, and taking it in and building stacks in the yard.

Where did the idea come from that you could also make silage?

It was going on down the country long before that. In fact there was a case in Sanday. They were making silage in the 1880s or sometime. With a horse and cart. It never was big but I think it was Colonel Harwood, when he was in Skar at that time, and he came from down in England. I think that introduced it but it, never was a thing taken up then I think at

119

any place. Maybe in Orkney. I think maybe you'd find something on the mainland. In a lot of Orkney there must have been something like that but it never took on. It was maybe too labour, too much labour, and the stocking wasn't as many then. There wasn't as much of the stock on the farm.

Did you employ anyone to help you with the work on the farm?
No in my time but I think there was what they called a hairst hand, a harvest hand helped out in the harvest when they needed more people to help tie up the sheaths. I think they had a harvest then for a year or two and most other places had that. Even big farms took on a hand or two to tie up the sheaves and cart them in. They required more labour. More people to do it.

Where did they come from?
Maybe off crofts. Something like that. They was making their living maybe working at kelping, working on the roads. They had a break at that time and they could go and help and be a hairst hand on a farm.

What did you do in the evenings?
We worked round the clock mostly. Built up dykes and did and repairs on the houses. Course I suppose they were working pretty hard all the day. They didn't work so much at night, but then in the summer time they were doing a lot and they worked on the farm at night. They would generally take down a load of hay or some turnips.

Did you have books to read?
Not very much. Not very much with that, early on with books and that but I didn't just buy very many. There were the Orcadian and the Orkney Herald. The Orkney Herald finished in 1960. I don't know why it finished. There wasn't another Orkney paper.

Did you get the papers to Sanday every day?
No, it was just weekly papers. They bought them at the shops generally and sometimes I think I remember here we were taking the Orcadian and our relatives only took the Orkney Herald and then they would switch them over. You were actually getting one paper free.

Did you or your parents have any musical instruments in the house?
No they didn't. I think there was the remains of an old gramophone here.

Did your parents tell you stories?
Oh yes. Very much a storytelling at that time.

Do you remember the stories?

One great story was the wreck of the Dutch ship here. The wreck of the Dutch ship they called it. The Utrecht. It was a very sad story that stuck with you all the time. The Dutch wreck took place in February of 1807. It was a time that there was war with the Netherlands and this Dutch ship rather than go through the English Channel, up past here by the north, and she was passing by up here in a snowstorm in February and the story was that she struck the shore of Runebreck and broke her rudder and drifted in here and there was 400 or more. We had 200 troops going out to the West Indies to save it from the British and the loss of the Dutch ship made Kuraka fall to the British because they couldn't get the troops out there.

The story is that they were going to attack the island. I think the word came up from Caithness. The volunteers, the Fensables at Caithness. That was the nearest they could do for the military information on this and they were told not to intervene or fight, and Sanday men left with pitch forks and scythe blades but they met them and they were no fighting there. In fact they had lost that many. I just don't know the numbers there. They surrendered there. They met them and they surrendered. She was supposed to have her guns trained on Skar but the ship lost it and went off the mark you see, and that saved Skar, but there were a lot of cannon balls I think came ashore here. I think there are one or two at Skar and I think there are one or two here gone missing through time. The bodies that came ashore were buried at the beach I think. That's what they did in the early days. Buried at the beach, but they dived on this Dutch ship away in 1985, I think, and they found a cannon on the bottom but they didn't want to lift it in contact with the air because I think it would rust even faster. I think it will be lying there yet. A cannon.

Did you use seal skins?

I never mind anybody doing anything with that. I think in the time of the krose lamp they did that to get oil for the krose lamp. Seal oil or something but I don't mind the krose lamp. I think maybe they were in use up to the end of last century. That's the 19th century I mean. I think they would have been used up til then. The krose lamp.

Everything you can use from the seal.

It would have been. I just don't mind scrubbing down and skinning a seal. There was something they called 'ribblings.' That was meat with seal skin like slippers. There could be an industry but then of course you're no meant to shoot seals. It was part of traditional life. Of course all the stories come into this.

Did you hear many of these stories when you were young?

Yes. Family history was the great thing that was talked about.

Relationships, family history and things like that. I suppose it was sort of, it was just told round the fireside.

The story of the troll. It's an old thing that's very popular in this district. The trolls were supposed to frequent the mounds. There's a mound there. I'll tell you how. Away at the east, a house in Burness on the very point, there you'll see on a map, and this troll was becoming rather something of a nuisance to the farmer. It wouldn't leave him and things happened and he got fed up with this troll and he was going to clear out and go to another farm, and he had all his gear and loaded it onto the cart. Away he went from the farm leaving this behind, and the story is when he came and he was ready to take over his new place, the troll popped out of the urn and said "You're getting a grand day for your flitting". Couldn't get away from the troll.

Telling Our Story was a reminiscence type-group based in Edinburgh, run in conjunction with the Salt Of The Earth Project. The participants recorded their experiences of facets of their past lives, and also individual life histories. Carmen was the tutor for the group, and she had her own story to tell, giving a fascinating perspective of life in Scotland within the Italian community over a large period of the 20th century, including the time of the Second World War.

First Father came over was...He was born in 1891 and he was the eldest of eleven and a few of them, my grandfather's brothers and cousins and so on, had come over here. But they were actually playing the accordion and they had the monkey in London. And my father's first time over here would be sometime in the late 1890's. And what they did was, they didn't want to pay a fare for him so they smuggled him through France on the train and they hid him under the wooden seats at Lyons and so on so he wouldn't be found. They got to Bologne, which must have been the longest crossing and the cheapest crossing from France, and he had no shoes so they bought him a pair of boots in a pawnbroker's shop there. And then brought him across to London, and he went round collecting the money while they performed for a wee bit. Then he went back to Italy. The fashion was, you came over, you made a wee bit of money and then you took the money back. He remembers vividly being on one of his uncle's shoulders and standing at Constitution Hill when Queen Victoria's funeral cortege passed. He can remember that.

That's incredible.
Yes. He would be about ten when he saw that, and he said it stayed in his mind. And then, because there were eleven of them and most of them were boys, there wasn't enough land in Italy to keep them all. So an uncle in Stonehaven wanted some slave labour – they used to take them for three years – so my father was sent over to Stonehaven. And he had to get up at three o' clock in the morning, chip the ice, do the freezers, you know, the usual story. Worked like a slave for three years and at the end of the three years, I think he got three hundred pounds or something. With that money, he didn't like up that east coast so he moved to Edinburgh and he got a wee shop in Portobello. The shop's still there actually. It was on the corner of Bath Street, a wee shop, and he got digs with a family of Faccendas up near the King's Theatre. And he used to walk from Portobello to the King's Theatre every night in the winter to save his happenny car fare, the tram car, because in the winter he'd be lucky if he maybe drew sixpence in a day. But in the summer, Portobello

Carmen's father Biagio Boni, 1909

was very busy and he did well in the summer. However, he was staying with the Faccendas and he fell in love with one of the daughters, who was my mother. But, my granny said that no way would she allow her daughter to marry him until he had a good shop, a flat and a maid for her. So, he slogged away in Portobello until he had quite a bit of money put by and then he started looking for a better shop.

The funny thing was that, although my grandmother was a Faccenda, she was married to a Boni – but it was a different Boni. There are two distinctly separate clans of Bonis and they're not related. And my father's mother was a Gizzi from the Glasgow Gizzis'. So, there was all this huge clan of people round about. It wasn't as if he was isolated you know. So, anyway, he was determined he was going to marry this woman, she was just what he wanted and he was very much in love. So there were two shops going – this must have been about 1910 we're talking now. 1910. Two shops on offer. One was where the Disney shop is in Princes Street now. It was the East End Café or the Royal Café, a lovely shop, and the other one was the Empress Café up opposite the King's Theatre. So, my father: bowler hat, striped trousers, gold Albert, went to look at both shops. And he would go in and buy a coffee and sit and watch how many people came in at certain times of the day, how it was stocked, all the rest of it and away he went with all this information, you see. However, he decided that the one at the King's Theatre was the shop he really liked. Because at that time the King's Theatre didn't have a kiosk for sweeties, didn't have anything at all. If you wanted anything, you had to come out across [the road]. And, of course, it was a great place in those

Carmen (seated), Rosebud and Ronnie. Edinburgh 1931.

Biagio, Ronnie, Nanny Shiela (standing). Rosebud, Maggie, and Carmen. 1933.

days for Variety and so on. Always busy. So, the man who owned the shop was also an alcoholic and he had really lost all his money and he had to get the shop sold. So, he wanted six hundred pounds, which in 1910 - I don't know what it would equate to nowadays - a huge amount for the shop. But it was well-fitted and there was a really good stock. So, my father, I think, had five hundred pounds but he was a hundred short. So he sent word to his father in Italy and asked him if he would lend him a hundred pounds to buy the shop because he said, "It's a good shop and I'll be able to pay you back with interest". So his father said, "That's fine, I'll send the money over through Zio Giovanni" – Giovanni Valente! So,

Giovanni Valente came across with a hundred pounds in gold – because in those days you didn't work in paper money – a hundred pounds and my father bought the shop! And it was a wonderful shop and he had all the people coming over for these four guinea boxes of chocolates and he opened the downstairs place into a beautiful restaurant with stained glass and lovely wall-lights and everything. It was really lovely! And he was doing very well, and by this time the young lady was sort of engaged to him, you know. But it wasn't official yet because her mother said she was far too young. She must have been too. But anyway, she and my father were an item and she used to help out in the shop.

She used to help out in the shop, you know, and got the feel of it and so on. And, the First World War broke out of course and Father was called up. He could either go back to Italy and join the Italian army – because they were allies in the First World War – or he could stay in this country and join a British regiment. So, he joined the Royal Scots and he went to Glencorse Barracks and when he first got there, of course he'd been brought up in the country and he used to watch the sheep out in the hills - he was great with a rifle. Because of the rules at that time in Italy, they were still...So, when he got there and he got a rifle in his hand he was showing off: bang-bang-bang! And this other chap said to him, "Are you wanting to die Boni?" He said, "What do you mean?" He said, "You shoot like that, they'll have you for a sniper and you'll last about twenty four hours in France." "Oh, I never thought of that." So, then he started bang-bang-bang all over the place. The sergeant said, "What's wrong with you now? You were good when you came." "Oh," he says, "I just cannae get the hang of this gun." So he just ended up an ordinary soldier, you see? However, they were shipped off to France and they were on the march to go to one of those big battles and they were told absolutely, they were not to drink any water. However, it was a hot day and my father had sneaked some water from one of these standing fountain things in one of the villages they'd passed through. He and two or three others and they took terribly ill, poisoned with the water. And they were sent back to hospital, in Liverpool I think it was. Somewhere around there anyway. The whole lot of the people that had been with them went on and were all killed. There was nobody left, they were massacred in one of these battles. But he survived. But his stomach was never really the same again. He always had a bad stomach. And my mother used to go down to visit him, of course with her mother, chaperoned all the way, when he was in hospital. During the time that he was in hospital and during the time that he was in the army during the first world war, my mother's brother Tom had been put in charge of the shop in Lochrin Buildings.

Uncle Tom was a real glamour boy. He was handsome, black hair, you know, moustache, big green eyes and a great lad for the ladies. And whilst he was in charge of the shop, he absolutely ruined it. He spent all the

Carmen.

First Holy
Communion,
Sacred Heart.
1937.

money, he used to give away boxes of chocolate to lady friends. He roamed around in taxis, had dinner at the NB (North British Hotel) and everything! Father said he just got back in time. The stock was all gone and the shop was just about on its knees. So he kicked Tom out and had to build it up again. And in 1919, he and my mother were married - on the 22nd of April 1919. And they moved into the flat at 10 Lochrin Buildings which was beautifully furnished, everything very fashionable apparently at the time, and she had a maid. So, he fulfilled all the requirements of granny and in 1920 my eldest sister, Rosalie Evelyn was born and then three years later Ronald Oliver. And he was the light of my father's life. His son! You know, he meant everything to him. And the two of them were spoilt rotten as far as I can make out...And they had a great time together.

Now, I know you lost your mother?

Yes, she died thirteen days exactly after I was born. It was quite a shock because there were two or three of the Italian women pregnant at the same time - there were seven years between me and my brother, my elder brother Ronnie – and my Aunt Connie had had her son Romano in the May and then mother had me in the July and she was fine. And Aunt Connie – that was Conchetta Crolla – she was to be godmother. So she'd come up on the Saturday to talk about the christening and so on and my mother had said to her that she really felt ill. She didn't know what was wrong but she felt terribly tired...and while Aunt Connie was there, she collapsed. She was rushed off to the Royal Infirmary, and she had a massive haemorrhage. And in those days, blood transfusion was in its infancy. So, they tried my father, they tried my grandmother, they tried everyone because it had to be a direct transfusion. Nobody's blood was suitable so by three o' clock in the afternoon, she was gone...

So, that left the family: my eldest sister, Rose, who was ten years older than me, Ronnie who was seven at the time, and myself. And, I think I told you about the funeral, how upset - my father was absolutely shattered that he'd lost his young wife. It was more difficult for him because at that time he had just changed from café to a biscuit factory and he was having trouble. Nobody had given him a recipe for making wafers and cones and he was finding difficulty in getting them to come out right, and between trying to keep the shop going and trying to keep the factory going and then having three children, I think things were *really* tough. So, he got an Italian woman to look after me. I don't remember her name at all. Maggie was her first name but I don't know what her second name was. She was a very fat, squat, motherly person and she was very kind. She didn't stay in the house because she was married and lived nearby, but she came in everyday and did everything and then went home at night. And her husband helped out in the shop because he boiled the milk for the ice cream and so on.

So, I don't remember much about the early days. Maggie didn't stay long – I don't know why, whether she perhaps had family of her own or what. And she was replaced by a Highland girl called Dora, Dora Lonie. She was only about 17 or 18 and she came specifically to look after me and she stayed with us until Father married again. But she stayed in the house and then there was another woman who came in to do the housework and general cooking and so on. Because Dodo – as I called her – her job was to look after me and that was that. And she was great! She took me everywhere! Even on her day off she took me with her and I really have very happy memories of Dodo and our life together. But, of course, you know what the Italians are like – they thought, here's this very eligible widower with children and a woman living in the house. So, the gossip started and it was decided that he should get married again. That it wasn't *seemly* to have the children being brought up in this way.

So, his sister up in Ardrishaig, Aunt Pacifica, knew a girl called Mary Arcari who she thought would be ideal. She was about 29, 30, which in those days you were really on the shelf! And she thought that Mary, nice woman, would make an ideal wife for my father. However, unbeknown to father, Mary was courting a Scotsman, Hugh McCann, who was not only Scots but he was Irish and had the family found out she would have been – I don't know what would have happened to her, something awful. She would have disappeared off the face of the earth! However, she wasn't interested in anyone else because she already had her fella....But she had a younger sister, Adelina, who was a bit of a soprano singer and travelled round the Highlands doing concerts and so on, which was quite frowned upon in those days. An unaccompanied woman traipsing about the Highlands and staying in digs and so on. And painting her face and all this. Well, it wasn't really on but er...they put her, er, before my father.

We all used to go out courting. Father, he had a car you see, which was quite unusual in those days. We'd all get into the car on a Sunday and go out and visit prospective females to pass judgement on them, you see?...So, the first day that I met Adelina, I disliked her intensely......I didn't take to her at all but unfortunately my father did. So, that was in 1935, '36 that the courtship went ahead. However, her mother was dying of breast cancer and she had to hurry the wedding on because she wanted her mother to be there and so, the wedding was in the December of 1936. Meanwhile I'd taken whooping cough. I was supposed to have been one of the little flower girls, I had all my frock and everything. In fact, I'd got two frocks because I couldn't make up my mind which one I liked better! And went off to the wedding, which was in December, in Lennoxtown. Miserable it was, and I was still whooping like anything and I remember I couldn't join the bridal procession but I watched this thing going on with this woman in the white velvet frock. ... So, Father came back from honeymoon. They went on a tour of the Highlands to visit all our relatives. We've got relatives all round the North of Scotland, and they went up to Aunt Pacifica's for their wedding night and Aunt Pacifica did not like Nina, never had liked her, and she was quite upset that Father had taken this woman instead of the one that she had recommended.

However, they came back from their honeymoon and came back to Edinburgh and when I walked in, of course, Dodo had disappeared, Father's bedroom had been totally done over – had all modern pink soft lights and everything - and I was banished to the boxroom. And I didn't take kindly to this at all! I remember telling her very clearly that I didn't like her and that it would be much better for everybody if she just went back to where she came from. Because I wanted life to go on the way it was! However, that wasn't to be! Her mother died in the January and in those days people went into mourning for a year. You wore black for three months and purple for nine months or something and then you came out of mourning. However, by this time, she was expecting a baby and she thought this might get my interest that she was actually expecting a baby. So, I was quite tickled about the idea, thought that a wee sister would be nice.

I had gone to the local wee school – I think it was St Thomas Aquinas but I'm not sure, but it was up near the Sacred Heart in Lauriston and father decided that I should go to the Convent because the other two had gone to convent schools as well. So, I was promptly moved, from a school with a teacher I loved, to the Convent. I didn't like it very much. It seemed awfully strange; I didn't like the nuns very much but I suppose I didn't like anything very much at that time. Life had become kind of peculiar... And worse still, we started going around looking at houses and we moved out from Lochrin Buildings to Juniper Green to a nice, big house - it wasn't the one I wanted. The one I wanted had a goldfish pond and I quite fancied the idea of the goldfish pond! – but no, they took this one. It didn't have a pond but it had a sandpit so...And we moved out because my stepmother felt that there wouldn't be enough room, with a new baby and so on, with all of us in the flat. It wasn't really big enough for us all. So, we moved out to Juniper Green. That would be in, it must have been about September 1937, and a month later, my stepbrother Mario was born. That was in October '37. I was really disappointed because I didn't want a brother, I wanted a wee sister, you see. So, things weren't really going my way at all! However, we were quite handy for the convent so we went back and forward to the convent.

But it was then that things began to get interesting politically because it must have been about that time that the Abyssinian thing was going on. And also, Father was having problems because the fascisti movement had started up in Edinburgh quite strongly and everybody was being urged to join. But my father was not keen because he wasn't a joiner. You know some people are? He wasn't interested in clubs and things so, he didn't want to join anyway... From what I gather from later conversations with my Dad, he, in the beginning he thought Mussolini was what Italy needed. He cleaned up things, he gave the Italians a presence again in international affairs and he appeared to be doing a lot of good for Italy and he...he didn't like him, he didn't dislike him, you know and that was the way it was.

However, by this time, the factory was well established but in order to make money he had to sell to the Italians, his wafers and cones. And, it was made quite clear to them that either he joined the party or he'd lose business because there was another biscuit factory in Edinburgh and they were really arch enemies of my father. Because apparently, just after Dad took over the factory, it went on fire and it was burnt to the ground. And when they heard about that, they went to the North British Hotel and had a celebration dinner because Father's factory had burnt down. And this got back to my father and it was enmity from then onwards. It wasn't a nice thing to do but it was, you know, it was typical of Italians wasn't it?

Anyway, in short, if Father didn't join the Party, he wouldn't get any business. So, he joined but he never used to go near any of the meetings or anything. We used to go to the Italian party at Christmas down in Fairley's and we used to go to the picnic at North Berwick or wherever in the summer. And that was about it. My sister went to the dances. My brother and sister went to the dances and that was about it. But, 1937 it must have been - '37, '38 I'm not sure about the date - one of the girls in my class had a birthday party and everybody in the class was invited, except me. And it was because I was an Italian and the parents didn't approve of what was happening in...so I never went to the party. And that was the first time that it suddenly dawned on me that there was something different about me.

Also, my mother used to say – we used to have pasta on a Sunday and she always used to say, "You didn't have pasta today, when anybody asks you at school what you had for your Sunday dinner, you had roast beef and Yorkshire pudding or roast chicken or something. You must never tell people that you eat macaroni." And so we didn't! And the funny thing is that, talking to Olive and all the other girls about that time, we all did exactly the same thing. We didn't talk about the things that we did that were different. We just kept it quiet. We tried to be as British as possible... So, I stayed on at the convent and things were quite difficult there because the nuns really didn't like the Italians and there were quite a few because you know Italians like to send their kids to a convent school. So they made things quite difficult for us and unfortunately, I was quite bright and I won every single prize that was going. And they used to give a book for everything. You'd come out with mountains of books. But they *grudged* giving me those prizes, it really hurt them that I had these prizes.

So that by 1938, '39 I was really unhappy at school and I got to the stage that I didn't want to go to school and so my mother said, "Why don't we send her to Holy Cross Academy?" They had just built a beautiful new primary school and it had a really good reputation but it was *miles away* from Juniper Green. But by this time I was nine, coming up for nine and they thought, well perhaps once I'd been taken a few times I could manage it. It was a great school and I could go from there on to secondary, you see. So, I was booked in to start, I think it was on the 4th of September 1939 when I was supposed to start at school! And of course, a little matter of the war came along and all the schools closed. Did you know that?

I hadn't realised that.
All the schools closed, there were no schools at all. People were in turmoil and it had been an absolutely glorious summer. One of those summers that just go on day after day, beautiful weather! And by the time it came to the september, Father had had a really good season, you know, everything looked great and this guy had come back and said there'd be no war in our time. That was fine. And then somehow when that announcement came on the Sunday that Britain was at war, it took everyone by surprise...

And the funny thing was that every Sunday, my father used to go up to the cemetery with flowers. We all went as a family, except for my stepmother who stayed at home with her child. So, this Sunday, for some reason or another, I can't remember whether I wasn't too well or something, I was left at home and they went off to the cemetery you see. Of course, the announcement came at 11 o' clock and about five minutes later, the sirens went! Well, my stepmother was yella' to the core and she *panicked*! And they had this special gas mask for babies, that they put them in and they pumped them, and we had gas masks as well. Well, she grabbed a hold of me and she grabbed a hold of him and she grabbed a hold of the gas masks and we had a cupboard under the stairs and we all – and I mean she was a large lady - we tried to squeeze ourselves under there. Now, all my life I've wanted to be in open spaces, I don't like enclosed. So I'm screaming the place down, she's trying to deal with this screaming baby and pump air into this thing! It was total comedy! And no sooner had the sirens gone, that the all-clear went - because I think it was a flock of ducks or something! By this time, father came home, found his wife hysterical, his child hysterical and the baby half-suffocated and that was our introduction to the war...

So, there was no school but then they started – some people went to school in people's houses, just a few people would go to a house and a teacher would come in. St Cuthbert's had a wee chapel school in the vestry and they got the children to go down there and we went to a sort of a school in the vestry there. Father thought it was too dangerous to send me all the way across Edinburgh to Holy Cross so he decided that it would be better if I went to the wee school. Because the convent closed down during the war. You either had to board at Aberdeen or do without and there was no way he was sending me to boarding school. I quite fancied the idea but anyway, I went to this wee school. And then... I mean I don't remember much about 1940 because nothing much really happened. I mean, Dunkirk happened. I can remember everyone being really upset about that, seeing the news bulletins and going to the pictures, Pathe Pictorial, and seeing all these men coming back exhausted but it wasn't really something that I was terribly aware of... And then, the rumour began to go around that Italy was going to come in to the war but on the side of Germany. Now that happened in, it must have been about June 1940 because it was particularly bad that when Dunkirk had happened, that just a couple of months later sort of thing, Italy went in on the side of Germany   And my father had seen it coming so he decided that Ronnie by now – 1940, he would have been maybe coming up, seventeen – Ronnie would take over at the factory because Ronnie had left school and gone into the factory with his dad and he was pretty good in the factory. So he thought Ronnie and Rose were both there, they would be able to take care of the business if anything happened. Because he was sure that he would be interned because he'd been - .

So he anticipated that?

Yes, oh yes he anticipated it. So he went to the bank and he dealt with the – what was it called then, the Commercial Bank or something? Anyway, he went down to see Mr Peacock and he explained everything to him and he gave Ronnie the right to sign cheques and all the rest of it, and he sorted out things for my mother so that she would be alright financially and she would get income every week and so on. Got another set of keys made and everything for Ronnie and primed him as to what he would have to do and all the rest of it. Italy – we went out to the pictures, my stepmother, she loved the pictures, and we'd gone to Poole's Synod Hall – I don't know if you know where that was in Edinburgh? It's round the back of the Castle, sort of in the area of the Caley Hotel, and there's a cemetery opposite where Burke and Hare, well just round there, there used to be a picture house called Poole's Synod Hall, a lovely picture house. And the man who owned it lived a couple of doors down from us, you see.

So, we'd gone to the pictures – I don't remember what it was – when all of a sudden, the lights went up and it was announced in the picture house that Italy had declared war on Britain, you see? And my stepmother: "*Let's get out of here*", you see? She grabbed me by the scruff of the neck and we belted out of that picture house. I mean, she'd have been better just sitting quiet but she wanted out of there before someone lynched her, you see. So, we made our way home and when we got home, Father said, "I'd better pack a few things into a wee case because they're bound to come for us now that war's been declared." So, he went off and he packed a wee case for himself and so on and he laid out all his keys on – we had a lovely hall stand in the hall – all these bunches of keys and chequebooks and everything, you see? Eleven o' clock that night they came and they took Ronnie! Left my father, ignored him! So, Ronnie was taken off and we didn't know where, just these couple of plain-clothes detectives came and took Ronnie away. So there was all this ceremony of handing back keys and everything. Father was totally gobsmacked!

However, my stepmother remembered – 1938 maybe it was, the Italian community got the young people to join the Balilla, the young Fascists it was supposed to be, you see and, of course, all the youngsters joined because this was great. They played table tennis, they went [to] tennis parties, dances, you know the usual thing. For the young Italians, all mixing together. But the thing, the carrot that got them was that if they joined the Balilla, they would get a fortnight in Italy for ten pounds...And Rose and Ronnie, I mean they pestered my father rotten until he said yes. However, unbeknown to them, what it meant was a fortnight under canvas at Anzio with daily processions, goose-stepping and "Heil Mussolini!" or whatever, up to Rome and all the rest of it. And it was extremely political and they got uniforms, sort of brownie uniforms, brownshirts and so on and cravats and things and armbands. The young Balilla. So of course, they had a good enough time, they had some fun and all the rest of it but they didn't take much to the political bit at all. When they came home, they were kind of disappointed about the whole thing. However, Stepmother suddenly remembered that up in the big drawer in the wardrobe in Ronnie's room, were two brownshirts. Middle of June, boiling hot, no fire on, of course, so she lit this huge fire in the kitchen – you know the old-fashioned range? – and she lit this huge fire and she put the flues on it full blast, you see. Down came these uniforms and she threw them on the fire and she's poking them and poking them and everything, making sure they were burnt to a crisp in case anybody came back to search the house. Because she felt that this would be very, very dangerous if they found these things. So, she got rid of *everything* that had *anything* to do with the Fascisti, you see. Even the postcards that they sent from Italy, she burnt all them as well. Everything! And Ronnie was marched off. We found out a few days later that he'd been taken to Saughton along with the first round of people that had been rounded up in Edinburgh.

And, I mean, we had nothing at all out in Juniper Green. In fact, our neighbours came to call. I remember my mother being very impressed because they came to tell her that, it didn't mean a thing to them. That they were still neighbours. One was a lawyer and he said, "If there's anything I can do to help, just let me know." And they were extremely kind. There was nothing at all in the way of breaking windows or anything like there was.......But apparently, down in Leith and so on, it was pretty awful. And we only heard about this; about the Deep Sea getting their windows broken and people going in and the Police going into the place to take people away, and opening tins of tomatoes and ransacking the houses and leaving a horrible mess behind. But Aunt Connie's husband was in the first wave away, and the Capaldis and old Alfonso Crolla from the Deep Sea [*fish and chip shop*] – I mean, *him* of all people....but he went away as well and, er, my father thought, "That's funny. What am I left for?" you know! However, time passed.

We went to see Ronnie in Saughton, I can remember. It was a horrible experience because he was actually in a prison and you were taken in and, you know, you had to wait and he wasn't allowed to get any parcels or anything. However, the man next door wasn't too pleased about this because he felt it was illegal because Ronnie was under eighteen and there was no way that anyone under eighteen should have been lifted. So, he was dealing with that.

It must have been nearly three weeks later before they came for my father. He was one of the last to be picked up, along with Guy Valente and, er, Peppino Demarco from Gorgie. And his brother, Joe, who had taken over our café in Lochrin Buildings had got naturalised! So he was fine, he was able to stay, that was alright. But he got a lot of heckling from customers and so on...but my father didn't think much of Joe when he got naturalised but it turned out that he was the wisest of them all. However, it was three weeks almost, it was a Friday afternoon and two plain-clothes detectives came to take my father away. And I was *really* upset...I remember. I just couldn't understand that they were going to take my father away, you know. What was going to happen to us all? But they were ever so nice! They insisted that he had a meal before he went away and they told my mother to go and help him to pack his things and get things and so on. "Where is he going?" "We don't know, we don't know yet, we're just taking him into the central bit." So, Father was taken away.

And my father-in-law here, believe it or not, although he'd been here for years – when they came for him, it was two policemen that came and they actually handcuffed him! And my husband couldn't forgive them for that because he felt it was a terrible thing to do to him. But nothing like that with my father, I must say. I think it was a few days later we found out that he'd been taken to a place called Woodhouse Lea, out at Penicuik and this was a tented camp that they'd prepared for these Italians...And they were out in the open, in tents, and there was a big sort of wire fence, barbed wire and then there was barbed wire and then there was another fence that had been hastily put up. And it was soldiers who were guarding the camp!

So we were allowed to go out – I think it was every Sunday – to visit Father and my mother used to bake ham and egg pie and this that and the other and we'd get the bus at St Andrew's Square because she couldn't drive and out we would go to the Woodhouse Lea, to visit Father. And that bus was full of Italian women going out because you only had, I think it was an hour, and then you had to get back again...

And then, not long afterwards, we went out this Sunday and the place was deserted. The camp was empty; the tents were empty, there was no one about. And oh mother! I'll never forget it. She went *absolutely* frantic. There was nobody even to ask. So all the women came back home and you were frightened to use the phone. My Mother used to be very scared to use the phone because she thought they could be listening in to what we were saying. And so we, Aunt Connie – of course her husband had been very high up in the Fascisti thing in Edinburgh so he'd gone off *very* early. She was frantic because she hadn't heard from him for weeks and he hadn't been at Woodhouse Lea. He had disappeared totally. And Alfonso had disappeared. My uncle Zio Lorenzo Demarco had disappeared, another lovely man, and nobody knew where they were.

So, we, by this time, my stepmother was told that she had to leave Edinburgh. She was an 'undesirable alien'. Because when she married she got the choice of either keeping her British nationality, because she was born in this country, or taking her husband's nationality, Italian. And she didn't think much about it at that time so she just thought, "Auch, I'll take my husband's nationality – it'll be handy when we go on holiday!" So she was bunged out of Edinburgh! So, of course, there was all the carry-on of who was going to stay in the house, what was going to happen? And, fortunately, Ronnie got out. So, Ronnie came home.

How was that? Was that because of your lawyer friend?
Yes. He was only seventeen so Mr Leese said "This is ridiculous", and he had gone straight to the authorities and dealt with it. And also, I think, he put in a good word for us as a family because they were a lovely family next door to us. So anyway, Ronnie came home and my mother said, "Well at least something good is happening here". So...she sorted out the house and she wasn't sure whether we'd be able to keep the house or whether something else would happen. So she put everything into one room and she left the house in such a way that, if the worst came to the worst, it could be let to provide an income, if we couldn't keep the factory going, you see. And we moved.

And Aunt Connie by this time had moved to Glasgow, she was staying in Bearsden, and so was Marietta, whom you've met, and Zia Carlina, Mrs Capaldi. All of them were all staying around Glasgow. Some of them had relations in Glasgow and were staying with them and so on. And she found us a flat in Clydebank, just a few days before the Clydebank Blitz. Now, my stepbrother Mario was a sickly baby. He never was well and he was very poorly and it really was a shame, to put him out of the house in Juniper Green and send him around the country. Because he had everything you could think would be wrong with a baby – he was chesty, he had bad eczema, he had all sorts of oddities wrong with him that just made it dangerous for him to have to leave home. But, however, leave home he did.

And we were in this grotty dump in Clydebank. Of course, the blitz started up, it was absolutely terrible...And it was a big tenement we were in and we spent every night in a basement underneath the tenement and, of course, you're terrified because I used to think, "What if this thing falls down and we never get out of here?" I felt like I was being incarcerated every night. Mario used to cry most of the night and annoy everybody else. But then, he couldn't help it; he was a sick baby. And then, you'd get up in the morning and go out and the place was absolutely full of debris and fires, just like you see in the [films]. It was absolutely terrible.

And my mother got in touch with Aunt Connie, she says, "Look Conchetta, I've got to get out of here". She said, "You've got to find me somewhere". She said, "Most of the women are going to Peebles. Can you not find me somewhere in Peebles?" "Well," she said, "I'm going down to Peebles and I'll certainly look out for a place for you as well". Because Mrs Demarco – who's still alive, Annie – Annie, she'd got a place in Peebles, and she was quite happy there because it was safe and there were no bombs or anything.

However, in the meantime, whilst all this was happening, we still hadn't heard *a word* about our fathers or anyone...Mr Leese had tried to find out, but a blank wall. Nobody knew where they were or what had happened to them – they'd just disappeared...So there was one Italian called Olindo Crolla, who came from Leith. He was naturalised. He had a nice wife, Antonetta, who was my confirmation godmother, but he was very much *in* with the police, up at the High Street...And a lot of people say that he was actually...a, what would you say, a 'stool pigeon'? That he used to carry information about the Italians to the police. And that was why he got to move about so freely and why nothing ever happened to him. However, they tried getting a hold of him to see if he could find out anything. By this time, people were absolutely frantic – can you imagine? Nothing.

And then, one day, my mother said, "We're going out. Get dressed, we're going out. I'm taking you with me because you've to look after Mario. You're to make sure when you go to this house that you keep him quiet, take him for a wee walk, anything. But you've to look after the baby and be a good girl." I thought, "What's new?" I was always looking after the baby. However, I said, "Right." So we got dressed and went along to this bungalow in Bearsden.

When they opened the door it was *absolutely packed*...when you're a wee girl, I thought, "What's happening here?" They were all in dark clothes and very flustered looking, you see? And they were waiting for Conchetta, that's my godmother, to come from somewhere. Nobody was very sure where but there was Marietta, there was Zia Pasqucha, Zia Carlina, Annie – oh, you name them, they were all in there. It was absolutely packed and there were Glasgow Italians as well that I didn't know. And, Aunt Connie arrived and she came in. It was a big sitting room, everyone was sitting around and I was sitting with Romano, that was my cousin, you see. Romano and I were always sitting together, arguing and, all of a sudden, Aunt Connie said, "I've got a letter that's been smuggled from Liverpool." And she said, "It tells us what's happened to our men folk." So, she said, "I want you all to sit round and I'll read this letter out." And it was actually written on Izal toilet paper – don't know if you remember Izal, it was sort of shiny on one side and it had little green writing. I can remember it like – this huge thing coming out, you know, this big piece of toilet paper. And on that paper were the names of the ones that had gone down on the Arandora Star, the ones that had been drowned, the ones that were injured and in hospital in Liverpool,

Palace Internment Camp. Isle of Man. Sept. 1940.

and the ones that hadn't been on the Arandora Star but that had gone to the Isle of Man. See, at that time, what had happened: Father had been taken with all the others from Penicuik, put on a train and taken to Liverpool. They had commandeered hotels in the Isle of Man all along the front and these were to be the internment for the less dangerous aliens. And they were being shipped across to the Isle of Man from Liverpool. But at the same time, a ship – the Arandora Star – was going to Canada with the 'undesirable aliens', the ones that they felt were a big threat. And they would be in Canada for the duration of the war. Some went to Australia as well, I think. But anyway, this was the Arandora Star. Of course, the Arandora Star, the Germans sank the ship. It wasn't just Italians that were on it, there were Germans on it as well, and there were Jews I think. There were a mixture of people that they thought were undesirable. Because Churchill had his back to the wall and he was absolutely panicking, so anything that moved that was slightly suspicious was being sent anywhere. So, that was what happened.

So, she started to read out the list and I can remember, you know, people crying and then Zia Carlina - she said that Zio Lorenzo had jumped off the ship but he had died. He had drowned - and she collapsed. And Marietta had to take her through to a bedroom and I was sent for a glass of water. By this time, we'd given up arguing, Romano and I, which was odd. And we were absolutely, we didn't, we couldn't take it in...it was like a moment in history that we were taking part in and we just felt the enormity of what was happening. And then Connie said that Uncle Achi had jumped overboard, had struck the raft and been injured – he'd cracked ribs and so on and so forth – but he was safe. And Romano who, you know, was a boy, he burst into tears and, of course, I burst into tears because I felt so sorry for him, you know. And then, she read all the ones from the Arandora Star...Serafino Capaldi had been hurt and Alfonso had been drowned, which was a terrible shame, he was a lovely man. And he wouldn't have hurt a fly, you know. He'd been drowned. Then she said, "And here are the lucky ones" – the ones that went to the Isle of Man. And, of course, my Dad's name was amongst them. Oh! My mother – oh, what a state we were all in! But we felt so *relieved* because we felt that at least he's alive and he's in the Isle of Man and with any luck, he's okay. So, I think we went...

Shortly after, we left there and went to Peebles. And Peebles was like 'Little Italy'. It was all Italians – and Poles. It was full of Polish officers. Have you ever seen anybody who wasn't an officer in the Polish army actually? They were all officers!

Oh I see!
Very handsome. And everywhere they went, they would click their heels and bow and all the rest of it. So, we went to this house first of all, with a Mrs Watts, and we had a room there and she had Polish officers there as well, you see, and it was really crowded. It was a big cottage but it was pretty crowded so Mother was still looking for somewhere a bit better. And eventually we found digs with a Special Constable who was also an arch poacher and to this day I think twice before I can eat grilled salmon because we lived on salmon, salmon, salmon. Every time you turned it was a big lump of salmon! Anyway, we lived with them and the funny thing was that, whenever the National Anthem came on the wireless, he used to make his family stand to attention and we used to have to do the same! Which we didn't feel – we didn't feel very British at the time, after what we'd been through. We didn't feel we deserved all this.

Meanwhile, back at the ranch, Mr Leese was working very hard to get my mother naturalised and to get my father home. And... I went to school in

Peebles and it was a two-classroom school. I don't know if you've ever heard of a school like that? It was a partition that divided the one room. And Mrs Dodds was the headmistress/schoolteacher and there was an assistant and she actually did the whole lot herself. So she had five groups, I think, in each class and she just gave each lot the work. And it was great, because there were the Poles there as well, and the Italians and the Poles got on fine and we had quite a nice time there.

So there were quite a few other Italian children there?
Oh yes! My Aunt Annie was there with Gloria, Teresa and Angela, and Aunt Connie was there with Romano. Vera and Ernie must have been grown up, they would have been looking after the shop in Edinburgh. Ronnie and Rose were looking after the factory...I can't remember any other ones. Just the ones that we particularly were close to. I missed home terribly. And that was one of the worst winters for snow that we'd ever had. The snow was piled up everywhere and Ronnie couldn't get down to see us and we were really pretty well stranded in Peebles. But, he...funnily enough Gloria and Teresa loved it, and Gloria now has sold her Edinburgh house and they've gone and got a house in Peebles. I wouldn't want to go back. I wanted home.

However, it must have been the January of '41. Was it '41? Aye, must have been...Mother was sent for to go to a tribunal for naturalisation. And she went and she was given her British nationality back. So we were able to move back to Edinburgh. We came back at the beginning of February and then in the Easter, it was Good Friday actually, my father got home from the Isle of Man. He was one of the first to get back. And he used to write to my mother every single week. They were allowed to write. And it was that typical Italian: 'My Dearly Beloved Wife', you know, and she used to read the letters out to us. They were censored, of course, but he used to write every week. And we could send parcels, and we sent Christmas presents to the Isle of Man and all that. So, that was fine.

And then we came back to Edinburgh. And the funny thing was, rationing was in full force by that time and Mother just couldn't get anything. You know, she just didn't seem to be able to get anything other than the basic rations. Father came back and the next thing we knew we had cases of apples and crates of oranges and all sorts of things as he picked up his connections with his friends and everything again. Life seemed to be an awful lot better once Dad got home. And actually, he never looked better in his life because he'd had about eight month's holiday, doing nothing, relaxing and it was what he was needing. Because he'd been working so hard with the factory and so on. He really looked very well when he came back and we were absolutely delighted that we had him back. And gradually after that, the ones that were in the Isle of Man filtered back home but, of course, the likes of Achi and so on, they didn't get home until the war was over because they went on to Canada. And the likes of the Coppolas, one of the boys actually stayed there. He became a chef and never came back. But that was the experience that I can remember of the war...

Did your Dad ever talk to you about internment?

Never! Never. The only thing he ever told us was, there was a professor there and he said he was a really odd man and he maintained that you didn't need to eat your food in courses because it was going to get mixed up anyway. So, in order to aid this process, he used to have his porridge and his bacon and egg or whatever, and his roll and his tea, and he'd mix it all up into a filthy mess and then eat it! And make everybody else feel sick because he said that that was healthy to have breakfast in this way! But he made a lot of good friends there, like my father-in-law to be. He met him and they became good friends. The ones that came from Edinburgh sort of stuck together...But he said that everyone was perfectly kind to him, that he never had any trouble or anything. But when he came back he got the chance to be naturalised, but he refused. Because he said, "What difference will signing a piece of paper make? I was born an Italian and I am an Italian and nothing's going to change that." And I admired him for that.

Is that why you said, was it his brother that had naturalised?

Oh he was very upset when my Uncle Joe was naturalised.

Because of those reasons?

Yes, he felt that you were, in a way, not true to yourself. He didn't like that at all. But it helped Uncle Joe because he stayed in the shop, made heaps of money and the family were kept together. But of course, the tragic thing was that Uncle Joe developed stomach cancer and died at 43. Leaving a wife and two young children, you know...So, it was difficult.

After I came back from Peebles, I went to the local chapel school because it was near, and it seemed a sensible thing because it was near the factory. So, what happened was: I used to go to school and then when school came out, I used to go over the Hutcheson Bridge, go into the factory, help out labelling or answering the phone or cutting wafers or whatever. Sitting at the machine, whatever was required. We were all expected to work. All of us. There was no such thing as not working. And so I would work there until the factory closed at five o'clock and then come back home with Father in the car.

Because he still had his car during the war and he was able to run it – don't ask me how but he was able to run his black Moseley. So I used to do that every day and then I went through the qualifying. But it was a year before I was supposed to and the headmistress had two of us that she thought were able to do the qualifying early. So, we actually sat our qualifying in her room, just the two of us. And I passed but Holy Cross wouldn't take me because they said I was too young. So, it was a waste of time. However, I had to sit it again the following year, which wasn't very fair. However, I got into Holy Cross and I did very well there. I wanted to go on to university but Father said no. University was for boys, not for

Carmen.
St Raphaels.
1951

girls. So...I was a bit miffed about that. Then...I got fed up working in the factory. I didn't like it at all. So, I went off to work at St Raphael's Nursing Home in Edinburgh. It was really slave labour. You stayed in, you worked from morning till night and at the end of the month, you got four pounds! So, anyway, I was there for a bit.

How old would you be then?

I'd be coming up to nineteen, twenty. I just had to get away from home because I wasn't very happy at home, my stepmother wasn't very nice and I just felt that I wanted away from her. I thought that if I got away and got into doing something where I was on my own, I might be able to sort things out for myself. I just wasn't happy. And then when I was nineteen I'd taken glandular fever and I'd been terribly poorly with it, hadn't got over it at all. So, my father decided that the best thing for me was to go off to Italy for three months, back to San Giuseppe, back to Aunt Carmela and that would put me on my feet. And it certainly did! I arrived there in the April and didn't come back until the beginning of August. And, of course, it was after the restrictions of home and not being allowed to go out without a chaperone and having to be back at half past nine at night and all the rest of it. This was heaven. I mean, Aunt Carmela was strict, sure, but every young man in that area came up to see the millionairess from Scotland – because, you know, they think that everybody in this country's made of money. And, of course, it was a succession of Vespas and what not, all these handsome young Italians coming up to court me. Bringing me wine and ricottas and torrones and you name it. All these presents, you see. And Aunt Carmela killing herself laughing at all this going on, you see. And Rosina, my cousin, she thought this was wonderful to see all these young men...One night I remember we went to bed.

As I say, this night we'd gone to bed, and Rosina and I slept in this great bed together. And suddenly, we heard this absolutely glorious music and singing outside. And it was in the middle, and I woke up and I said, "What's that?" "Oh," she says, "you're getting a serenade". "A serenade! I'll go to the window". "Oh no, no! You don't go to the window. You don't look, you don't do anything. You just listen to it. And then tomorrow – I know who it is," she says, "and we'll thank him." So, that was fine. The whole she-bang went on and the next morning we got up and Aunt Carmela never said a word, she never said, "What was that din outside?" or anything. The following night, the serenade came back again and I got another dose of beautiful music. And on the third night, same again. Apparently, this was the deluxe model – you got three nights. This was a professional serenade. But I was determined on the third night, I wanted to see who this beautiful singer was, because the voice was lovely. So you had the wooden shutters – they'd no glass in the windows – and I opened the shutters just a wee bit and I looked out and here was this three foot tall wee bauchle with a few chromium plated teeth. A real ugly little monster with this lovely singing voice! And so of course, I got back to bed, and Rosina and I were just about wetting ourselves laughing over this, you see? So, what I had to do was: I had to go and buy liqueurs and biscotti and things and on the fourth night, invite them to come back and have wine and biscuits and so on - with Aunt Carmela in the corner of course – and thank the person for the serenade who came along. You see there was this chap from Cardito, very handsome chap, who'd taken a fancy to me and had this serenade lined up. But I got two serenades and on the night before I was coming home, they came along to serenade me and wish me a safe journey. It was absolutely lovely! I mean, you know, coming through the war and all the shortages and the upset and everything, to go to Italy and suddenly be exposed to the sunshine, and the fruit and the lovely people and the language. It was just heaven, it really was! I think they were one of the nicest three months of my whole life...

And we came back to – that was 1950 – came back to Rome because it was Holy Year, and Rosina came with me to see me on my way, and we stayed a couple of nights in Rome. And we went round the basilicas, through the holy doors and saw all the sights in Rome and so on. Stayed in...what do they call it? It's not a hotel...a sort of place there, lovely. And then, she saw me on the train home to Britain. And I was heartbroken to come home. I would have been perfectly happy to stay there. There was just something about the life that was just lovely.

So, anyway, I came back and it was that that decided me that I had to do something with my life. I couldn't go back to Juniper Green, back into the house, back into being a servant for my stepmother. If she was ill, it was up to her to find somebody to look after her. I was just fed up with it. So I went to St Raphael's and I stayed there maybe about, nearly two years. And then, there was an advert in the papers, it said that Jenners was looking for young ladies with a view to training them to management in different departments and I thought, "Oh Jenners!" You know, I knew the shop well so I thought, "Right, Jenners, that sounds nice." So I went to Jenners, got an interview. There was another girl there, she was a schoolteacher who was fed up teaching in school. She fancied this idea of going in and learning about retailing. So, we had a nice sort of informal interview with Mr Kennedy, who was the head of Jenners at the time, and both of us started in Jenners.

Meanwhile, Gloria Demarco, and Teresa, we were all going to the dances by this time, you see. But it was more formal in those days. You didn't sort of just grow up and start going out and all the rest of it. You had to go to your first dance and you had to have your family with you and then you had to sort of graduate on from that. So, Oreste had come to one of these Edinburgh dances, had seen me but hadn't had the courage to come over and introduce himself or anything. So, he'd asked his cousin Gloria who the girl in the lemon dress was and Gloria says, "Oh that's Carmen Boni, I know her well. She's working in Jenners at the moment – I'll take you in one day." So, he came in, pretending he was looking for a present for his mum. Came up – what was I on? – I was on hankies and scarves and things at the time. I had eight weeks in different departments, you see. So, he came in, but I wasn't very well at the time. I'd had a bad bout of flu and I had a sort of swollen gland in my neck so I was wearing a very natty scarf you see to hide my neck! I was as pale as death. However, he came in and Gloria introduced him, and he bought a box of very expensive hankies for his mum and then, Gloria sidled away, and he said, would I like to come out for lunch with him one day, you see? That he usually came over to Edinburgh on a Tuesday. He was a professional musician and he came over for music and reeds for his saxophone and blah blah blah. And I thought, "Demarco? Now, maybe my father will approve of a Demarco." Because he'd vetoed several of what I thought were promising young men. And I thought, maybe this one will do. So, I said, "Yes that'd be lovely to come out and have lunch with you." I could have lunch, you see. I didn't have to ask anyone's permission. They didn't know where I was going for lunch. "Yes that would be fine." So, the following week I had lunch with him and he took me to an *absolutely awful* place...It was near what was the Caley Picture House – I don't know what it's called now – and it was downstairs and it was a kind of vegetable soup-fish, chips and peas-and steam pudding and custard kind of a place. And, he took me there for lunch and it was a horrible meal. But we hit if off and we blethered away for ages, had a great time. And he took me back to Jenners. He had a very posh car, by the way, a beautiful big black car and it was his. Not lent by Mummy or Daddy, it was his own car, you see. He was about twenty nine, coming up for thirty. He was a good bit older than me. You see he was a nice, natural, easy-going person. And then, of course, he started phoning me, so I thought I'd better tell the family. So, [they] said, "Who's this on the phone for you?" "Oreste Demarco from Cowdenbeath." "Oh!" my father says, "That's a lovely family." I thought, "Thanks be to God!" "Lovely family, I know the family well. He's an only child. You're alright there." I thought, "That's great."

We married in St Cuthbert's, Slateford. Beautiful. It was the first Wednesday after Easter and it was a lovely day, sunshine and everything. We had the reception in the Adam Rooms in George Street. They were very swish in those days. And, as we came along Princes Street, it was a twenty-one gun salute because it was the Queen's birthday, wasn't it! So, we spent our wedding night in the Caley Hotel in a suite, which was a disaster! I was greeting all the time wanting to go home, and he wasn't much better! We'd planned a three month honeymoon which started in London, went down to Naples, Capri, Rome, Florence, Venice, Lucerne, Paris, back to London. Wonderful honeymoon! My husband had six gigantic pieces of luggage – he had everything but the kitchen sink. And he even had a suitcase with card games and board games in it...draughts and chess and I fell apart when I saw this. I thought, "What, on honeymoon?" Anyway, that was how innocent he was. He was a really genuine, caring, gentle man. And he thought that we might get bored and that having a game of draughts or that would be fun. However, we had a great time on honeymoon. We went everywhere. We went to Capri, we took donkeys. We went to Naples and had great fun there – the biggest pizza we'd ever seen in our lives. We had a wonderful time in Rome. We went up the mountains to see our relatives. We had a week in Rome, so we disappeared for a couple of days, went up the mountains, collected a wad of money which Zio Giovanni Valente had put there. Because at that time you were only allowed so much money you see and for a honeymoon of this length it wasn't going to last. Not the way he was spending it! We went there and we visited all our relatives up in the mountains.

So, we arrive back in Cowdenbeath and we settled down and within a year I had Lawrence and that was, oh, such a day! Because my father-in-law was over the moon that I'd produced a *grandson*, you know. And then about fifteen months later I had Angela. And then I had several miscarriages, never managed to have any more children after that. But I had my son and I had my daughter. Unfortunately, the old couple died quite early on. She died at 69 and he died six months later...So, we lost them both quite quickly. And, of course, for years, I didn't have anything to do with my own family. I'd had enough of her and for several years, I just kept well away. I didn't have anything to do with them. We made peace later but I was always very wary because I just didn't want to get caught in that trap again, you know... And we had a very nice life here. He was a musician. He went out every night playing in bands and so on and I looked after the shop. But I was never very happy, there was always something missing. And

Oreste, Carmen, Baby Angela and Lawrence.

Oreste on clarinet with Dixielanders, 1957.

when I got the chance to go and do a course at Stevenson, to go as a mature student to university, I took it. Went back to university and did an honours degree...which was really good because it gave me a different job and it gave me an interest that I can still maintain now, which I wouldn't have had if I'd stayed in the shop.

So, your questions?

Yes, just finally. I'm just quite interested all the way through, what you've told me, there seems to be quite a big social network in a way. When you talked about your father finding a second wife and even yourself, when you were going to get married, there was always a lot of people, you know, putting people, Italian people, your way. Was there, did you feel you were part of a -?

We were part of a family, yes. It was important for us because we were still foreigners in a foreign land. So, the Italian parties, the picnic, the dances, godmother, godfather and so on. This was a very important networking that we had...We had to be there for each other because at that time there was a strong opposition *to* Italians. I mean, that's why you didn't say you ate spaghetti. You were, if somebody got drunk or a

148

bit obstreperous, you were 'a dirty Tally', you were an 'Eye-tie'. You were 'those funny people.' They made fun of our parents because they couldn't speak the language very well. They would make fun of the fact that you ate spaghetti and things. These were all *foreign* foods, nowadays everybody's learnt pizza and spaghetti but at that time, nobody drank coffee! If you went for a coffee, you got a spoonful of Camp essence and a cup of hot milk! I mean, no, young Italians nowadays I don't think could understand what it was like. I was lucky in that I was a fair-skinned, grey-eyed Italian so I didn't stand out like a sore thumb. But the frizzy–haired, brown-eyed ones with the sallow skins, they got really a lot of stick because they were *obviously* foreign.

And I don't care what you say and what they say on television and everything but the Scots are very racist, really they are. It's not just about race, it's about religion. So you were a Catholic, you were an Italian and you ate funny food – God help you in an argument...And all you could do was fry fish and chips or make ice cream. So, they had a very poor opinion of us. That's shifted now and the Pakistanis and so on and the Chinese, they get most of the brunt of it. Because the Italians have sold their culture to pacify another culture that I don't think was worthy of the sacrifice.

How would you describe your own sense of identity now?

I am still Italian...I admire a lot about Scotland and my father used to always say that he came here of his choice to make a better life than he could have had in Italy and that, to him, he always used to quote, "When in Rome, do what the Romans do" and he used to say that about paying taxes and so on. But, at the end of the day, he was still an Italian with a culture that stretches away back into the mists of time, and it's a culture that I'm sad to see it dissipate among the young ones nowadays. I mean they don't have the same – when we went to the Italian party in our wee frocks, it was like a big family. There were the Coppolas and the Crollas and the Pias and the Bonis and the Gizzis and so on, and we were kept like that. It was always hoped, that's why my father made such hard work of our getting married, because he didn't want us to marry outside of our own families. Because he said that marriage was a difficult enough thing without putting the obstacles of race, of religion in the way as well. And he felt if you ate the same food and you went to the same church and you had the same background, that these were great things for a strength within a marriage...I think he was right. And why be ashamed of a culture that has given so much to the world? It makes me mad when you see people on television implying that the Italians are cowards or making fun of the way they speak or making fun of the food they eat and so on. I think that's extremely insulting. And it still maddens me. If Italy and Scotland are playing football, there's no doubt who I'm cheering, after all these years, I'm still cheering for Italy.

This location in, the North East, hosted another of the pilot groups, learning recording skills and eventually interviewing independently. They produced a fine collection of recordings and looked broadly at the land and the sea as themes. The following interview depicts the unique dialect of the area and a fascinating working life.

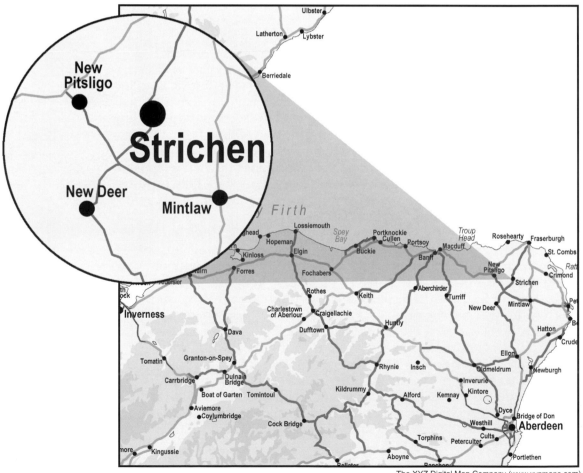

Can you tell me yer name and when you was born?
Well my name is May Hutchinson and I was born on the 27th August 1916.

Is that yer maiden name ?
Stephen is ma maiden name.

Now fit aboot yer parents, far where they born ?
I dinnae ken where ma father was actually born, but he was country, cos he aye spoke he landed in Turriff, and I think long ago fin he'd been young he must a workit on the fairms, and then he cam doon tae the Broch (local name for Fraserburgh) and he was workit on the coal for years and years, aal ma young daes till he was ould, until he died. My mither was Belger. Her father had a yawly, a canna talk, a canna talk, a yewly.

What's a yewly?
The sma boats, that jist ging inshore, three mile aff. That's what they did in them days, was him and anither man had a yewly and they jist gaed three mile aff and, of course, the bigger boats sterted tae come and they gaed awa further oot, ye ken, the Seine net boats. He was an inshore fisherman, ma Dide.

What kind of fish was he fishing for?
Well just haddock and cod. They had a hoose in Belger, ma Granny and ma Dide, that's what they ca'd him there. So they had their ain hoose in Carnbulg. He was awfa weel aff, my Dide. I used tae hear ma mither say he had a watch an a'thing, which was somethin then. He lived till he was over 90 that's fifty year ago, 60 year ago, cos my aaldest quinie was jist a baby fin he died and she's now 63 this year, ken, and so it must have been a gye lang time ago. But he had a hoose o' his ain and a watch 'fore he was 21 or somethin, I used tae hear ma mither say it, so he was coonted nae bad aff.

Well the fishers were poor
Verra, verra poor at that time, till before the war. It's only since the war that they started tae climb. Because my father's boss, the coal man, an awfu nice gentleman, he was blind, he really was a gentleman, Mr Grey. And they hadnae money tae pay their coal, ken. He says well, they cannae dae withoot it, so ma father and Peter an them, that's the driver, had tae ging oot wi coal tae them. He was an awfu gentleman, Mr Grey. And then of course efter the war it started to get..... They were verra verra poor. So tae hae a hoose o' yer ain then was somethin.

So was your grandmother fae Belger as well?
I think ma Didie was fae St Combs. But the bit I mind was in Belger.

Noo how did yer mither come to be bidin in the Broch.

Well, cos she mairrit ma father. They were aye followin the fishins, you see. My mither aye gaed oot tae Yarmouth and Lowestoft, and so did I actually, and then ma father came doon tae the Broch tae work. Fit wey they actually met up I dinnae ken, but he cam doon tae work in the Broch, they met, ye see, and that was it.

So you dinnae ken where yer faither was born?

That's one thing I dinnae ken. But I ken that his father was cottar'd and then he was a gardener tae the doctor in Turriff. They spent a lot o' years in Turriff. But he bade in the Broch. His brothers and sisters was up there, but my father made his life wi' us in the Broch, and a very good father he was too. He was a gentleman.

Did he have a coal lorry?

No, he workit under Mr Gray, coal merchant, ye ken? He was, if ever there was a gentleman, it was that man. He was a very very nice man, he bade doon fae the West Kirk, ken, up fae Victoria Street towards the school well see the hoose there before you come tae yon home, well that's where he bade. He was an awfu nice man. Then George Mair took that ower, a Brethren man. I will say nae mair aboot that. (laughter)

How aboot yerself? Fin did you get mairrit?

Well I was mairrit on the 25 December 1934.

That was Christmas Day!

That was nae Christmas Day. I cam hame fae Lowestoft fae the fishin.

Was that your job tae pack the fish in the barrels?

Well I jist traivelled. I was one year in Stronsay up in Shetland, and I was one year at Yarmouth, and one year at Lowestoft, and then I workit here in the Broch an a' for one year. When I cam hame fae Shetland, I workit in a yard cos it was a busy time. The Shetland fishin is earlier, it's in May, than it is here cos the herrin is comin doon, ye see, the herrin gings roon and begins tae come doon. So they are earlier than us. Then it comes doon tae Broch, and then it gings awa doon tae the North o' England, and then it gings doon tae Yarmouth, the shoals, ye see?

It would hae been gye hard work at that time?

Well, but I liked it. Fin I think on't it now we went doon tae Yarmouth in the October November for six weeks, and we was workin ootside see, like the sands, like a beach they ca'd it, the deens in Yarmouth, and it was a' just oot in the open, the barrels an a'. The gutters, I think, some o' them, no them a', had a thing ower the tap o' them. The packers jist workit ootside, ye ken.

In a' kinds o' weather?

In a' kinds o' weather, ye had hoodies, yer ileskins and that was jist it. But I was doon on holiday there a lang time efter, years like, it was nice and warm in Yarmouth, and when I cam up here to go doon the toon I was on West Road, it was bitter cald. The change in the climate wisnae real, it was so mild doon there twas, in November, but up here I was standin' there in West Road waitin' for a bus and I was frozen tae death till I got used to it again.

But workin doon there - I was one week we was the best in Yarmouth, ma mither in Chrissie Westie, ken the Westies, aye, well Chrissie wis my neeper an my mither in her in me. We had so many barrels that they cam up fae the big yard tae see fa they could crew us. It was nearly at muckle herrin tae pack ye ken, ma mither wis an awfu good gutter and so was Chrissie. It was an awfu barrels we did that week. Cos sometimes they had what they ca'd a glut o' herrin. Ken what a glut is? A great lot. There always seems tae be a glut when they're just overpowered wi' herrin, ken? And that was the week, we was oot in the early mornin and workin till late at nicht, and things like that.

And you had to work till a'thing was done?

Oh aye, you had tae work till it was done nae maitter fit time o' the nicht it was. You jist had tae work till it was feneeshed ye see. I've seen me gaein up efter tae ma mither's yard at yin or twa o' clock in the mornin till they were feneeshed, ye ken. And then ye was oot at six o'clock in the mornin and fillin up the barrels because they sunk wi the saat, ye see. You had tae top them up. Ye had tae flatten the bellies like that and you had to put two in one. You had tae pit the hieds in a row like that. You had to mak it awfu bonny to top up the barrels because the man used tae come roon and taste them, the Russians and the Germans used to come and taste them and they used to eat the raw herrin. They used to taste them like that you see. They'd open the barrel to see fit like the herrin was and then they branded them. If they were first class they branded them first class, they got mair money the curer, you see. So you had tae do yer best.

Did maist o' the herrin go abroad?

Aye, aye. To Russia and Germany, that was the main places. It was a busy busy time here in the summertime. They used tae come doon fae Moray aa doon the East Coast, aff a Shetland, fae Stornoway and that way for the fishin here. They used tae bide in huts. Ken aa the huts were up abeen the yards. They were a made o' wood. Aa the yards had huts that their crews stayed in, aa them that didnae bide in the Broch. Fin we was in Yarmouth we had tae bide wi landladies, we keepit intae the hooses and they made wir food. Ken we bought wir food and they made it. Oh it was a busy busy time. The first time we went awa we didnae ken whit we was in for. I was only 16, 17, aye cos I was 14 fin I had to gae awa intae service. I must be getting auld.

No, no, this is interestin

Well, see fin my mither gaed to Yarmouth, we wis aye puttin oot for us tae bide wi somebody. She had tae pay for it. We wis aye puttin oot tae bide wi somebody. The last time I was fourteen and ma sister workit at the Morrice the Lawyer, an that's yon Nor wood as you come in tae Strichen Road, ken? Ma sister workit there and he was a lawyer. His wife telt ma sister tae take me oan tae help her because they had a big hoose. So I did that. Well it was comin on time for Yarmouth, you see. Well I was too auld for ma mither tae pay for. So she took me through. I couldnae get a crew tae go tae Yarmouth, I was too young, you see, I was only fourteen. So we gaed oot tae college registry in Aberdeen, ma mither and me, and at the time there was a lady there, it was the County Hotel in Stonehaven was wantin a kitchen maid. Well of course, ma mither telt me tae ging and the lady bade in the Broch. Her husband was Thomson the curer, but she was through there for her mother, for her mother was hersel in Stonehaven for her husband had died. So away I goes doon there. Ah I was hamesick, terrible.

Well I did ower weel, I was helpin the cook, I was brought up tae work, you see, wash and everythin, and nae washin machines. We had tae scrub. But onyway, I was helpin the cook and I overdid it, should a' been awa ben tae Mrs Duff tae see aboot fit was for the meal the next day, but I was washin up the dishes. Well what did she dae, she put the housemaid awa. She telt me tae get overalls, and I had tae get lacy overalls wi a lacy cap and she put me up the stair. I did ower weel, that's the God's honest truth. And I was put up the stairs and there was fourteen bedrooms up there and two bathrooms and two flights of stairs. I was just goin on for 15. Well I was fifteen months there and I just aboot killed masel because I just did ower weel and Mr and Mrs Thomson gaed up tae see ma mither and telt her "Oh Mother's upstairs is spotless" and so it was. I was shinin, the loaby ken, she had broon kinda linoleum, and it had a big windae in it and it used tae shine. They were awfu nice tae me. Well I stuck it for fifteen months and I had tae take mattresses doon the stair, up and doon the kitchen stairs, great big lang stairs, roon the back and beatin them and cairryin them up again. And I did a dose in the one mornini ken at spring cleanin time, and I was killed. So I cam hame tae the fishin efter a. Now I wasnae lang hame fin Mrs Thomson was doon again seekin me, you see, I wasnae wantin tae gang, but ma mither says gang, you had tae dee fit you was telt, you see. Doon I goes tae Stonehaven again, but she was bidin there this time, she gave up her hoose here, and she was doon in the hotel. I dinnae like her, I did not like her at all. She made ye feel little and small. I didnae like her, and they were mad at me, and I gaed tae the Salvation Army, you see, and I gaed doon tae Stonehaven. There was a woman came to the door and offered me her daughter's place in Aberdeen. She had an awfu good place and she was leavin and she thocht that I wad maybe like it but I said "No I'm goin awa hame tae the fishin." They didnae believe me. Noo efter aa fit I cleaned and did for them. I gaed ben wi their meal, but Maggie Thomson she bade in the kitchen and she kept her heid doon and she says "Religion 's alright but when it comes to telling lies I don't think much about it," I never forget her words. I had no intention of gaein tae Aberdeen tae work. I was gaein awa hame tae the fishin but they didnae believe me, so I cam hame onyway and I never got dole cos I had left ma job. And I never forgot her words, she didnae believe me, just thocht I was tellin lees. And the best o' it was fin you are speakin aboot the curers it was John Dunbar, Jim Thomson, and Airchie Watt, ye didnae ca them Mr Watt and Mr Dunbar. And, of course, when I was there I ca'd him Jim. She says "Its Mr Thomson to you, May". I just felt like that and I says I'm no stickin here. And another thin she says "Don't give them two courses, put the beef in amongst the soup", this is Maggie. Well I was starvin, I had tae ging tae the doctor when I was there, I really was, I was starvin, see the cook had onythin she could pick at, the waitress she had cakes and biscuits and a'thing, I had nothin. I was starvin, I had tae ging tae the doctor, ken, ma period was comin a' the time. It was too hard workin, I never telt ma mither, ye see, ye just thocht at that time ye just had tae dee it. And that was ma sojourn in Stonehaven, so I left and gaed tae the Yarmouth, the fishin in Yarmouth. And then I got mairrit fin I cam hame in December 1934. And it was no Christmas Day, no decorations up and no holiday or nothing. Oor decorations didnae go up till two days before New Year. That is just what it was then. Then it started tae creep in Christmas. It's a lang time ago, 1934. I canna believe it maself sometimes, do ye ken, it's a lang time. Tae me its just like yesterday.

So fin did Christmas Day start being official?

I dae ken it was a gye file efter that, Isobel. Ma bairns were beginnin tae grow up, ye started giein them their presents and then they wouldna be bothered in Aal Year's Nicht and they'll get back tae sleep efter a late night. And that's what they sterted tae dae. Gie the bairns their presents at Christmas. So it just began like that, you see. Fin I was young they just gaed in droves fae hoose tae hoose on Aal Year's Nicht. Its nae sae popular noo, so they say,cos I'm never oot, you see. At that time you never see a hen. Fin I was young the only time we had a hen was fin ma granny in Turriff would ha sent doon a hen for New Year. And noo you can just ging doon and get a bit hen when you're needin. But we never went hungry, cos my mither used to sek tatties on a fairm and you got a dreel, if you ken fit a dreel is, or two dreel, and then come October ye gaed oot and gaithered them up cos the man wi the tractor thingmied them up, so we had always plenty o' tatties. And you had yer barrel o' herrin, ken, and we used tae cure eggs.

How did you do that?

In a some kinda glass, something glass it used to be. I hinna din that for a lang lang time. But we used tae dae that, cure eggs, fine country eggs. That's one thing we got at the time o' the war fae a fairm oot here, fresh

eggs and butter. We were no supposed tae dae it but we did get it.
I think it was all supposed to be rationed. We aye got that onyway.

What about your vegetables and stuff?

Well my father had plots. He had two plots and he grew our vegetables
and flooers. He used to sell flooers for the men comin hame fae the war,
for the fund. My daughter used tae gae roon and sell flooers, lilies,
daffodils an a'thing. There's nine year atween ma twa. And my mither
used to bake oatcakes. The Welcome Home Fund, that's what it was. My
mither used to be an awfu good baker o' oatcakes. She used to make
oatcakes and sell them for the Welcome Home Fund. You had to try and
dae yer bit.

Is it two quines you've got?

Nine year atween them, aye. Ma second yin she just bides along there.
My ither yin bides in Peterhead. She's got five of a family. They are a'
daein well. They are a' grown up and mairrit.

May, second from left, with husband and daughter

Far did ye meet yer man?

He kent me. He minds when I was at the school. I didnae ken him then.
It was his brither I kent because he was in the army and Danny was in
the army. But I didnae ken him. It was Johnny I kent, his younger brither.
It was when I cam frae Stonehaven, he was in the band in the army. He
plays the trombone.

Fit regiment o' the army was that?

Oh no, the Salvation Army. So he asked me oot, ye see, and that was it, ye ken.

So far, when ye was coortin what did ye dae, did ye just gang for walks?

We just gaed for walks and then we had the meetins tae see. I enjoyed ma young days in the Army, we had a rare time. We just gaed for walks an that. Maybe a walk efter a meetin, and things like that, ye ken. I was mairrit for fifty one and half year, he died twelve year ago. He took a heart attack doon the shore. I just said cheerio till him. I was just off for a bus efter dinner time. I said "I'll hae yer tea ready when ye come back up again. Five o' clock and here was the doctor at the door. He'd had a heart attack doon the shore and just died. The police was up. An awfu shock. We had a happy marriage.

What did yer man dae?

He was a cooper. He was a cooper and a fresher. He freshed herrin. He put herrin intae boxes and sent them awa tae places like Southampton and London.

Did they gang in the train?

Well they used tae gang on the train, and they used tae hae tae flee tae catch that train if the boats was late in comin in, and he had tae flee. He was rushin and caught his leg atween the platform and the train. He was aff for seven weeks wi his leg. It was oot like that. An awfu leg. We had tae poultice it every four hours. But that's what he was. He used tae gae doon tae Plymouth and Girvan. He was six months in Girvan, cos he was freshin there. They did that in the summer time and in the winter time they were cooperin. Makin the barrels in the winter, you see. And that was when they used tae shed an awfu lot o fat, cos they were so hard workit. And then in the summer time they were in the yards, and they put it back on again. They were awfu hard workit coopers, ye ken.

He workit wi the masons a wee whilie in Pitsligo in the time o the war. Mind Benzies was bombed, well ma man was workin wi him. He was knockin doon the great big high wa', a jerry flew richt past him, ken. As sure as daith he lost his pocket book and his curl, he'd a curl aff o' his hair when he was a baby. He'd awfu curly hair when he was little. He lost his pocket book and his jacket ower heids o't, ye ken. And he's runnin. Fit way he got doon oot o' there he disnae ken. One o' the workmen says "Fits a dae ?" He was deef. "Run" he says "the germans". Because they were bombing the convoys, you see. The convoys always gaed past up there. We were the last hoose in Marconie and there was a dyke and then it was the park and the sea. And they used tae cam ower oor hoose and cam oot again and doon further, ye see, richt roon the coast. I had a bullet hole in my windae fae ane o' them. An ma mither was cleanin the box far you keep the brushes for cleanin sheen (shoes), at the back, it gaed richt ower her heid an aa. The sheddies in the next block was aa blown up. They left aboot six bombs but the maist went in the park . The sheddies were a blown tae smithereeens.

There was a bit o' bombin in the Broch. We'd a lot o'bombin. A terrible time. A strain, I used to sit in my bed listenin, just listenin for the drone. For the size o' the Broch.

What was the target in the Broch?

McConnachies, and they were aye tryin for Tooley's but they never got it. McConnachies got it and my brither was in o't. I mind ma father pacin at the door, he didnae ken, pacin up and doon if ma brither was killed. But he was OK. But there was a lot o'folk killed. But I dinnae ken really fos foo much gaed oan there till I read in the Herald in this past year or so, there's been an awfu lot written in the Herald aboot the bombin by folk that's awa frae the Broch. They bade in huts there, they've been tellin their tales. I wannae gae intae details aboot it but it was forty year since I was doon the road — so I was — for aboot three year wi ma spine and so I missed an awfu lot. I was hame in 1939, the year war broke out an I was nae aboot tae ging oot an aboot. So I can only say fit I saw fae ma ain door. Ye used tae tell the bairns storics tae try an tak their mind aff o't. My sister's quine was there an aa. She'd tell them stories in ablow the stair, ken and in a ablow the table sometimes. An the nicht that Benzie Millers was bombed, ma sister and ma brither were baith in the picter hoose across fae it. You wouldnae mind o'that Isabel. It was a bonny shop fin I was young. We didnae ken fit was happenin there. Ma father was in the coalshed that was in the back o't. So he gaed awa doon. He cam back up govie me. We heard this whistle in the loabby, it was a lang loabby at Marconie. We was a lyin there when this whistle started, ye ken. What a bang. It landed richt in the corner o Corbetts Park, just aside the road ower fae wur hoose. I thocht was just ootside oor door, ye ken. What a crack it gaed oot. I'll no forget that crack. There were nae hooses there at that time, you see. It was verra near, I mean it could o been his, ken, could a been his. But it fell ower a bit, ower at the park. It was a big bang, whistlin bomb.

So it scared ye for a lot o'times ?

Oh you've nae idea, and I mind ma father and Jock up the stairs and ma man gaein oot tae see fit was goin on, ye ken, and they saw somebody signallin fae a bit o a hill in Corbetts Park in the gut factory. They saw somebody signallin there once, aye, they did that. They saw somebody signallin, ye ken. Gut factory used tae be doon there, well it's a gradual slope comin up, see oor hoose was here, it was the last hoose, and they saw somebody there. There was somethin there then. But I'm readin in the paper an awfu lot o'it happened here, at the time o'the war that I never kent. There was a lot o'folk killed. Ma sister would a been killed.

Ma sister got ma mither's hoose in Forside Street fin we got that hoose in Marconie. The bombs landed in Commerce Street and then the postie was in Forside Street and he was in his bed and he waukened up tae daylight and there's a great enormous boulder gaed richt through the roof o ma sister's hoose, richt on the tap o'the bed. Noo if they'd been there there would a been serious damage o'some kind, and somethin on her sideboard an aa. So there were a lot o'escapes.

Did you nae hae air raid shelters?
Ma father dug an air raid shelter in the gairden. Just dug it oot in the green, ye ken. Aye.

Was your man at hame through the war?
Aye, he was grade three. I was richt gled cos I wasnae a well woman. But we aye managed.

Your bairns must just a been little at that time?
Oh aye, Stella was four fin war broke oot. And I lost near three year o her life. She was nine fin Irene was born. And Irene just bides along there and she maks ma food and a'thing, you see. Ma faimily's been awfu good tae me. Grandchildren an aa, they are just special. Just special. Our Pamela worked in Simms, doon there at Simms the chemist, she's a pharmacist.

Is that your grand daughter?
My grand daughter, aye. And she's gaein awa, she's finishin this week, she's gaein awa tae work with George Ellison, Peterhead Dispensary. She's gaein awa tae bide there. I'll miss her comin in, ken. It was fine, just kinda newsy, ken.

That's just hoo life was then. (Laughs) I'm laughin, I cannae help it, the three o them was out the night that bomb gaed aff. And we'd a press fin you gaed in the door and ma father got in, we heard the whistle, you see. And Jock got in and ma father got into the door and Danny came in and went smack intae the door and the door intae the press opened and it near broke his fingers. So funny things happened in times o stress like that. Ah weel, ye need somethin tae brak the stress

Bargin into the door an this thing came doon see. It was a funny thing. It was awfu stressful though. Nicht efter nicht, it had a certain bum (humming noise) the jerry aeroplanes. You just sat up like that listenin and listenin.

You could tell them apart?
Aye you just seemed tae ken. It was awfu fine when the all clear went, you could relax then, you see. It wasnae fine for the convoys fin they came along, for they just cam oot and oot intae them and richt doon tae Belger and that, ye ken.

See fin ye was new mairrit far did ye bide at?
I bade in 77 Shore Street.

In a room?
In a room fae his mother. His mother had a flat. We had a room, and a wee room aff o't far I kept ma coal. It was a' bonny and clean, it was nae like a coal shed, it was kept in a big tea box, ye ken these big tea boxes you used tae get, you'll no ken aboot them, but you used tae get big tea boxes and the caol gaed in there and your brush and shovel and things like that. I had a bonny room, me.

And his folk were fisher folk as well?
Aye, his father was a sailor fin they were young. They had twelve o'a family, my man's family, there was twelve o'them. And she raised up all o them. He was the eleventh one. Johnnie was the twelfth one, he was a seventh son.

You should have had seven sons. (laughter)
She had a hard life though. I dinna think its fair. My granny had thirteen but she only brought up four. My Belger granny, ken.

My granny was the first yin tae hae a hearse in Belger and they a bade in St Combs fin I was a young. Fin I was a young quinie my granny died, cos my sister had tae be lifted up tae see her, and I was just a young quine and I managed tae see her, and they were taen on a larry ower tae St Combs. My granny said afore she deed that she would like a hearse. She was the first yin tae hae a hearse.

And when did she die?
Oh I was just a little quinie, I'd be aboot nine or ten. Then my Granda he lived tae 90, and Stella was aboot nine or ten yer old, ma first lassie, when he deed. He lived a lang time, a lot o the 'our the water' did, they lived a lang time. And I'll tell ye anither thing, it was the weemin that hauled the boats up oot o'the watter. They had rollers tae haul them up. The weemin did that. They had tae haul them up.

This was oot in Belger?
Aye, the weemin had tae cairry the fish up tae the train oan their creels, ye ken. The weemin had tae work, ye see.

Was it your man's mither that used tae go and collect mussels?
Aye, ma man's mither. Course he was a deep sea sailor, and then some o' Danny's mithers folks had a'boats, ye ken. So Freddy gotten a job in there, ye see, fin he stopped gaen awa tae sea. He used tae go tae Russia and a'road. He got a job sheelin and baitin, reddin the lines and a'thing.

161

They did that in the hoose?

Aye it was a'done in the hoose. Sheelin and baitin his mussels. And I was with ma mither's auntie when she was in Yarmouth one time wi ma sister. My mither would never hae allowed it. She couldna be bothered, wi bairns in her road. And I says to her "I'm dyin tae open these mussels", cos they had tae dae it, ye see. "Weel, weel sit doon there" she says tae me. So she gave me a futtle, a certain kinda knife. And I got to open a mussel and hand it ower. I don't think she was beatin. It was awfu good o'her. I got a poisoned finger wi a great big bealin in't. I never forgot o't. And I aye mind her takkin a haud o ma haun like this. They had a lang steel in front o the fire. She burst it tae me. She was awfu good tae me. And I was dyin tae open these mussels. It's just little things.

Then I bade wi her ither auntie fin ma mither was in Yarmouth. She says tae me " Wash James' face" "No" I says "I'm nae washin James' face, I dinna wash ma faither's face and he is in the coal, I'm nae washin James' face" and I never did. I think I mind my Dide getting his face washed. Aye, you see that, that was what they did, its true. (laughter) Ye had tae pamper them, tak aff their rubber boots and a'thing. I said I never did that tae ma ain father . I says "I'm nae daein that"

I was aye puttin awa tae bide wi somebody. And I'll tell ye anither thing. We was bidin in Strichen and I hated the name o Strichen for years, and I'll tell ye for why. I had nightmares aboot it. We were supposed tae be bidin, me, ma sister, and I'd be aboot 11 and ma sister was........the school, she'd be aboot six, Edith, and ma brither was aboot two. There was five year atween us a'. And the wifie that was goin tae tak couldnae cos her quinie took diptheria. So she got this woman tae tak us and it was in Water Street. Bit it is knockit doon noo, you see. Its at the beginnin o Water Street. She wasnae mairrit but she had a boyfriend, who was in India in the army. And she used tae play a record, somethin aboot the hills. I never forgot o't for years and noo I canna mind it. And I saw her once when I was a bitty older leanin ower the railin at the beach and she was going wi her boyfriend.

We bade in this little wee squary roomie aff o the hoosie. The toilet was awa up the gairden. This little wee roomy was aff o' the livin room, you see. A little wee roomy. And it had a wee windae and a sill like that, ye ken. And there was table base on it, and when I lifted it up, and my brither was only two, it was full o'forkytails, full o'forkytails. It was a nightmare to me, I used ta take them off o the bed and throw them on the flair. And it was a nightmare, cos three o us were sleepin there, ye ken. And oh, I hated that place. It was a nightmare tae me for years. The school wasnae sae bad. I wasnae too bad wi the school, for Edith was at the school and must hae been aboot six, and the wifie skelpin her backside. Funny bit o't fin ma mither cam tae collect us and was comin up the brae, and Edith says tae ma mither "I'll aye dee fit I'm telt noo". (laughter)

She'd learned her lesson. The lesser o'two evils, "I'll aye dee fit I'm telt noo". What a laugh we got for years ower the heid o'that. But for years, even fin I was goin doon tae Yarmouth and I passed it in the train, I hated the name. But my grand daughter has a bungalow in New Deer, so I'm passin through Strichen a lot now , but the hoose is awa. And I can aboot thole it now. It was yon forkies I hated. I hated that place for years. It was massed wi forkies. It was just aside it, there was naethin but a bed. I was terrified of them gettin intae their lugs.

You must have been little at that time? What age were you?

I think I must have been about 11, my sister was just been new at the school. Cos I aye mind o'goin tae the Academy on the next year which was twelve. You gaed tae the Academy fin you was twelve. But oh, I wasnae happy there. It wasnae a happy time at a'. We was aye puttin oot wi somebody.

I was goin tae say was that the normal thing if your folk gaed awa tae the fishin?

Aye, your mither had tae pay for it, ye ken. But she aye gaed every year unless she was expectin. Ma father aye gaed tae Yarmouth, ye see, followin the drifters. It was a' drifters then. Gie ye a laugh, Stella's father-in-law telt me this. He was a butcher, but at that time he was just a message boy. The Harbour was like this wi drifters, one here and one here across, like that, there was that much o'them, ye ken. And Jock was a message boy wi the butcher, as I say. He saw the coal humfers wi a bag on their back takin coal tae the drifters, and they jumpit wi this thing fin they were walkin along this plank, it was aboot this breadth, was three things jined together, and of course it gaed richt ower a' the boats, and of course Jock saw this and thocht "I can dae that", you see, cos the coalmen never fell in. Onyway Jock wad dae that, ye ken, and a hale basket o beef fell in. (Laughter) I says "Jock its awfu". He couldnae work it at a' wi the thing, ye ken. Funny things happen.

Ye ken they hadnae much lang ago. And oranges used tae come in a certain box long ago, wi a partition in atween. A lang box aboot this height. They used tae come intae the shops. And a lot o folk used it for their pots and put a screeny in front o't. This woman in West Road was tellin her faimily this and they said "Was you tinkies?" You see, they dinna understand, because a'body jist had one room long ago, just what ye had, ye see. Well I had a bedroom suite fin I was new mairrit, a bonny bedroom suite and a bed. We just had hard chairs. Well, we'd a' the Aberdeen mannie, which Isabel would ken aboot, Lawson's o'Aberdeen, a'body had Lawson's o'Aberdeen. Well fin I got my first easy chair I thocht there was naebody like me. We hadnae room for nae mair. We sat on the steely ye see, then we got a bass. I was talkin to Jane White yesterday on the bus, she was laughin, she says "That was what it was like for a'body, ye ken." A'body had Aberdeen mannie, it was the only way ye got things. Ye had tae dae it tae get stuff for your hoose and that.

Did ye just pay up every week?

Every week, aye. I was a good payer cos I liked tae pay a'thing, I still do. I hinnae got Aberdeen mannie noo like, I stoppit years ago. But it was verra verra handy.

Was it everything, like stuff for your hoose?

Everything, claes and a'thing. Made lovely suits. I mind ma man when he was single had a suit. He had that and he was single! He had a lovely suit and his boss asked him fa made it, it was so bonny cut, it was a lovely suit. It was Lawsons o'Aberdeen. But a'body had Aberdeen mannie, fin you got a new rug you thocht there was naebody like you. As sure as daith, I thocht there was naebody like me.

Changed days noo.

Its different a'thegither noo, ye ken. But my biggest blessin is the automatic washin machine. I aye mind my faimily gied me that. And I aye mind my brither's wife died and ma sister was nae weel and I was gaein up their bed sheets and that and I wasnae able tae scrub you see. And I had an ordinary washin machine, a twin tub, and they gied me this and I didnae ken, ye see, and I said "Fit way are they sae lang ?" I was ower in Irene's. "Theyre awfu lang in comin for their supper." And I'm goin on like this. They were a' congregated in here fixin this machine up. And they took a photo o me and I'm goin like this. (laughter) Oh me that's the biggest blessin I have. I'd give up onythin afore I'd give up that.

It has changed women's lives.

It did. We had to scrub sheets and blankets, and take them through the mangle and hing them a' up and things like that ye see. Course there is nae blankets noo. But how easy it is asides afore. We still moan aboot it Aye, ye have tae pit it oan and aff noo. (Laughter)

So did you have a wash hoose?

I had a wash hoose, it was aye doon the stair and roon the back. My mither's was a rare yin wi a great big laft, doon in Forside Street, for hingin the claes in, nae need tae worry whether it was a fine day or a coorse day. But we had na laft in Marconie. Ma man used tae pit up tows in his yard which was up, nae Kirk Brae, but the ither brae off o North Street, Duke Brae, up Duke Lane. His yard was up at the top o the lane. He put tows up there. We used tae cairry oor claes up there. There was naebody took them awa. It was different a'thegither.

But I've had a washin machine for a lot o years. I had ane first, a metal ane wi gas in ablow it, a fire in ablow it, I canna mind. It was somethin, Lawrence the Baker bocht it . Mind Lawrence the baker ? They had a tearoom. They bocht it, I put it intae papers. And I got the twin tub. And then ma faimily gied me the automatic. A great invention. I think that's the thing that's changed women's lives.

It was a hale day washin. We had tae help ma mither tae scrub, tae brush in the board. We'd tae get the first water. Then ma mither took the second water and turned the ootsides in and scrubbed them. Then white claes would be put in the biler, then into bile wie Omo, then into bleach in front of the taps. We had a rare washin hoose in Forside Street but I had a washin hoose on the shore. We had tae share. Then what I was goin tae say wis "Oh no, there's ma mither takin doon". Long ago we had bed pans, nae bed pans for in ablow but curtains on yer bed. Mind o'them? There were curtains at that side o the bed, nae curtains ower the bed, like that and along the fit, feather side an a'. Do ye no mind o'that ? Well see, ma mither had that. I would only been aboot twelve. I dinnae ken hoo lang they kept it on. Well did she nae ging awa and ter a' that stuff doon and ging awa and wash in the afterneen again. She'd aye tak extra doon in the efterneen. I used tae hate it, I est to wish she wis deen at denner time, but no no, doon come the things.

Did she dae her washin a' on the one day?
Aye, cos there was four days for four tenants. So efter that you could ging in anither day, Friday Setterday if you wanted, ye ken. But you had tae licht a fire and pit oan the biler,which ma father did, fill the biler and get the water heat.

Well I mind ma mither sayin she didna get educated because she was the aalest daughter and she had tae bide aff oan certain days tae dae a washin.

Well we did that too. A woman said to me the ither day "I didnae see your photo in my class at the school", I says "Oh I'd be aff". My father used to write excuses tae the school, "She's in the wash tub". Somebody had tae watch the babies, you see, because it was a' doon the stairs and awa roon the back o the hoose a'thegither and awa up anither sair to get tae the wash hoose. Well we had tae bide aff , ye see.

Were you the eldest o the bairns?
No, ma sister was aulder than me.

Hoo many o you were there?
Four. Three quines and a loon. She lost one quinie, which she blamed the midwife for, because she said the midwife put her into too hot water. The baby jumpit, loupit up in a kinda fit fin she was washin her. Fit they did then was they washed you efter they washed the baby. Cos you had tae lie for nine days. Fin I had Stella I lay for nine days, and fin I had Irene I was up that day. (laughter) You bein bleedin and that, they used tae wash you, ye see. My mither said that water was far too het for her and the baby had been bathed in't. It shocked the baby, ma mither blamed that for lossin the baby.

Two groups ran in Aberdeen, one looking at the social impact of the oil industry in the city, and the other concentrating on language and dialect. With the latter subject the participants interviewed in several rural locations, where they felt the local tongue had been better preserved. The following is an extract from one of these.

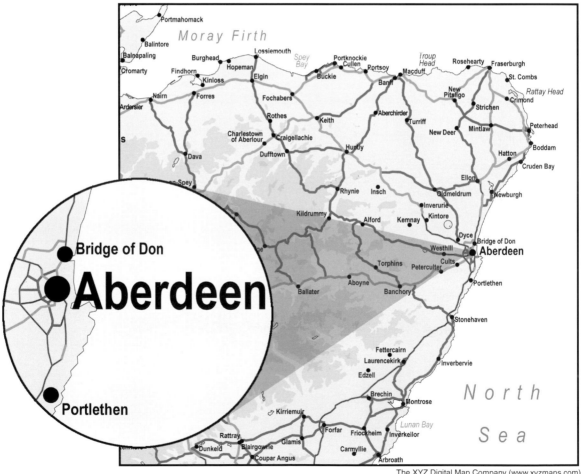

The XYZ Digital Map Company (www.xyzmaps.com)

ANDY and MARGARET LESLIE

This is Andy Leslie speaking, fae Westside, Kingsford, Alford. I've passed the 65 mark and decided to run down the farm and enter business so that I can take care of my health and enjoy a bit of life eftir working hard all my life. I first came here up here in 1956 I would say, to see my wife Margaret, and I've been here ever since eftir.

As a boy I was at Alford School for the duration of my schooling. The dominie, he was called the dick, Mr Ritchie. He was a hard task master. A bit of a disciplinarian. Some liked him, some didnae. That was the way it was. I had a short period at college, Agri college eftir that. Didn't shine at that but got passed. Fae there I had another spell in the army and eftir that was by, I came back and started ferming. The ferming was dairy, milking coos, but that was machine milking. Aberdeen Angus Bulls and I've seen the full circle on them. In the sixties they were up at a high level and they went very near extinct. Now they're gan back up to this very high level with the folk needing good beef. Aberdeen Angus, aye.

And then there was cropping which I mind it was a binder at that time, and you had to gie roond the ootside of the parck with a scythe and ridd the rods, and eftir that you got going with the binder and you had to stook up. It was a windy day, which you often got end of September, the stooks could be doon at your back and they a had to be stook paraded again.

The biggest change I think I've seen in ferming is the weather. You used to get terrible winds end of September October, and did a lot of damage with shacking the barley et cetera, but that's changed noo. You dinnae

get that terrible winds seemingly. Same in the spring time. You used to get devils of storms o'sna and the road totally blocked here and that hasna happent for a lot of years and they dinna want that back again either, because I've seen the sna nearly half up the telegraph poles here so that's come back to that. It was 60s and then gradually the seasons totally changed.

And then in the cropping business the binder gradually wore oot the first combine. It was a con tractor wi a bagger. He stood on her and bagged the barley and that was one devil of a job. I'd say it was one of the worst jobs I've ever been, wi her rocking aboot and you trying to get the bag tied, and you didnae ken and that had to be lifted back on again tae the certt and then gradually got a combine wi a bulk tank on it and that improved, made life a lot easier, butI would say the best tool that come on to the farm was the big roond baler. Without a doubt it saved man handling, hard graft, than ony tool that's ever come oot o the ferm.

Fit did you dae afore?
Well you had the little sma bales, ken the little sma square bales, so there was a lot of different ideas of hoo tae collect them and, we'd went a' through the process and that was some of the worst tools I'd ever worked. The bale grabs and accumulators werena fine to work. They sooked in the rain, the little square bales. But as roond bales keep the rain oot, you see.

You didna hae a mill did you?
I missed oot the mill business. Fan we come to the end of the binding we had a road mill. It was a Garvey Road mill and she had big iron wheels we caed her we a Marshal tractor. That was happy days that, fan you had a squad of about ten of us going, a bit of fun.

Fit was it the mill did exactly?
She separated the grain fac the strae.

What did you call the knife?
The lousing knife. You had twa lousers. Ayc. Usually the very youngest or the very auldest got the louser job because it was a michty job, but it wasn a heavy job, and the stronger men were aye at the back among the oats, but the hardest job was on the forking up because again if you had the wind in your face you had a fair job.

Was it tied with a strap in case it fell into the mill?
Aye. It was on with a strap. You had to watch that aye.

So we're coming up to gye near the present time and this is the worst time in farming that I've ever seen because they're destroying folks interests. Ifter the BSE there's been such a downturn in all the markets.

Were you oot o the cattle business afore BSE?
No, no. I'm just newly out of the cattle business. We were, we had coos and calves when the BSE started and it affected the price badly. Just native coos and calves with a Charolais bull. Never had a black bull since the sixties cause thae went oot o'favour and they've come back the full circle and they're in favour now but they're scarce to get the good enes. Did you see the man at Kemnay got £28 000 for ene?

And is this to bring back quality rather than quantity?
Quality. Get away fae this great big benes that the Chavolais. Get intae fine quality beasts.

Fit what breeds did you use for the milking?
To begin with they were Ayrshire, and they went oot of favour again like things de. They were an excellent coo. My favourite coo. They lested well, they had good feet, excellent coo and fit you did, you'd get mair milk out o'a Fresian that's what it was, but this was Dutch Fresian at that time. Real Dutch, and you crossed that with a Dutch bull and then you got a cross and eventually you landed that with a pure Dutch Fresian.

They were good, good cattle. And the calves aff of them made a good premium and also they were into this Holstein Fresian and they're just one business, milk and bull calves have to be shot at birth because they're nae use for onything. Nae value avva and that's a distressing thing. So that's the dairy business.

And your milk was collected?
My early memories was gan doon to the station in wi the cans in the morning and went intae the train to the co-opie in Aberdeen and they were best at putting back clean cans. They were beautiful washed oot and you could have put the milk back in without touching it again, whereas when it went into, fit was the other place, the milk board I think, you got it back, gye middling they were at Kittiebrewster. There were a lot of old firms in the toon at that time. Agricultural firms you

see. Wilson was a long time, James Wilson. Feed firms, tattie merchants and all that but then they were just gradually taking over the bigger anes.

What happened when you were snowed in with the milk?
Well you just had to get on with the horse and the sledge, tak the cans doon.

Margaret:
We're talking about a firm now that was nearer Alford, this was Greystane that Andy's parents were in then and the dairy was going then. That was nearer Alford, so you were just aboot a mile fae the village so it's nae here that we're speaking about.

Andy:
Up at the shiel when it was richt stormy he came doon at nicht afore wi his horse and sledges, maybe twa pair of horses, and bid the nicht in the Maughton and did his roond the next day and the horses were plunging up. See we're nae getting that storms now. That was ane of the things I used to like fan we came oot o the school fan there was that big storms, you used to see the sna ploo fit you cald the Bammy, she was a steam sna ploo and Bert Taylor was the auld driver and he couldn't get a second man to bide with him because he was aye tied down the steam release valve to get mair and she was some sicht when he was going I can tell you that. He was some one, he was that.

And your father and the pony trap Margaret?
My father, he delivered milk to Rhynie and Huntly with the horse inte Hazelheid, he had a place there. Kidd was the man that delivered milk there. Kidd, he was a character. There was mair characters gan aboot. There's nae time to be characters noo.

Your father was the milkman?
No, no. He took the milk in, in the cans. It was bottled there and then it was selt. And he did a', what was their scheme, the dividend? The co-opie divi, a dividend book, the very same, with stamps to try and compete to the co-op, but it was a gye uphill job you ken. That was his thingie there. And of course that was the time just afore there was the milk boards, and they've done awa with the milk boards noo and its just the big conglomerates like Wiseman et cetera, and they're dictating the price to the dairy ferms and they're haeing a hard time wi it.

They are getting into bigger units. They have to be big big units. 200 coos or they're nae much use but the milk board was an excellent thing. You were guaranteed at.......a certain price was agreed. It was a fair price but noo they're just cuttin it as far as they can get aff with it.

The co-opie bought your milk direct. Didn't come through the milk board?

In the end it would have dene. Aye, oh aye. The milk board was the distributor. At that time then they came on to the milk tanker-collected. The earliest wagons, the man who'd had the first concession for caing the cans, the milk cans was Charlie Alexander fae Aberdeen and he caed fish too . Well he caed the milk but then the milk board got their ain wagons and it came on to, I think Wisely also caed the milk.

You ken a lot about a horse?
Ronnie:

I remember as a loon I stayed up by Kingsgate and there was a small holding there and he used to come round with his own milk wi a little sheltie and it's now all houses. I think this was maybe before the folks started to worry about their health. You could almost do what you liked and we used to skim the milk.

Andy :
There was some gye bad businesses that came oot o that.

Was there health problems aboot the milk?
Brucellosis went through a bad spell.

Ronnie:
I remember my father drunk milk during the war from a cow that had aborted and he got milk fever and he almost died.

Andy:
It wouldnae have been milk fever, it was brucellosis,undulent fever.

Ronnie:
Aye, and he just went down to skin and bone.

Andy:
A lot of vets got it. The health-wise has improved greatly. Absolutely.

The sheep dip has caused a big problem recently. It affected my health greatly. Organo-phos. I was really quite ill eftir that business. When they found out hoo serious it was they stopped makking it compulsory and a lot of folk dinnae dip ava.

Margaret:
It was the organo phosphates that caused that problems which was used in the Gulf War wasn't it?

What happened with it?
Well I got inflammation of the joints and I got bad vision and got

depressed. In fact you felt bloody awful and you wondered fit it was because previous you'd dip sheep and kent nae different but this was a new dip. It was made compulsory and we didna realise fit we were deing.

So it was the new dip that was the real problem.
Exactly. The previous dip was easy to handle but it did damage to the birds and that. It killed the insects and a'thing so they stopped this and came in with this organo-phos, the same as they did oot in the last war, oot in the desert, the Gulf.

That boys are suffering. It's the same thing.

What happened noo?
What happens noo? Well that is the problem. You're getting the sheep scab now and the sheep are suffering. There is injections now. There's still dipping contractors but they tak ill. At times they have to tak to their bed for a day or twa just to come back to life again. There's been far mair damage done wi that tae folk than there's ever been wi BSE but it's been swept under the carpet. They've never tene responsibility for it. The big firms that was selling it dropped it like a hot potato as seen as they saw the implications of it. That was Coopers Red Label I think. Micht have been an American firm. I'm nae sure but I can tell you it's lethal. I've had first hand knowledge o'it, I can tell you that, but saying that some folk can work and never touch them. It a' depends if you're susceptible to it.

Margaret:
I dinnae feel I can add very much tae that. My name is Margaret Leslie. I was born in 1933 near Aberdeen. My father was a ferm worker. He worked in various places in Aberdeenshire and eventually landed up here at Westside in 1945 just at the end of the war in May, beginning o' May. I can mind I was just at Alford School a few days when we got the holiday to celebrate VE day. I went aff til Alford School until this third year. Went to Inverurie Academy eftir then went to university for three years and then did a secretarial course in Glasgow where I worked for just a few years until we got married in 1958. And that time Andy's father rented a ferm near Craigievar, that's where we started our merried life, and oor family were born then. A son in '59 and a daughter in '61. A few years later we moved to a cottage near Alford on the Greystone Ferm that Andy's father owned at that time and then my father decided to retire. My mother had a heart attack so we came here to Westside in 1970 and well, we've been ferming here ever since, as Andy said, it was coos and calves then while he was still continuing dairy then it was quite a heavy job for him. He was getting up at aboot four o'clock in the morning to dae the dairy at Alford and some gye long days. That went on for several years until the dairying got too much and he selt af the

dairy coos. The golden handshake. And I dinna think you were very happy at seeing your coos gan down the road but it was something that had to be faced up to. It was the end of an era and then the Aberdeen Angus. Had you your Aberdeen Angus still at that time?

Andy:
Well they went oot of favour.

Margaret:
In the '60s maybe

Andy:
But as you grow aulder you should never put athing awa. You should aye keep a nucleus of something. Ene or twa. Age does beat you.

Margaret:
I think I have to admit I was never a member of the Rural or onything like that. A lot of fermers wives are or were although they're finding it difficult now to get memberships now to Rurals, whether that's because a lot of the wives are working during the day and just dinnae have time in the evenings to go to that kind of thing I'm not sure, and I cannae honestly say that I did an awful lot on the farm. My main job was just keeping the books and deing that sort of thing. I think that's about my..

Andy:
But you're ging in the morning to get your 75.

Not quite. My ambition at the moment is to get my 75 blood donations dene so I can get my Caithness glass paperweight. I'm nae quite that length yet. I'm doing my best before my 70th birthday. If you dinnae manage afore you're 70 you're disqualified.

I use to do it but they cut me off at 65, being a man.

Well I'm still allowed. I'm 66. As lang as you're in good health.

I met a lot of good interesting folk when the Prisoners of War that came to work on the ferm. Italians and Germans. I can aye mind their names yet. There was a big camp in Monymusk and Cameron and Gibbon had the concession for caing them oot, ken in his wagon but then eftir if some of them were trusties, they got to bide in the bothy on the ferm. In fact they were treated better than the ferm worker, the local farm worker. They seemed to get mair, I dinna ken. They were a'good workers. Some of the Italians were extraordinarily good.

The project in this former mining community in West Lothian involved a group of residents who were interested in local history. Some of them had been astonished and upset when it became obvious that many of the schoolchildren had little concept of the town's industrial heritage. The Salt Of The Earth tutor began working with the group in the Community Centre and Miners Welfare Club. Some were interested and enthused enough to learn recording basics and tackled interviews themselves, supported by tutors. The primary schools were involved at the time in a community arts project involving the children in local awareness through history, poetry and song. In a collaborative venture, several of the Salt Of The Earth group were invited along to the school to share with the pupils their personal experiences and recollections, and links were formed with the school staff for further development work. Plans were initially made for the primary pupils

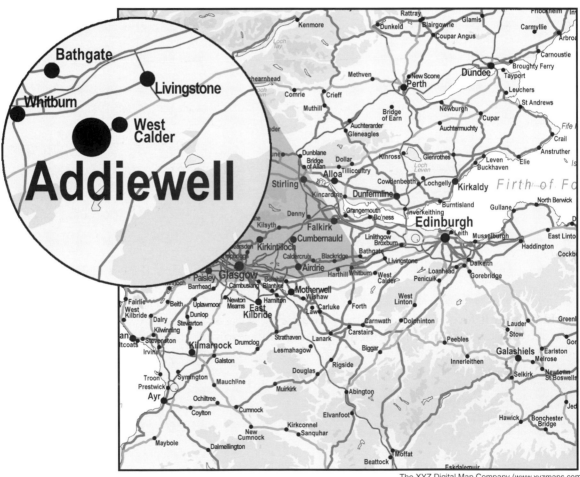

The XYZ Digital Map Company (www.xyzmaps.com)

to perform a play based on the recordings that the project group had made, however time and timetables ultimately conspired against that. We modified the outcome to a series of five monologues written by Danny Lambie based on the Five Sisters of Addiewell, the landmarks being the legacy of the mining industry waste. The monologues feature local events and characters of the recent past, revealed through the group recordings, and we hope to see the published work performed locally.

Foreword

When I first became involved in the Salt of the Earth project in Addiewell I have to admit I knew very little about the village. What I did know was it was a place down on its luck.

This I could empathise with. I too come from a small community struggling to find an identity following the demise of the industries which were not only the lifeblood of the community, they were its purpose.

Addiewell muddles on. It is the most deprived settlement in West Lothian. It's children find little promise for the future, little enthusiasm for the present and little interest in the past. Its parents struggle to make a living in the great industrial estates and retail parks of Livingston. It is left to its grandparents to remember the former glories of a village which has always fought (way above it's weight) to influence the civilisation and history of Scotland and beyond.

The village has many stories to tell, per head of population probably more than any other in central Scotland.

The following is an attempt to capture five of them. Through the last 150 years the village has been born, grew old and weary, died, been resurrected and now once again finds itself tired of the cards that it has been dealt.

The stories focus on five women, narrators who recite tales of their lives as they see them. They illustrate how the turbulent history of Addiewell and the world around it forced the community to develop a consistent ability to produce characters with great principle, courage and resolve.

Very little remains to remind visitors to Addiewell of its original purpose. One of the few relics dominates its skyline to the north east. Five massive spent shale bings, characteristically red, have been sculpted to look like the Five Sisters of Glenshiel. Though these man made monuments are nowhere as grand as the real mountains, the lives of the people who have grown up in their shadow are just as dramatic.

Danny Lambie

Monologue 3

They come in the house ever other hour. Moaning and greeting. "I'm hungry." "I'm tired." "I'm cold."

I don't want to be a grumpy old woman, but I do get annoyed. They take so much for granted these days. Don't know they are born.

When I was their age I lived next to the greatest women who ever lived in Addiewell. At that time we knew real hardship. But you always got the feeling with a neighbour like that, somehow you wouldn't want for too much.

"Ma" Moore became a folk hero some twenty five years ago, between the wars, at a time when towns and villages across the nation were crying out for change. Industrial unrest had reached epidemic proportions, a worldwide recession had made mass unemployment a fact of life, households teetered uncomfortably close to a level of poverty unknown to us today. All of this and the poor housing, health and education, meant that during the hot summer of 1926 Great Britain was a tinderbox of social unrest, waiting for a spark to ignite it.

Some folk would say I'd be exaggerating to suggest that Ma Moore was responsible for saving Britain, but it is fair to conclude that she did douse the flickering flames which if left unchecked could have spread and might just have caused irreparable damage. What is without question is that she was, as we all came to know her, the Mother of Addiewell.

Mrs Sarah Moore was a remarkable woman. By any standards her achievements would be considered outstanding. At a time where women's suffrage was still a fresh memory, her place and influence in society was almost unheard of.

She became Scotland's first female County Councillor, and the Labour Party's first elected member from the west side of Midlothian (of which Addiewell was then part). She was a pioneer of the Labour Movement, and was instrumental in turning the ideology from a fringe doctrine to that of the elected government.

She was convenor of the Public Health Committee, a member of the Licensing Appeal Court, the Joint Committee of Midlothian and Peebles Hospital and of Saughton Prison Visiting Committee. She was active in Council Chambers, working on issues from health to education. She tirelessly attended to the needs of her ward and its residents, campaigning for better housing (Moorelands is named after her) and social well-being.

She was an accomplished poet, and she counselled her neighbours on topics from rent arrears to the threat of asylum committal, she was and remains a peerless inspiration. Not least, there was the small issue of a husband and nine children.

Ma Moore was elected Councillor for Addiewell in 1929 and remained in the post until her death in 1947. During this 18 year reign she was returned to office, on all but one occasion, completely unopposed. Her notoriety as a witty, resourceful and spirited leader grew to legendary proportions during this time, but it was over one weekend during the general strike of 1926 that her name became an immortal part of Addiewell folklore.

Our village had become a strong bastion of left wing politics long before Ma Moore. Many of our ancestors – your great-grandparents - came from Ireland to work in the Paraffin Works; their camaraderie galvanised the working class community. This spirit had remained through generations, and was strengthened by the perpetual struggle to make ends meet. After the Great War, those who had survived the years of attrition had returned to a nation poorer and more fragile than the one they had left to fight for so gloriously. Most who did come home did so without brothers, sons, neighbours, lifelong friends. The naivety with which they had taken up arms had long since been replaced by scepticism.

Thus, Addiewell, as with so many communities during the 1920s, was angry and disillusioned. A national general strike which broke out in 1926 was an exasperated attempt to express this depth of feeling.

In the days before the Welfare State, people relied on the Parish when times were hard. So, when West Calder's People's Parish Administrator Duncan Hay decided to withhold money which means-tested miners were entitled to, Ma Moore took it upon herself to make a stand. She sent local children chapping doors across Addiewell and Stoneyburn, calling on miners' wives to mobilise. By the Friday a group of between thirty and forty women marched to West Calder Council Office to register their protest.

Duncan Hay decided the troop was hostile, and called on the police. When they arrived they found the women camped peacefully along the pavement outside the buildings, singing and passing sandwiches and tea. The police decided they posed no threat, and let them be.

The next morning, the men arrived as reinforcements. The day wore on and the men, hot under the summer sun and frustrated by the lack of progress inside, overturned a car parked by the kerb. The police moved in and a violent riot ensued. Neighbour fought neighbour, children scattered across the streets and women screamed. I was there, crying.

Duncan Hay watched from his office, smug in the knowledge that his suspicions had been founded.

Ma Moore mounted the steps outside the Council Offices and surveyed the scene. With all the might her lungs could muster she screamed for the fighting to STOP!

"STOP! Stop!" She commanded the men to go home, and when they had shuffled off, Hay and union delegates called on Moore to come inside.
By the Sunday evening they had negotiated to call off the siege, and in return all due monies were paid the following morning.

The unrest which might have started an unimaginable catalyst had been chastised and sent to bed by a stern mother as if it were her boys squabbling on the drying green.

The events of that weekend, and the way in which Ma Moore managed them, came to define her. But there was much more to her than this one instance. She was a deeply compassionate woman, with an uncommon understanding of human nature, and an unshakeable loyalty to her principles. Her energy and enthusiasm, and her pursuit of the righting of wrongs, became her life's work. She died whilst still heavily involved in local politics.

And her spirit is still evident in the village today. Long after her demise, Addiewell continues to fight against the odds for a better future. A lesser village may have rolled over and died, but Addiewell stubbornly stands its ground. You sense it might be frightened that if it did give up, those screaming lungs might call it indoors, and send it up to bed without any dinner. The world is a poorer place without Ma Moore, but Addiewell is a richer one because of her life.

Text and photograph courtesy West Lothian Libraries

"The Five Sisters" shale bing.

The "Five Sisters" Shale Bing, near West Calder, is one of the many monuments of the shale mining industry dotted throughout West Lothian.

For it was West Lothian in the mid 19th century which was the pioneer in the production of oil. The district did, albeit for a short period, dominate the world oil scene. And it was all due to one man - the Scotsman James "Paraffin" Young - who was undoubtedly the "Father" of today's industry.

It was he who succeeded in producing oil from the abundant shale deposits underneath the rich West Lothian soil.

Sport had not manifested itself in any significant way within the project so we attempted to address this. Rather than look at professional sport, much of which has become dominated by business interests and has lost much close community involvement, we concentrated on Scottish Junior Football. This is not – as the name might suggest – for young players, but is the level below the Senior leagues. Many of the most successful Junior teams come from mining and manufacturing towns in Midlothian, Ayrshire, Lanarkshire and Fife, and there still seems to be a real sense of community identity within these areas for the teams, with social clubs providing focus and financial support.

The Salt Of The Earth group from Gorebridge, all women, were primarily interested in photography, but learned interview and

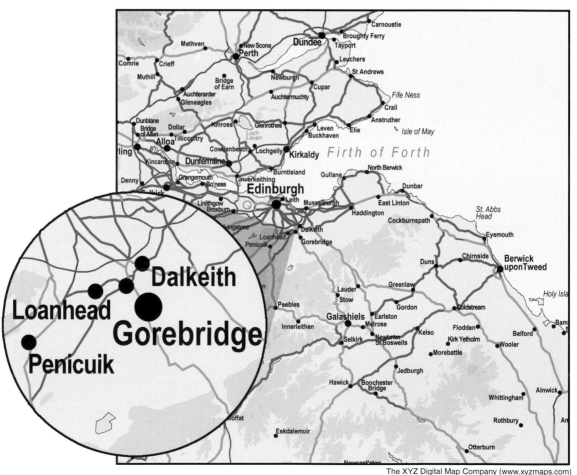

The XYZ Digital Map Company (www.xyzmaps.com)

recording techniques. They then photographed at matches and clubs and recorded not only interviews with key people but also ambient sound. The results were combined in a photographic and sound essay, presented on CD Rom and video, utilising the three elements.

The following is part of one of the interviews accompanied by a selection of the photographs.

What's your name?
John Darling Grey.

Where were you born?
15 Nine Street. In that corner where you're sitting. I was a twin.

Did your mother only have the two?
My mother actually died through childbirth, through having twins. We were the last of the family. I had two brothers and three sisters and I'm the last of the Mohicans.

What is your date of birth?
21/6/32. My father was a miner all his days.
My grandparent was the gardener at Cockaromansis Gardens. I don't really know what he was head of but he was the head man in the village in these days.

What did your parents do when they were first married?
I think my father was just a miner. I've no idea what my mother did, I'm sorry because I never ever seen my mother. I've heard stories.

Can you describe your family home?
It was a happy home. We were all pretty close. This is the house here that I was born in. Four apartment.

What did your father do outside work?
Fisher. He was a great fisher. That was his real hobby was fishing. He went everywhere. To the White Ladder and the Esk, Ettrick, fished everywhere.

What transport did they have?
One of his friends, in the latter stages, had a motorbike and he used to go on the back of the motorbike to the fishing.

Did he catch many?
Oh yes. I can mind coming on a Sunday morning and 'I'm going away to the Esk.' You can be told a lot of funny fishing stories but this story was true. I can mind when we had a big sink and a wee sink. Most hooses had that in these days and he used to wash in the big sink, but I've seen the big sink with no water in it right up with troot. I could bury my hand in the troot, and he was friendly with a man fae Peebles and he used to bring the salmon to the house here and the living room was always lined with salmon. A carpet of salmon. Oh yes, you were always well-fed. My faither went oot fishing if they couldnae catch fish they would always come home with a hen or eggs or something.

Were you taken out visiting friends and relations when you were young?
When I was young I had a lot of relations, actually that weren't related at all. The circumstances being twins was very rare in those days and my mother died with twins. Everybody had a... for the first year of my life I was next door with a Mrs Pride, and my brother for the first year was at the other side with a Mrs Weston, and really they brought us up for the first year of our lives. And my sisters took turns but as they got married off it finished up with my youngest sister and she was just 11 years old when she started looking after the twins and it curbed her young life. She couldn't go out dancing or out with her friends or anything so there were a lot of people that knew us and I cried auntie and uncle, that was no relation at all because they had so much to do with us.

Most of your relatives lived nearby?
Oh yes. The furthest away was Bonnyrigg. Jessie. My oldest sister stayed in Bonnyrigg. Jessie.

Who did you play with?
We used to hae gangs. We used to play in gangs and they had a character in the village. She was a very nice woman. Mrs Gowrie. She used to just have an interest in our gangs. If we did anything brave we used to get a medal fae her and we used to go into a committee room in her front room and they used to present to you ribbons for if you'd done anything brave. Brave. That was like fighting the council house, if we maybe hit one of them it was a victory to us.

Where did you play?
We played mostly on what we called the banking. The main strip in Newtongrange when you go up the main strip you used to go to a banking, because the trains used to run from Lady Victoria to Ladywood, right round the village and cross the main road where Derek stays and in where Moffat was, was the gas works and they used to wire the coal to the gasworks so this was a bing that went round, a railway line that went right round to Easthouses, Linewood and the Lady Victoria. I got hurt a thousand times. I can't tell you how many times I was hurt.
The railway's away now.

Which school did you go to?
Newtongrange. That's the one at Six Street. That was the primary place and after that we went over to the 'big school' they used to call it, where the new houses, where the community centre is.

What kind of school was that.
Just a secondary school. A Mr Wallack was the headmaster.
He was pretty fair. He was one that was aye frightened. When he saw us

189

we used to draw ourselves up, ken. He had something. He could get people to do things the right way and that was good for him.

Did you enjoy school?
I think I did. I wasnae very clever at the school but I quite enjoyed the school. I liked the morning. We used to go to the school an hour before the school in the morning to play football in the school playground.

Did you play football after school?
In the park and places like that. I was never a football player.

Did you support the football?
Yes I supported the football. I supported Newtongrange Bluebell. They were a Juvenile.

When did you start supporting Junior Football?
As far back as I can mind. When I was a lad it was Newtongrange. I used to support Newtongrange as a wee boy. Newtongrange Star.

Did you go to the matches on your own?
I went on my own but I met mates at the football match.

Did many youngsters go to the matches?
Oh yes, yes. I think every youngster in Newtongrange used to go and follow Newtongrange Star at one time.

When you were a man did you go to most of the home games?
I went to home and away for years and years and years.

Did you find many changes as you got older?
As I got a bit older, and of course the reason I stopped going to football was that it was too commercialised, especially in the senior games. I thinks football players get too much money for doing a thing of pleasure. The more and more it was going and going it got to the stage where you couldn't afford to go to the football.

What about the Junior.
It wasn't pricey when I was younger and there's a lot of times that there were a lot of them went through the fence and stood at the gates to see the football.

Was it always the old park that you went to?
Yes. It was the best Junior Football Park in Scotland at one time just due to the fact that it was the Coal Board, and Mackay and all of them that were to do with it and it was the best that could be bought in these days. There weren't many football grounds that had stands to start with. Newtongrange always had a big stand and a big park but there were an

awful lot of the football cup ties. I suppose it would be to try and make money but, the bigger the park the bigger the crowds, so they used to play an awful lot of the ties in Newtongrange park because it was, the capacity was 14 thousand or something like that at one time.

Why does Newtongrange have such a good park?
The Coal Board, at one time it would be the Lothian Coal Company. They'd put money into it. It was the Coal Board who built the stand at the Stars Park and all that. They wanted it to be a village.

At one time every miner or pit worker had a penny taken off their wage every week, and that was to keep the brass band, the Institute where there were snooker tables. Anything like that, community-wise, got paid through this penny that the miners...

Did the miners agree to this?
Yes, they had no objections. That's why a lot of the things in the village are no longer crisp because there isnae the penny from the miners.

Even though Newtongrange wasn't in the final they still played the games at Newtongrange?
No, no. In the final of a cup they would maybe go to a Senior Park but most of the ties, like Arniston played a lot of the ties in Newtongrange Park because of accommodation and all the facilities it had.

Did you ever take a girlfriend or a wife?
Aye but she had to hold her tongue because she was an Arniston supporter. I don't think we had very much arguments through the football. If Arniston won, well hard lines.

There was one stage in my life I was that dedicated to Newtongrange Star that I wouldnae go out that night if they got beat in the afternoon. I just wouldn't go out. Just that they got beat. That I was that upset about them getting beat. And I think that's partly was why maybe when I stopped going to football, because I got right excited about it and I just..

Did Star play against many of the local teams?
Aye, all the local teams. Dalkeith, Bunnery, Arnison, Rosewell, Whitehill now. It's in the Second Division I think.

Was there much rivalry between local teams?
Oh aye. Between Newtongrange, all the local teams. They all wanted to see their ain team win. The Star and Arniston was the big rivals in those days. We aye called them the Germans.

Why call them the Germans?
Because they were the enemy I suppose, and then if the Star won they

John Grey

would talk about the pie grease running doon the Toll Brae fae Arniston because they'd bought all these pies and they had nothing to celebrated. They'd been defeated, so they spoke about the pie grease coming down the Toll Brae.

Her mother never missed any game of Arniston in all her young life. She was a great supporter. She was home and away every match.

Took my young brother and to every match, everywhere. In fact I was on the phone to her today and I said this thing about football. I said I can mind going to Kirkintilloch and it was pouring rain and we were soaking wet and we needed the toilet and it was in the housing scheme. And they went to this woman and they said to her and said "Can we use your toilet" and she said "Indeed you can and come in here and get your coat off and get a plate of soup in you." That was the type of things. I used to go to the football long after Derek was born. When Derek was born and Hearts won the Scottish Cup for the first time I was at the game and my wife was in the maternity having Derek.

And I said "I might be a while getting back from Glasgow so I might not be in to see you the morn." She said, "Well that's all right, I understand".

But when I got home I was in time to see, well I was late to go and in these days you had a card to go in and the man at the door and I said I'm sorry, I missed my bus and everything and made all the apologies for being late and instead of handing him the ticket for the maternity I handed him the half ticket for Hampden and when he seen this he said "Get away up the stairs, she'll hae plenty to say about it."

And I said "It's ok, I'll understand if you'll no come in. I'll understand that you've no got home in time," and I cried my eyes oot when it came visiting time and he wasn't there. Of course when he came in it was great.

Did you go to away games and how did you get there?
Yes. Usually bus and very often the train. They put special trains on.

They made a special outing of it with friends who were equally supporters. We used to go up to Aberdeen and that.

It all depends where Newtongrange was in the cup tie. Maybe Ayr, well it would maybe be a special bus that they would arrange. Buses or maybe a special train to take us through there. The train used to go over the bridge. Did you see the big bridge when you were coming in? The trains used to go over that to Edinburgh.

So a lot of people went to away matches.
Oh yes, Newtongrange was a well-supported football team simply because in thae days they were in the top three. If they weren't the best team they were the second best or the third best team. Everybody wanted to beat Newtongrange.

What was the atmosphere like on the way home if they won?
It was great. Celebrations all the way home. Celebrations with singing and just anything with a wee bit drink in our hand. Quite happy.

Was there a difference between a win away and a win at home?
Oh aye. You're a wee bit dejected if you're coming away fae, especially if you're up at Ayr or away up in Aberdeen. You just got feeling that you want your team to win up there instead of lose.

Was it a long journey home?
No, we didn't make it a long journey home. By the time they sit doon and play cards. Take packs of cards and have a card school. Eight packs of cards. We did a lot of things.

What was the furthest away that you ever travelled?
It was Aberdeen I think. I cannae mind the name of the team either. There were maybe some of the supporters stayed over night because they were arrested for misbehaving. They were a well-supported team. There were instances when folk got a wee bit wild and the Police, and they got released the next day. That match they were standing there and they were saying, "God, Newtongrange'll take ten goals off the two of them," and that gave us a wee bit glee.

Does any game stand out in your memory?
Well, the Scottish Cup. We played a team called Auchinleck Talbot in the Scottish Cup, and five times we had to go to Cowdenbeath because Cowdenbeath was where it was getting played. We played it at home and it was a draw and they played it at Auchinleck and it was a draw and the next three times it was at a neutral ground, and they picked Cowdenbeath so we had three times to go up, back and forward up to Cowdenbeath cause it was a draw the first game at Cowdenbeath, a draw the second game at Cowdenbeath and then Newtongrange won on the third draw.

What would you say is the role Junior Football plays in the community?
Well it was something for us to really get interested in, plus the fact if you were a young laddie it was inspiration for to go in and see your Junior Team and, well, that's how you start. You see your Junior Team and you're aye wishing to play for your Junior Team, so its quite a do with the young ones in the village.

So do you take much part in the community?
Just the folk club. It's held in the Dean on a Thursday night.

Tell me about the Dean Tavern.
It's supposed to belong to the village. It's run by a committee that's accountable to the village. The Gothenburg. They were all Gothenburgs.

I remember when I used to go through to Fife my cousin said to my mother "I'll take Lilly doon to the Goth" and my mother said "Indeed you will not," but the Goth there was a picture house. Gothenburg. My mother thought she was going to take me to the pub. I was about 12 year old or something.

The Dean is a Gothenburg pub. I dinnae ken the significance of it.

They started in Germany first, that type of pub for the local community.

It's run for the local community. That's why they gie gifts. They're always wanting to give back to the people and you ken how they give gifts at Christmas time and they donate to the gala day and they donate to everything. The band and different things.

How long has the Dean been there?
It's been there as long as I can mind and I'm 67 year old.

What kind of place is Newtongrange to live in?
Newtongrange was a great place to live in. In fact there's a saying going "A day out of Newtongrange is a day wasted."

Tell me about your job.
I retired in '82. I was 39 year down the Lady Victoria. I started my work in the Lady Victoria and I was the last one oot of the Lady Victoria.
I'm in the last cage coming up and it was the last cage, and in the paper the last cage, the last cage came up with the coal, and it wasn't the last of the coal. I came up in the last cage months after it was in the paper that this was the last.

What did you do?
I was a rock splicer. I used to maintain the haulage ropes, the winding ropes and cable belts. In fact I used to come to Newbattle. Other pits used to send their apprentices to us to learn off us. We had a top man as regards to rocks. Robert Bryson and he was a right authority on it.

The Lady Victoria was the deepest pit in Scotland, for long long years it was the deepest. It was the biggest steam engine in Scotland and in fact in Britain at one time.

Do you think it's a good thing having a mining museum?

Yes, I think it is and I've seen it. What they're doing, they're doing a marvellous job, what I've seen of it. I've been up and had a visit to it but I've no been up lately. I gave them a lot of stuff for the museum up there. I gave them records, with being the last person to be in the pit. There was me and an engineer Willie Dixon, and that's all that was in the pit. We closed the Lady. And they were coming in and taking things away. They were coming across fae, they were breaking in and taking, away things. Sherwood. There were nobody there to stop them of course so I taken a lot of stuff they didnae really want. But I took it because it was going to be stolen and after they established the museum I got in touch with Wullie Hall the engineer. And I got in touch and said there'd be a lot of stuff they'd be interested in and the oil cap, the grease cap in the engine. They were made of Thistles and they were made of brass and they were really beautiful, but I took all the brasses off before somebody else took them off, and I brought them home and then I got in touch with the curator, and the curator and Willie Hall came doon and they'd taken away a lot of stuff.

What about the brass band?

I was never a player or anything like that but I like to listen to the brass band music. I've been at Blackpool, London, the Albert Hall with them and I was in Germany, France. They're a great bunch of lads and a grand holiday.

The village has changed immensely since the pits closed and since everybody was able to buy their own house because now young couples here can't get rented accommodation, so they're automatically in debt with mortgages at the start of their marriages. It isn't as good a start as we got. When we were married this was John's house and I think the rent was about 4/6d or something.

And with me being in the pit the same as my father, my father was in the big explosion that killed four miners in the Lady Victoria. It didn't kill him then but it eventually killed him because him and my brother, my oldest brother, were the last oot the gas and everything after rescuing folk, and he just wasn't the same man after that. So he put the house in my name, so the rent was coming off of my wages with just being in the pit and of course, when he died the house came to me. Of course I was only paying rent and then years after that we got the chance to buy the house.

An impressive aspect of the project has been the number of partnerships and collaborations established with other agencies and institutions. One that has worked very well for both parties has been that between The Salt Of the Earth Project and the Borders Memory Bank, a Council funded initiative established to collect, archive and present local and oral history in many forms. In providing training and advice we formed a relationship that has allowed the project to represent the Borders region through the Memory Bank's now extensive collection. The following interview and photographs, copyright of the Memory Bank, is a fine example of another disappearing facet of Scottish life.

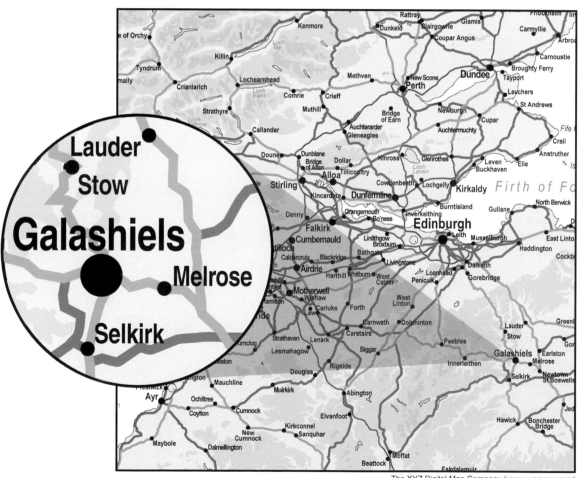

The XYZ Digital Map Company (www.xyzmaps.com)

This is Mary Drysdale interviewing Mike Brydon at his home in Clovenfords on Thursday 16 December 1999. Mike was born in 1937 in Galashiels. His family owned and ran the Brydon's Dairy for five generations until it was sold on in the mid nineteen nineties. Mike has already recorded some of his memories of Galashiels from the time he worked with his father on the doorstep delivery round. Today he is going to expand on these memoirs of a milk boy over the years from the mid-forties to the mid-fifties.

The dairy and the byres

My family have been involved in the delivery of milk in Galashiels and district for... over a hundred years, and it was into the fifth generation by the time the business was sold on. As a little boy I was always... I lived right next to the dairy in... just in houses fronting onto the dairy yard, which at that time was the bottom of Gala Terrace, St John's Street in Galashiels, and therefore from the time I could recognise anything the dairy was there; and, was always a source of activity, and so on. And when I was quite small I started going in the van, out to the farms, the local farms where we uplifted the milk...which we subsequently processed and then delivered. The farms to me were absolutely wonderful. I would go in and... we would arrive at the farm and if we were lucky the milk was already ready to be uplifted, and it was in large ten-gallon churns, which we uplifted. But quite often the milking would not be finished, the dairyman, the baillie[1], would be getting to the end of his milking session and I would then be able to walk into the byre and watch all the cows... standing quite contentedly in their stalls. This was long before the days of herring-bone parlours where nowadays... where the cows sort of come in, stand in a compound then go in through this milking parlour then go out into another area. These were all tethered

Mike's grandfather

Mike's grandfather second right, Michael Brydon. Mike's Uncle George first right.

cows and they were all milked by putting the teats[2] of the milking machine onto the cow and invariably these were made by a company... these milking machines were nearly all Alfa Laval. And the milk came off into - I suppose they were five- or six-gallon containers which were part of the milking set. This was then taken through to a clean area where the milk was poured into the top of a cooling tower and simply flowed over the top of... more-or-less a radiator to take the... the milk of course comes off at more-or-less blood heat and before people would... milk is very unpalatable when you drink it straight from the cow, it's horrible - at least *I* think it's horrible - and it had to be cooled and of course in those days it was cooled, as I said, by water-cooled coolers. As progress went on they became refrigerated, chilled coolers and were a lot more efficient. The water-cooled coolers were inclined to be rather warm in the summertime because a lot of the water pipes were quite near the surface and the cold water coming into some of the dairies was not as cold as it might have been.

Processing and bottling the milk
Once we had uplifted the milk we then took it back to the dairy in St John's Street, and we then cooled it further, if it required that. And then we put it into a machine which allowed us to put it into bottles. Of course the whole process of glass bottles was another facet to the

business. We brought the bottles in and of course the bottles made several trips - I think they were supposed to make something like twenty to thirty trips to be economic. But these were washed in ... they all came in dirty from the customer... were then put in to steep in a big tub. They were then... we had a machine with three rotating brushes on it. You picked up the milk bottle and you pushed the neck of the bottle - onto the top of these rotating brushes and you had to hold - make sure you held onto the bottle, because if you lost it the whole brush... the whole bottle started to spin and it was then you had to duck because the thing would fly off if you were not careful - unless you were lucky enough to pick it up again. The bottles were then rinsed and then they were turned upside down to drip. They were in... the bottles were held in metal crates, and they were then stacked up and they dripped and dried. Then you took them from the, the, the washing area - from the washhouse - into the bottling house and you had to turn them over of course; and then the crate sat in a moving, a sliding trolley arrangement and the... you pushed it forward, you pulled on a big handle; this lifted the crate up and it bottled, as far as I remember, about five bottles at a time, depending on the size of the bottles, I think. And you pulled it down and the milk filled the bottle.

Bottle tops - cardboard and aluminium

Now in the early days when I was quite little, about five or six or maybe even less, the design of the bottles was quite different; they had a lip which you pushed in a cardboard cap, which was roughly about an inch and a half... two inches in diameter. It had... in the centre it was kind of punched in and when you were going to open the bottle you pushed in that little half inch diameter circle, and then that allowed you to put... use your pinkie to lift out the cap. And I used to stand there helping, in the dairy, with a handful of these little cardboard caps plopping them on - I became quite expert at pushing the caps into the bottles. Now some years after that it was realised that that wasn't particularly hygienic, in that the lip of the cap on the top allowed the dust... if the milk was sitting on somebody's doorstep and it was a dusty, windy day, the dirt was coming onto that and when the person took the... unless they were careful taking the cardboard cap out there was quite a risk that a bit of dirt would go into the milk and contaminate it. So we then moved to a different type of cap which was an aluminium foil. And we bought these in in big boxes and they were about... about the same size, but they fitted *over the top* of the bottle and you then had to put them all on... the same way you had to put them over the top of the bottle, but we had a machine - a small thing that you held in your hand that pushed over that crimped the edge of the metal foil cap and put it into a groove on the bottle; and this was obviously a much more hygienic form of closure. The only problem with that is when you put these silvery bottles down on the doorstep in the wintertime... they are a great attraction to the sparrows in particular... and the sparrows used to peck through the cap and drink the cream. If the weather was particularly cold it was actually possible... if the bottle was sitting on somebody's doorstep for a few hours - maybe four hours, the top of the bottle froze and the milk expanded and actually lifted the cap off, so you had about threequarters of an inch of a column of solid milk - solid cream - with a cap on the top, and that's possibly how the sparrows learned that the milk was good to peck. Anyway, that's just an aside. Once we'd bottled all the milk and they were all stacked up in crates... they were in different sizes - we used to go from a - quite a big bottle which was about a pint and a half - I suppose the equivalent of a litre almost now - but mainly it was pints but we also had half pints... and, in fact when I think about it I think we had two pint bottles - they were huge ones... which *were* equivalent to a litre.

Delivery vehicles - austin twelve - ex galashiels ambulance - ex-army pickup - ford van - the beetle - electric milk floats

And we then... you loaded the van... The vans were either just standard delivery vans or they were converted from something else; there was a period, just after the war, when it was very difficult to get transport - it was strictly rationed, there were very few vehicles being made; and my father had all sorts of vehicles including the old Galashiels ambulance, which was an Austin, a big Austin Twelve with, obviously a long, thin vehicle because it had room for two patients in the back. And this had been used in Galashiels from the early thirties until the late... the mid-forties and had then been replaced by a more modern vehicle; and this was the only transport that we could get. It was a very awkward vehicle

Mike on roof of "Old Nellie" at back.

to deliver milk out of because it was quite high. You had to go up about two steps to go into this thing and the milk crate... sat in crates where the patients had originally been laid, or the space up the middle where the attendant would have walked. Another vehicle I remember my father getting was an army... an ex-army surplus pickup truck, a half ton track - truck, with a canvas back... which we used for quite a few years. But it had a hard life in the army I think and wasn't always the most reliable of vehicles. But it *was* versatile, and I remember on one occasion we actually went on a holiday in it, a camping holiday; with... my mother and father and in fact I think it was probably four brothers at that time[3], and... disappeared away up to the north of Scotland, up to Kirriemuir and round about there, and we thought this was wonderful. Some of us slept in the back of this canvas tilt and some of us slept in the tent. Anyway, that's an aside. We also had a funny little old, I think it was a... Ford van with characteristic back windows which were oval shaped; and my father called it "The Beetle". It figured - it was a well-known vehicle in Galashiels and in fact featured in a comic... a series of comic films which were made by a guy call McLauchlan, called "Where's Pete?" and I was quite amused when I saw these films some years later and recognised this vehicle that we called The Beetle. It was quite a few years until we got proper milk vans, and only in the latter stages of the business - by which time I was not involved, that my brother actually had electric milk floats as they did in the cities, which were much easier to deliver from - very slow of course, but much easier for deliveries.

Getting up in the morning for deliveries - bantam coffee
Right, when we loaded the... we used to start delivering milk about five o'clock in the morning and this meant getting up at half past four, quarter past four, and as I got older I absolutely hated getting up - it was *hell, pure hell*. My father would get up at half past four, quarter past four, and he would cough noisily and... get himself dressed and go down the stairs; I'd hear the sounds of the... and he'd shout "ARE YE CUMMIN !?... ARE YE NO CUMMIN? - THE COFFEE'S ON !". Down we would go, and we drank very strong coffee... it was called Bantam Coffee. It was tiny little beige-coloured tins about an inch or an inch and a half high, by about an inch in diameter, and you only needed... it was a *tiny* spoon. The spoon would now be about... I suppose it was about a quarter of an inch in diameter and you only needed one spoonful, or one and a half spoonfuls of this tiny... so the coffee essence was really, really strong. I suppose it had the merit of waking you up.

Delivery round - in the dark
Then we would go down to the dairy and start loading the van with the crates which had been previously bottled the evening before, and obviously depending which round we were going on you had a recipe of different sizes of bottles that you needed, and off you would go. And I used to sit on a piece of old carpet or a folded up raincoat at the back of

the... on the back of this van, and we'd drive through the town, in the dark, in the wintertime. I hated it, absolutely hated it. There was no street lights in Gala at that time through the night; street lights didn't come on until, to the best of my memory, about half past six, so when you first started off the street lights were not on. Some of them were gas lights anyway at that time. They weren't all electric, some of the main streets were electric. So you had to have a torch, you had to have a torch and of course we were... the type that was favoured on the dairy was the kind that fixed on the front of the front forks of a bike. It was a fairly squat sort of thing with a lamp about three inches diameter or something like that, and you carried that in one hand. And of course you had to go up all these back stairs and into dark lobbies. And one bit I used to absolutely hate was when we did the round down to Tweed Road and the houses on one side of Tweed Road backed on to the cemetery. And my fertile imagination used to run riot and I would imagine... particularly if you happened to see an owl or something like that - it scared the hell out of you! And I used to hate doing that bit - I used to do *very* fast deliveries on that part. There were a lot of other bits like that as well, where they were a bit unsavoury

Delivery round - in the rain

People got used to you coming with their milk at a certain specific time and if you were early you weren't so bothered but if (...other than it maybe waking them up with the noise) but they *hated* if you were late - if you were half an hour late, oh gosh! Some of the wet mornings - obviously on a wet morning, when it's tipping down... you had a series of raincoats, old gaberdine raincoats And my father had a contact in some of the mills who would put them through the waterproofing process in the mill. You would get old raincoats from somebody roughly about your size - the old sort of beige-coloured raincoats - and they would be treated in the mill so that they were a bit more waterproof than they had been when they were discarded. Some of them were torn a bit - you weren't the most tidy-looking person, and you would start off and a raincoat would last about an hour and a half of heavy rain, of bucketing rain. And you wore a woollen bonnet on your head of course - the standard cap. And the caps were treated in the same way and they lasted about an hour and a half as well, so you had a series of horrible old bonnets to wear, and caps, and inevitably of course, with a bit of spillage and that, these raincoats got milk dripped on them, they started to pong a bit, so you were pongin a bit if you had your raincoat on on a wet day and, of course, you didn't get on so quickly on a wet day. So if you were on a round that took maybe two hours to deliver you were probably half an hour late by the end of that round. And all the wifies would be out girning - "I needed the milk for the bairns' breakfast", or "my man likes his tea in the morning with fresh milk". Oh it was a nightmare.

Delivery round - gauging the time, without a watch

But you knew whether you were running... it was like a race against a clock, it was like a time trial.... You saw the clock at various points, obviously at the war memorial, and things like that - you actually saw the clock. Those days I didn't even have a watch probably. But you knew by the time the trains were coming up the valley - there would be a train about the back of six o'clock, maybe, coming up - it was the overnight train from London, King's Cross. And it would... quite often, if it was a wet morning particularly, it would slip quite a bit as it came up Ladhope Vale, and you'd hear it slipping and they'd use the sandbox and the thing would grip a bit. No, as it came up it used to... looking from the back of the houses in Magdala Terrace you'd be looking down on these sleepy people sitting in a train looking at you, as you were delivering milk. And you'd think "Oh, hell, I should be four hundred yards further up the road - I'm late, I'm late, *I'm late*! - oh my god, I'm late! And you'd start to try and work a bit harder, and work a bit faster, and get back on track.

This is Mary Drysdale interviewing Mike Brydon at his home in Clovenfords on Wednesday the 22nd of December 1999. Today is a continuation of his memories of the milkround, starting off with the collecting of the money at the end of each week's deliveries, and going on to describe some of the farms they collected milk from, and the people on them.

Delivery round - which days worked

I used to work mainly on a Saturday, as an additional helper on some of the rounds, because... each van had usually two people, two adults - the vanman and his assistant - and I went along, as a young boy I went along as an additional pair of running legs. I got the high ones to do and the ones that were awkward... and that was mainly on a Saturday and sometimes on a Sunday and then, of course, when the school was on holiday you worked every day, and throughout the seven weeks of the summer holiday you worked probably five weeks, as we'd go for a fortnight's holiday.

Delivery round - collecting the money

It was useful having an extra pair of legs on a Saturday because that was a bigger day, because that was the normal day that we collected the money. People paid for their milk on a weekly basis. The people that had their milk delivered in... in the early morning usually put their money out, and it was always coins, it was... very seldom it was notes in those days; it was coins which were, ideally were put under a, hidden under a a flowerpot or something like that, some hidden place where they weren't obvious that there was money there. I used to hate the people... absolutely *hate* the people that put their half crowns and florins and pennies, and so on, into the bottle because when you rinsed a bottle out - very often they were just rinsed, they weren't washed clean - and then at the bottom of the bottle you'd get this mixture of coins and greasy, milky... horrible, cheesy... eugh, horrible! And the sure way that we used to... teach people not to do that - we used to pour that out on the doorstep - pour the milk and the water out and then take the coins out and of course it left a greasy mark which, if the housewife was at all proud she wasn't happy about it and no doubt we got a swearing for having done that, but at least it stopped them doing it, from putting that in, because if you can imagine a frosty morning, six o'clock in the morning, a frosty morning, maybe four or five degrees of frost and you've got to pour this icy water out. On your hands you're wearing mittens - we didn't wear gloves we wore mittens, for you had to be able to handle the money, handle the bottles, so you ended up with these woollen mittens... with the mittens inevitably if you were pouring milky, watery, stinking, horrible, and of course my mother would wash them, maybe once a fortnight or something, so you wore those horrible, smelly wet mittens. So that was a way of teaching the folk that it wasn't ideal to get your mittens wet. The money was carried in leather bags. My father used to get these made by the saddler, Jamieson the saddler in Gala, and we wore them across the thing and of course you kept the notes in one bit and you kept coinage and the different size of coinage. And you got to know the whole town; eventually somebody would mention a name, you know "Thomson" or something like that "I think they live up..." "Oh, yeh, yeh... Jimmy Thomson, lives up 30 Magdala Terrace" or something like that; "round the back... the money's put out under a... a flowerpot... Puts out dirty bottles". So, you sort of, you had a rote, as it were; you could recall... you could sit, could close your eyes, and think of the whole round, the geographical location of the whole round.

Identifying parts of the town by smell
As I mentioned earlier, there was certain places... different parts of the town had different smells and it was quite interesting. You would, for example you would put in milk in to McQueen the printers, where Menzies is now in Channel Street[4], and there would be a beautiful, almost antiseptic smell of printing ink which was a, to me, was a really nice smell. And that was, that was a lobby that you liked delivering into. You would go up to places like the sawmill, where Comet and so on is now, up at the old Brewery buildings - there was a sawmill there - there would be a beautiful smell of sawn wood and depending whether they might have been sawing a hardwood or something like that, a beautiful aromatic smell. There was, let me think of some of the other smells; just the smell of different types of businesses; you could smell the stables of the store[5] milk, I mean that was the big rivals. You tried to get up the street before the store; in my youth the store actually had horses.

Model T ford
In my time we never ever had horses although my grandfather had horses - but I think my father probably had a horse. But we were one of the first

businesses in Galashiels to actually have a motorised lorry; and I still have a photograph of my grandfather with his Model T Ford lorry and it's taken at Stow with my Uncle George (still alive in the States) and he's with members of the Gala Angling Association and he'd been involved in taking fry to stock the River Gala for the Angling Association, taking them up to Stow to pour them in, put them in the river; and obviously they used the milk cans as the transportation for this fish from - presumably they had a hatchery somewhere. But I've also got a photograph of my grandfather with his four-wheeled milk cart up the high road at a house that still exists called Lyndhurst. I think he was courting my grandmother at the time and she was a maid in that house, and that's how that photograph came to be taken.

Types of milk sold

When I first got involved with the dairy we had several different types of milk that we sold. We had what was called standard milk, and this was milk which wasn't - not from a Tuberculin Tested cow, its just from an ordinary cow, and it wasn't treated in any way - it wasn't pasteurised, or heat treated in any way. And a lot of people preferred this milk because they thought it was more natural. But of course it had the risk and milk... tuberculosis was very often contracted from milk from a tuberculin infested cow. So gradually the Tuberculin Tested milk, which was a penny or two dearer became much more popular. We also had Jersey milk which we got from a special... from a Jersey herd up at Tolquhan near Stow, beyond Stow; we sold a small quantity of that and this was milk that was particularly rich in cream. It's a bit ironic nowadays when we're all living on skimmed and semi-skimmed milk, half-fat and all the different names that they give it, that at that time people were deliberately trying to get milk that was particularly rich. There were other dairies in Galashiels as well which sold special milk - from Stagehall for example, from special cows that the doctor, who was the farmer there, used to keep a particular breed of cow - which I can't remember just right offhand, they were maybe Ayrshires - but they were particularly rich. And we used to be very annoyed when some of the doctors in Galashiels recommended that people moved to Stagehall because their milk was better. But after the war... during the war we weren't allowed to sell cream but after the war milk became much more plentiful and my father used to... then bought a cream separator which separated the cream off, and we sold single and double cream, and I find it ironic now that we used to pour the milk that was left, the skimmed milk, the "blue" milk, which my father used to say was virtually water. That's the same stuff we're now buying in the supermarket to keep our figures nice and trim.

Pasteurisation

At the beginning, early days, in fact until probably the early sixties, we didn't have, we didn't have a pasteurisation plant because the early pasteurisation plants - the Co-operative creamery in Galashiels which was out the Edinburgh road - they had a pasteurisation plant but those days, and I mentioned the chilling, the refrigerated chilling, those days the milk was simply cooled after it had been through the pasteurisation plant and been up at quite a high temperature, nearly boiling, it was then cooled by going once again going over a radiator, a cold radiator. But the milk was left with a custardy taste, at least we thought it always had a custardy taste, and if the pasteurisation plant guy hadn't been very diligent the milk would be quite cooked in fact. A lot of people did not like that cooked, pasteurisation plant milk. But by the sixties, the problem of brucellosis had arisen and there was a campaign to eradicate brucellosis. Brucellosis is a very nasty disease that gives you horrible 'flu'-like symptoms and keeps recurring - a bit like malaria - it keeps recurring and it's really pretty nasty. An awful lot of vets suffer from it - because you got it from dealing with cows that had brucellosis. And there was a big move - in Scotland we were very early in eradicating brucellosis - but one of the key areas of eradicating it was to have all the milk pasteurised. So latterly all the milk was pasteurised, of whatever grade, and of course the Tuberculin Tested cows became the norm and they developed a test for the cows which reacted and carried tuberculin and these were all slaughtered. These were always forward looking policies and actually the milk became a lot safer.

Refrigerators in homes

The other big change that occurred in my lifetime was the advent of refrigerators. And I recall that the first houses in Gala that had refrigerators were the prefabs. When the prefabs were erected - I think it would be about nineteen forty-seven forty-eight, they were the first houses and they had gas-powered refrigerators and we thought this was wonderful. We didn't have a fridge ourself in those days, in fact we didn't even have a refrigerated cold store, we just had a well-shaded cool room that the milk was left in. The net result of this of course was quite laughable in that in, perhaps, July and August when you got thunderstorms, the milk would inevitably... when you've got hot, thundery weather milk goes off if it's not kept in a fridge. And inevitably - it was quite laughable - the following Saturday after a period of thunderstorms about twenty percent of our customers would migrate to the Co-operative, to "the store" as we called it, and about twenty percent of the Co-operative customers would come to us, so there was an exchange of people who didn't keep their milk properly. Now, of course, I suppose virtually eighty percent or more of the population or more have a fridge or access to a fridge and milk keeps much better, it keeps much longer. And we've even of course got the phenomena of long-life milk which has been blasted with some kind of radiation to kill any bugs, and keeps in its revolting state for several weeks. I think it's the most revolting taste there ever was, I can't abide UHT - ultra high temperature treated milk which is absolutely horrible. But, as I say, refrigeration has now become the norm and that's really changed - in fact that's the reason that doorstep delivery has become almost a thing of the past - it's almost a thing of the past in Galashiels and is probably the reason that it declined so much that my brother had to sell the business about... when would that be, let me see - about nineteen ninety-four or ninety-five, he sold the business on to somebody else, and I don't think it's going at all now. But, of course, with refrigeration people can now go, pick up their milk from a supermarket or a corner shop where it's kept in a refrigerated container, and take it home and put it in their fridge; and it keeps, and it's date stamped, and it keeps much better. In my day, unless you drank the milk the next day the milk would go off within a couple of days, certainly it would be soor... soor I say and not sour. My grandfather interestingly enough used to deliberately make milk sour, he made buttermilk. He would put a pint of milk down every night beside the fire, at the side of the fire so that it got heated and then he would leave it for a couple of days by which time it had gone into... it had separated out into butter and milk and he poured that buttermilk on his porridge - I don't know what he did with the creamy bit, at least I don't think he drank that. But that was one of his idiosyncrasies.

Can I ask why it was you were not allowed to sell cream during the war?

Because there was a shortage of liquid milk. There wasn't enough milk, as milk, to go round and of course by taking off the cream fraction you were then discarding... I don't know... something like threequarters of the liquid content was being discarded and there was a shortage of milk because there was no milk being imported, I don't think, from Ireland or... and certainly any other place. And of course there was the big push on where children under five got free milk, or cheap milk; mothers - expectant mothers - got milk, and that carried on for a long time. And of course children at school got a third of a pint and the... eventually by about... nineteen forty-eight or... forty-seven, forty-eight, much more milk became available; there were more herds coming onstream, or whatever, and we were able to make cream. And initially it was illegal; and my father used to make it illegally and - big secret - and hand it out. People would buy it - there was no crime in it in the sense it was still... you weren't allowed to do it but there was no... they weren't harming anybody; there was nobody being put out or deprived of milk. But my father used to refer to it with the code name of "julep". So-and-so was getting a carton of julep, not a carton of cream.

Finance

The whole finance aspect of running a dairy was quite interesting. During the war there was a great concern that there wasn't going to be enough liquid milk supplies. And the Milk Marketing Board was set up, and I think I'm correct in saying the whole of the south of Scotland was run from Glasgow and then there was a Northern, or Northeastern Board based in Aberdeen. But we were under the Glasgow thing and really for a government department run by civil servants, it was actually very, very well run. I suppose you'd say it was a quango now, would be the word that we would use. But these people determined where you would get your milk supply from - that's if you didn't have your own cows obviously - and we got our milk from three or four farms and they regulated everything; and we sent a cheque to... the Milk Marketing Board would tell us how much we were owing them, we would send a cheque and then they would pay the farmers, so it was a system that worked extremely well, because the farmers got their milk cheque absolutely on the line, it came in regularly, and it was an incentive to us; we couldn't be in debt. In other words we couldn't let bad debt build up and... because we had to pay our cheque, we had to pay for the milk whether the people paid us or not. There wasn't a lot of bad debt at all. We actually... most of the money, the milk money, was collected weekly or fornightly, or monthly. Some people came into the house and paid my mother, paid my mother at the door. Other people we went back to - if they weren't available we went back to them later in the day. I'm thinking particularly of people that got early morning deliveries, which was about two thirds of the people, I suppose, got their milk before eight o'clock in the morning. The money would be either, as I think I mentioned it earlier, would be in the bottle - I absolutely hated, because you'd get this greasy money with... still with a wee drop milk in and cream on... and I hated that - greasy, greasy. Or it was maybe wrapped in a piece of paper and hidden under something or in behind a stone, or under a vase, or so on. I remember one man, that I greatly annoyed... my father used to say "They havena' paid, get them up, knock him up! knock him up!" So I remember knocking up a man at eight o'clock on a Sunday morning to say, you know, that "I'm sorry, but you haven't paid your milk for a month" and this man was so irate, jumping up and down in his dressing-gown, and said "I could buy and sell your tinpot dairy a hundred times ower!" However he paid up and actually he didn't stop the milk, and the money always came in. The only people in fact ran accounts were people like hotels and maybe big houses.

The farms supplying the dairy's milk

We collected milk, as I mentioned before, through the aegis of the... arranged by the Milk Marketing Board, but our main suppliers were Caddonlee, at Clovenfords; Mossilee, up on Meigle Hill; and Netherbarns, out the Selkirk road out at Gala. And we collected milk for, I suppose, twenty, thirty, forty years from some of these farms. And I have, you know, happy memories. As a boy we used to love to go - Caddonlee was probably the furthest out and we went from Gala up, up Wood Street and out... and that was quite a long hurl. This is of course - I was a wee boy in the period when people didn't leap about in cars as they do now, because petrol was rationed and you simply did not go for pleasure trips. Petrol was there to be used as an essential service, so a trip on the milkvan, sitting on the milkvan, it seemed such a long way, you know, it's only about a ten or fifteen minute trip from Galashiels from the dairy and St. John Street out to Caddonlee, and we used to, used to love to go out there. Even when we weren't working on the milk, if we happened to be home from the school and my father was going to collect the afternoon milking - because we went twice a day to these, to these farms; picked up the morning milking and the afternoon milking. And this was a way of ensuring that the milk was always fresh, because it was taken from the farm already cooled, and it was more or less bottled within an hour, probably bottled almost within an hour of coming from the cow. So it also ensured that, that each particular batch of milk, from each particular farm were more or less quarantined; in other words if there was going to be any problem, any health problem - and we were always mindful of the fact there was a public health problem - you could say that only a small section, from one - maybe three or four cows would, in fact, be in one particular set of bottles. It wasn't all mixed together as it is now, where it all goes into big, refrigerated machines that hold the complete milking, two milkings for a day - or hell maybe even two days over a weekend, I'm sure - in a refrigerated container. Which then goes into a huge milk tanker and sloshes around being driven along roads, sometimes for a very long way. So that was an aspect of the... of the collection of the milk from the farms. And, as I said, we went to Caddonlee and Mossilee - Mossilee was nearer, it was just up the hill and the Pate family - who are still in that farm - old grandfather Pate was the guy who was running that. It's interesting that a lot of the dairy people were actually what I call Galloway-Irish. They were really of Irish descent... and had come from that area, the big dairying area in Dumfries and Wigtownshire and Stranraer and Castle Douglas and all these places. And up the Ayrshire coast, and they were, they were super people; hardworking - amazingly hardworking folk - used to hard graft. Working at dairy's a cold, hard job, because you're working... scrubbing things, washing things; dealing with cows you've got to be pretty meticulous and my memories of all these families were that they were, they were extremely hardworking, they were very good. In my boyhood a lot of these people - it was the same people year after year who were there - and you got to know these people very well they were good friends, you know, and we struck up a very warm relationship with these people. But they were, they were rough diamonds as I say - I mean the... I learned a lot of swear words that I didn't shouldn't have known, in my youth, just from going to the dairy, or going to the byre. Netherbarns was another farm that I liked, mainly because just next to where the byre was where we collected the milk was a great big barn, and in the autumn it would be full of straw, it would be full of baled straw, or it would have hay; and we used to love to climb up these square bales and dive off. The only thing about it was they often seemed to have tramps... vagrants... slept in the barn. I don't know whether it was just because they tolerated it or, or whether they were actually particularly kind to these people, but I remember once or twice we would dive off into a pile of straw and there would be a very irate tramp would come out and chase us; we would rush back and sit in the van in case he came and got us. We went further afield at times as well; I remember going - a long trip was going away down to St. Boswells, beyond St. Boswells to a farm called Magdalene Hall, and they had a lot of cows, a lot of Jersey cows there... which... and very good quality Ayrshire milk there. And I don't know why we went there, it was something to do with maybe a particular farm we went to regularly had a problem and the Milk Marketing Board would divert us. In fact I think these people used to send us milk on the train, they would put the milk on the train at St. Boswells and we'd pick it off the train at Galashiels. And I remember being intrigued by the fact that the same train that came in with, with our milk churns on it had... had two calves which were parcelled up in hessian sacks; just a calf sitting on its backside with its neck sticking out. Obviously a calf being sent by train to somebody; I mean, you certainly wouldn't see that sort of thing nowadays.

The co-operative creamery
The other times we got milk from the creamery, from the Co-operative - they had a big creamery on the Edinburgh road out of Galashiels - which has been demolished within the last couple of years. It was an interesting building; it actually started work, started life as a steam laundry and then been converted to a creamery. But it was a big place and ... and the British Road Services, which were a nationalised transport business... run in Gala by the Brown family, Arthur Brown the rugby player's people, used to, used to be the people that ran this, and they picked up the milk in cans, in churns... and took it to the, to the creamery. And if we needed, say for some reason the milk supply had dried up, if the cows were calving or there wasn't as much grass as there should be, and the quantity went down below the amount that we could get off the three farms near Gala, we would have to go up to the creamery to pick up milk. We also, if we had surplus milk, we took it there, there was kind of a milk pool where we could, we could give the creamery milk, or we could get it from it depending on the supply and demand; and we had actually, there was a gentleman called George Douglas was a manager of the, of the Co-operative creamery and we had an excellent relationship. Although the retail side of that business was actually competing directly with... with the family, we had a very good relationship with the actual wholesale bit of it, with the creamery.

Racing a lorry to the creamery
An aspect of taking the milk to the creamery was that... if you were unlucky and, and, and ended up in a queue at the loading bank, in other words there would be a big British Road Services lorry, probably loaded with, with something like sixty or seventy ten-gallon cans in front of you - it took him a considerable time to lift these off onto the loading bank and then for them to be poured into the, into the big milk tank and so on. So we always tried to time things so that we were before a

particular lorry coming from a particular area. And I remember on one occasion... coming up Bank Street, now this is in the days when Gala had two-way traffic on Bank Street, Channel Street, High Street, Sime Place, these were all two-way traffic; and as I came up... up Bank Street behind this Co-op... this British Road Services lorry in front of me I thought "If I nip up Sime Place I can beat this guy, he'll take longer to go up the High Street than I will to go up Sime Place", so I shot to the side up past the Harrow Inn, round past where the Police Station now is and up onto Bridge Street and nipped in in front of this lorry - just nipped in in front of this lorry... and thought I'd done really well and went belting up the road, unloaded my four or five cans and came down the road. As I came down the road into the town, across Bridge Street here's a large policeman who held his hand up, pulled me into the side and gave me a great row - who did I think I was, did I think I was Juan Fangio; and how dangerous it was, I was exceeding the speed limit in a built-up area, etcetera etcetera. So that gave me a flea in my ear. Another aspect of, of, as I got older and reached the age of seventeen and got to drive on the milkvan and that was quite an experience in itself. I remember when I was learning to drive out at what is now Langhaugh Gardens, and the Melrose Road coming in to Gala; and I wasn't very good - the van, the clutch in this van wasn't very good and it had a gear that jumped out - and I came up from Langhaugh Gardens which was still a wee bit of a hill onto the Melrose Road and I didn't just quite stop at the edge of the pavement, I went in perhaps... oh, quarter of an inch further than I should and this car coming the other way struck the front of the van. It didn't do anything worse than the fact that it broke the string on what was an enamel L plate, an L-plate, a standard L-plate, what's that about a foot square; and it broke the string, it didn't really damage the car - it didn't scrape the car, car's were, the paintwork was good in those days. Oh! what a fright I got; stopped, and this big farmer got out, this big Berwickshire farmer got out and he had these kind of boots that stick up at the front, and he gave me a blasting - what did I so-and-so think I was doing and so on, and the guy that was sitting beside me, a qualified driver, a chap, a Polish chap Tadek Awlson, who worked with my father and he started arguing with the farmer. Oh dear, it was a whole bad scene. That gave me a considerable fleg[6]. But at the end of the day the very same van, when I eventually became a student and... went to the Heriot Watt in Edinburgh, I eventually got that van, my father gave me the van and I used to use that to travel out and in. In fact I did my courting in that van... we called it Old Nellie and... it was a very reliable Morris Ten van, I think it was a Morris Ten. It was a bull-nosed sort of thing, the van boy, or the person sitting beside the driver, sat on a little dickie seat - there wasn't a proper well, there must have been something under the floor, part of the engine I think was under the floor. And that van served me for many a year, in fact I decided I'd eventually never get married unless I could sell this van because it cost me so much to run. And my younger brothers were quite horrified when I came home and said that

I'd bought an engagement ring and showed them the ring on my wife's - my now wife's - finger. They couldn't believe I'd traded this huge piece of hardware in for this insignificant thing on my wife's - my fiancee's - finger. That was Old Nellie, a very reliable old van.

Customers - hotels - restaurants - Tadek

Among our other customers there were... nearly every hotel in the town got milk from us and... we used to visit them... sometimes they phoned up to tell us how much milk they wanted. And we had smaller... as well as the ten-gallon cans we had smaller cans - we had eight-gallon, six-gallon, four-gallon, two-gallon, and we could deliver various... and of course we could augment it by using bottles but the hotels preferred to get it in... in a small milk can... and... we would check their cold store and see how much milk was in it and go into the kitchen and see the chef and say "There's... you've got, you've got three gallons left and it looks quite sweet - are you, how much more are you wanting?" and he'd say "such and such, or such and such" and we would maybe put another couple of gallons in. But it has to be said that not all chefs were, at that time - I think the regulations were tightened up enormously - but some of the kitchens were gey so-so in those days, and I remember going into some of them and you'd go round the back and they would be... they had a potato peeling machine and there would be potatoes peeled... they would peel a fortnight's potatoes, and they'd be sat there in something like about five or six cracked enamel buckets... with, you know... sitting in water with the... and gradually over the course of the week the water would evaporate and you would see the tatties turning black on the top, and I used to think "Oh my god!". The... and you would see jelly or trifle made in pretty cracked, enamel dishes or pretty so-so crockery dishes - oh pretty horrible. There were certain kitchens - that there's no way I, I would've eaten in that particular hotel. I'm not naming any names. But Tadek - I spoke about Tadek before... Tadek loved when he went in and found that some of the milk had actually gone sour because he would then go back into the kitchen and say to the chef "Excuse me, there is... three gallons of milk there which... which has gone sour, will I just take it away?" and of course the chef would say - unless he particularly wanted it for some... some dish he was going to make, maybe scones or something, he would say "oh take it away" and the next morning Tadek would come out with a smile from ear to ear and offer me a piece of this wonderful cream cheese crowdie stuff that he made. He *loved* it. Tadek had come from a... a peasant family in, in Poland - obviously what we would call a crofting family and, and he loved this sour milk cheese, absolutely loved it. He was, he was an amazing guy, he... I remember when he used to go round the back of Abbotsford... he would spot the fact that there was a lot of leaf mould or something lying under the beech trees on the, on the Abbotsford estate, and he would get permission from the guy at the estate, and he would get permission from my father to borrow the milkvan and he would go out and he would dig leaf mould.

He had the most wonderful garden at his house in Galashiels. He was quite a character. I can think of another... restaurant, it wasn't a hotel restaurant, it was just a restaurant in the town that got milk from us. And it was pretty... oh goodness... not just the world's best place. I had an aunt worked there and she claimed that she was given a basin to wash the stairs down and it was the same basin that later in the day they made trifle in... which kind of beggars description. In the main though... I'm painting a kind of black picture, but in the main most of the hotel kitchens were, were fine, they were exemplary really. But it's amazing how you can judge people's attitude to hygiene. We were always horrified at some of the people that put out bottles that weren't even rinsed. I mean they just poured the milk out of the bottle and put it straight out, and of course by the time you'd picked the bottle up it had maybe been sitting for ten hours or something and the milk, the cream of the milk would be on the inside of the bottle and it would be getting gey cheesey, and pretty horrible actually.

Sterilising the bottles

The actual bottles and crates and everything... the... the... when we washed them - I mentioned in the earlier part the, the rotating brushes that we had, that was the early days - but then latterly we had a proper machine that... the milk, the crates and the bottles were all washed; the bottles were inverted and... they were... everything was washed clean and it was washed in virtually a... type of detergent which was, was like Milton - you know that detergent that they use for kids' bottles and things. The other thing that we had, is that we had a massive steaming machine; we'd a very big boiler; and we'd a massive steaming machine and all the cans, and, and all the utensils that were used, all the pipework that went from the milk holding tank to the bottling plant to the pasteurisation plant, that was all steamed - absolutely cleaned with... by being steamed in this huge steamer up to... and it was virtually sterilised - it *was* sterilised. We also, there was lots of O-rings, rubber rings that are in part of the connection, part of the joints in the pipe; they were, they were actually literally... steeped in Milton-type stuff for an hour or two. So hygiene was, was, it was pretty good.

Public health, and milk recording

The public health people were very diligent as well and... they came regularly and took tests and if, by any chance, some of the milk had a, had a bad test - that there was e-coliform as they called it - in that milk, they would come back and back... and these... you couldn't, you didn't know exactly when they were coming, they just came on their own behest; random checks. You might get a formal check and, and, and not see them again for six weeks; you might see them three times in a fortnight. And that wasn't necessarily because you were getting a bad, a bad sample, it just meant that... the way the thing was randomised. The, the other feature I think, did I mention it earlier? was the, the milk recorders, who came and they checked the milk at the farms. This was quite a feature; that milk from every cow was checked for its butterfat content and it also was checked to see what its yield was. And this would be charted; the farmer would get reports. This was done by ladies - I don't remember a man doing it, it was always young ladies - some of them very attractive - who used to come and do these tests. And it was quite a common thing for farmers to marry, marry the milk recording lady; I mean that happened in many many cases. Some of them are from a dairy background and some of them were not. They'd mainly all been trained, as I recall it, in Ayrshire I think, was the big centre where they were trained in some of the, the colleges in Ayrshire. And these girls came round and, and checked, they checked every aspect of the milk and I think they were probably involved in some of the Tuberculin Testing. I'm a bit woolly about that but certainly when the Tuberculin Testing came along the cows were, were tested on a pretty regular basis and... that made sure that TB was eradicated eventually, I mean TB's almost unknown now apart from immigrants bringing it in and spreading it and so on. That is almost, it was unknown almost in the population and yet it was terribly common in the thirties and right through up until I suppose the forties; people went to TB sanatoriums and things, it was a big thing. It's interesting that my family must have worked with cows and with milk as I said for, oh, well over a hundred years and nobody, and as far as I know - and I'm quite keen on... on my family history - I'm not aware of any of the family ever dying of tuberculin... you know, of tuberculosis. So we must have had a... a natural immunity or something of that nature. The hygiene... nowadays is probably even more stringent. You end up with you know different types of devices as well, things like ultra-violet and so on are available... there's lots of different sprays and things. In fact I have a theory that perhaps our domestic kitchens are almost... some of them are almost *too* clean and, and, and people are not exposed to the natural run of germs and, and if they take something they take it very badly. Kids get much more severe doses of certain, certain types of things and I, I don't think the population in general has the same resistance to... you know... salmonella and that type... these types of things as, as maybe earlier generations did. I might be wrong, it's just a, just a feeling that I have that you can actually sometimes be too clean. Kids are not allowed to sit on the floor and play on a carpet and so on, and ingest a little peck of dirt now and again.

This is Mary Drysdale interviewing Mike Brydon at his home in Clovenfords on Wednesday the 5th of January, 2000. Today Mike is going to conclude his memories by describing how his family's retail milk business changed with the advent of supermarkets and the growth of larger milk businesses from other parts of Scotland.

Upgrading dairy premises
By the time I reached the age of... seventeen, eighteen, I was only working occasionally on the, on the round because by that time I was... in

Edinburgh studying at the Heriot Watt and so on although, in the holidays, I used to be quite glad to come home and work the... the two or three months that we got in the summer. It was all good money - and all students need money. Those were the days of course when... tried to burn the candle at both ends... I would be out at parties and things and probably get home about... three o'clock or half past three in the morning, my father would be getting up at half past four. I think I remember one occasion when I worked right through... I... I just literally came in and went straight to work. I think it was about thirty-odd hours before I'd... I'd had a sleep and I decided that wasn't a good idea. Anyway after... my milk days I... I went to Edinburgh, worked for Ferranti for a long time... and eventually joined the South of... what was then the South of Scotland Electricity Board as a... a... an electricity supply engineer. The dairy then outgrew the premises in St. John Street, Gala Terrace and... the volume of milk that was being processed plus the fact that we needed to upgrade the... the... the machinery and so on and... we needed more room for vehicles and so on; the dairy then moved out and moved back to Scott Street, the bottom of Scott Street where it had originally begun... where my grandfather had moved out to Tweedbank Farm sometime in the... in the middle twenties... by that time... in the interim the... the yard had been a d... a builder's yard and... they moved back in a brand new premises - nice, clean, custom-built premises were built, with much better facilities for cold store and so on, and a big pasteurisation plant went in and... it was a much big... bigger operation and... and the volume of milk being processed... by my brother Bruce and my father... rose considerably. The town of course expanded, and little dairies gradually packed in... in until there was... latterly really there was only the Co-operative, the store as we called it, and ourselves delivering milk in Gala. There's little things... but the hygiene regulations and so on pushed these out eventually.

Supermarkets and Wiseman's

However, over the, the period, sadly, the whole retail thing changed; we had the advent of the supermarkets. There was a period when milk sales were expanded and... we had, for example, we had milk machines situated in shop doorways and things all over the town. Now I think it was three or four of them. And we... we sold innovations like flavoured milk, raspberry flavoured milk... and that type of thing as well as more than one grade of... of... of ordinary milk and people used to come and... and put their sixpences in, or whatever it was to... to... to buy the half pint of milk... I think it was a half pint, it might be a pint. These were in cartons and that was really the first of cartons coming along and... but these machines got vandalised and things and, and gradually... supermarkets and shops were open late, they all carried milk; my brother in fact ended up supplying a lot of the shops with milk. But I mean, the profit margins on that were so small that it was... it was almost uneconomic and to try and - you couldn't sell the milk in bottles because you didn't get the bottles back and you lost money that way. The cartons

223

were expensive so that was another factor, and gradually that changed and then if... the supermarkets came along they started selling milk as a loss leader. And in fact some of them were selling the milk la... at certain points, they were selling the milk almost cheaper than we could buy it wholesale because of the sheer volumes that were involved. And then of course latterly... we had the... the... huge companies like Wiseman's and Mackie's and so on in... in Scotland. They came along and, particularly in this area it was Wiseman's, and they bought over lots and lots of retail dairies and they... they've gone in for huge modern plants. The only thing about it... what seems strange to me was that they were bringing milk in cartons or whatever, bottles, all the way from Glasgow to Gala you know... I don't know... sixty-five miles or something like that. The milk itself - we no longer had to pick up milk from... from the farms; that whole aspect changed - all the farms had a refrigerated tank - if they didn't they more or less went out of... out of production. And the lorries were now tankers... they weren't flatbed lorries picking up... milk churns they were... they were actually picking up... the milk as liquid milk and it was kept... it was kept in good order. But on the other hand you had all this milk from all these cows all mixed together all churned about and... and while it was processed it went through the... so the milk was then delivered to the dairy... in Scott Street by tanker and, and kept in a refrigerated tank and so on and processed... but gradually it became less and less economic. My brother tried various things to try... tried delivering morning rolls and this type of thing along with the milk delivery but the profit margins in all these things is driven down and down, and the supermarkets can always buy in bulk and sell cheap. And gradually I... I don't think there's any... doorstep delivery of milk in Galashiels and district... as far as I can...know - I certainly haven't seen any... there might be one, maybe the store have one or two, but it's almost finished actually and... it's interesting how in the span of my lifetime I've seen it go... get very much bigger and then finally fade away. So I think that just about concludes my milkboy memories.

Mike Brydon

1 The interviewee comments that the word "baillie" is a northern word and would not be used in Galashiels. It was used inadvertantly by him as a result of his 29 years living in the Buchan area (MD)

2 "cluster" is the usual word (MD)

3 Mike is the eldest of seven brothers

4 In the latter part of 1999 this became a W H Smith store

5 refers to the Co-operative

6 Fleg: The interviewee comments that this is another Aberdeenshire word, acquired from his time there, but as a Borderer he would normally have used the word "gliff"

One of the first substantial productions to come from Salt Of The Earth stemmed from a collaborative venture with the Scottish Maritime Museum. We provided training, equipment and guidance for one of the museum workers who then did a series of interviews with ex merchant seamen. These recordings contributed to the Bringing Home The Bacon exhibition that was resident in the museum in Irvine, and the work ensured that the experiences of these men are preserved as part of the Salt of The Earth Archive. One interview in particular was the basis of an evocative illustration of life at sea in **'Frank's Story'**. This video used the edited sound from the recordings supplemented by still images, archive footage and dramatisation from museum workers to present a stimulating treatment of oral history material.

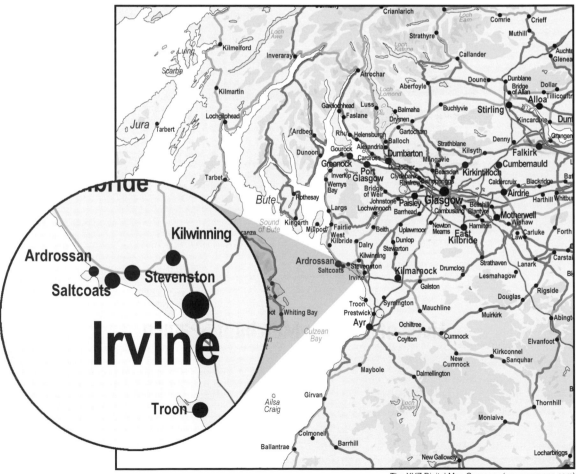

The XYZ Digital Map Company (www.xyzmaps.com)

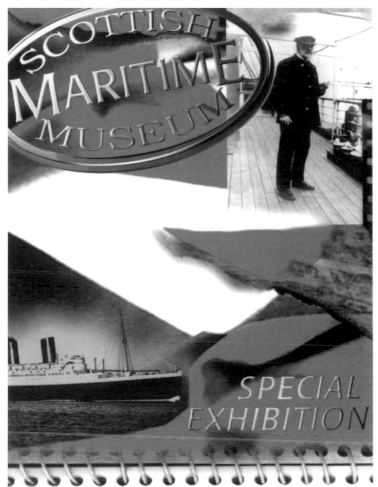

BRINGING HOME THE BACON

Lives of Scottish Merchant Seamen

What would you do with your dobi? How would you arrange for 500 reindeer to sail to America? Would you know how to survive if your ship was torpedoed? And what is the Merchant Navy anyway?

Join us as we travel the globe with captains and cabin boys from 1898 to the present.

The Salt Of The Earth group in this area of East Renfrewshire had been meeting for some time for reminiscence sessions. When they started with the project, they were inspired by meeting a CSV (Community Service Volunteers) group from Craigmiller in Edinburgh who had constructed their own web page.

Few of the Salt Of The Earth group were at all familiar with any aspect of computer work, but with the help and guidance of the WEA, they managed to build an attractive web site based on their recorded contributions and were thrilled to be able to communicate in this contemporary fashion. Their tutor observed a remarkable enthusiasm as the group tackled what could have been a daunting challenge for the mainly elderly participants. Being able to enter the technological age and

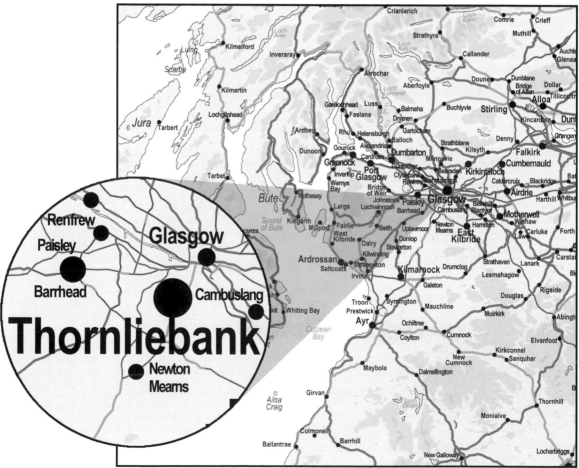

The XYZ Digital Map Company (www.xyzmaps.com)

discuss computing with grandchildren and great grandchildren provided a marvellous stimulus and platform for lifelong learning.

The web site was launched in Thornliebank library with the Provost and press in attendance.

Web site launch

Video conferencing with the Alness group

In the Argyll village of Dalmally, the Salt Of The Earth Project initiated what must have been one of the most inclusive of community ventures. The setting was home to Stray Theatre Company, led by producer David Lightbody with whom we made initial contact. The local Historical Society became involved and, after training, conducted a series of interviews with local residents. Local writer Ruth Black then formulated a distillation of the recordings and produced a script which was taken by the Dalmally and Loch Awe Amateur Dramatic Society for improvisation and rehearsal under the direction of David over a period of months. The oral history interviews suggested that the focus of many significant events in the village during the 20th century was the railway line and station. Subsequently, the set of the play was the local railway platform and presented a hundred years of Dalmally events through the eyes of the stationmaster.

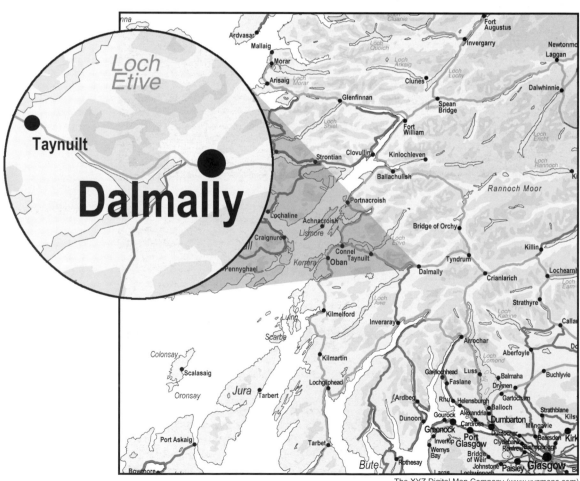

The XYZ Digital Map Company (www.xyzmaps.com)

The various stages of recording and production involved many of the people in the village and there can have been few other Dalmally inhabitants who did not attend the two local performances. Subsequently the play was performed at a drama festival in Oban and at the final Annual Gathering of Salt Of The Earth participants where it was very enthusiastically received.

Play performance

Dalmally village hall

The Kingdom of Fife hosted two Salt Of The Earth Groups. The first was based in Methil Heritage Centre and undertook an impressive number of recordings within the town. Titling themselves Levenmouth Strikes Back With Attitude, they produced an audio CD and museum display which toured venues in the area.

The second initiative involved people who were either disabled themselves, in some way, or were carers for someone with a disability. The group discussed a variety of topics over the first few months and then planned their presentation of the material. They decided on an interactive sculpture that would communicate experiences of disability. The group then did more recordings and started to build the sculpture with the help of artist Jan Miller, and the complex audio technicalities were

The XYZ Digital Map Company (www.xyzmaps.com)

tackled. The resulting figure has buttons on various parts of the anatomy, which when pressed give an audio account of an experience of disability affecting that area. It is certainly an impressive and innovative achievement and another example of imaginative use of oral history testimonies. The figure was initially displayed in the Royal Museum in Edinburgh.

Fife sculpture group.

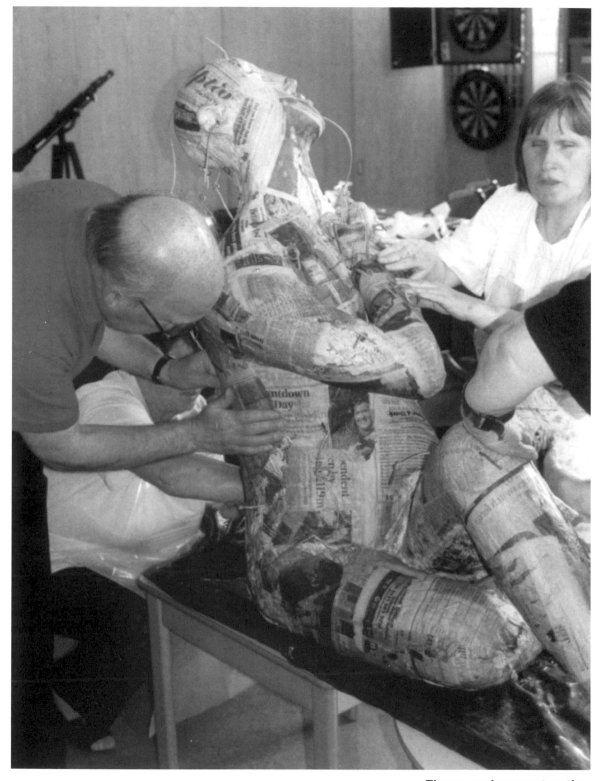

Figure under construction

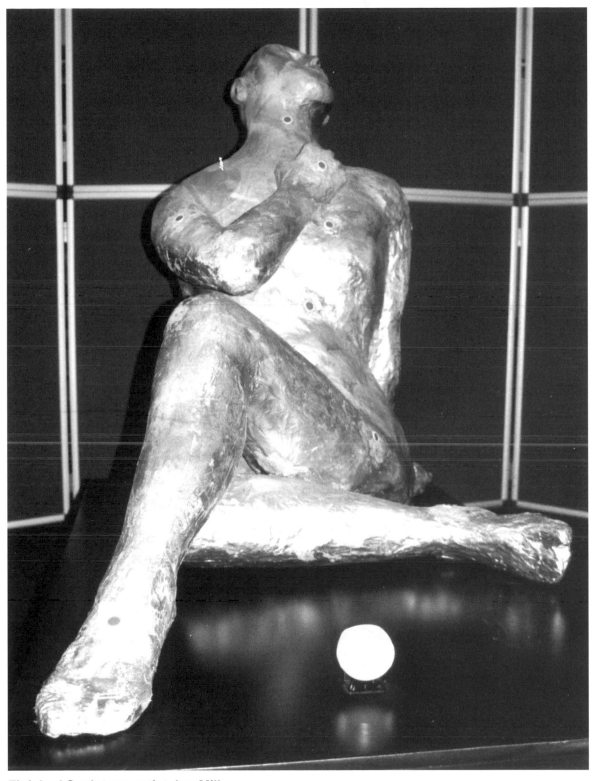

Finished Sculpture, artist Jan Miller.

The focus of the group based in Ayr was the mining industry of which most of the participants had some firsthand experience. They met within the premises of The North Ayr Partnership who provided help and support. The outcome from the recordings was a video - An Ayrshire Mining Story encompassing the experiences and poetry of one particular ex miner.

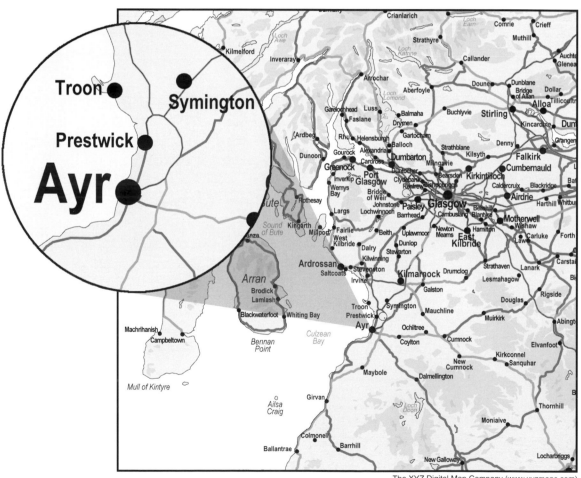

The XYZ Digital Map Company (www.xyzmaps.com)

The group in Logan in Ayrshire worked very hard and often quite independently to produce an impressive publication entitled 'Logan: Fae Big House Tae Wee Village' based on their recorded interviews. They then progressed to a photographic display combined with a launch of the book.

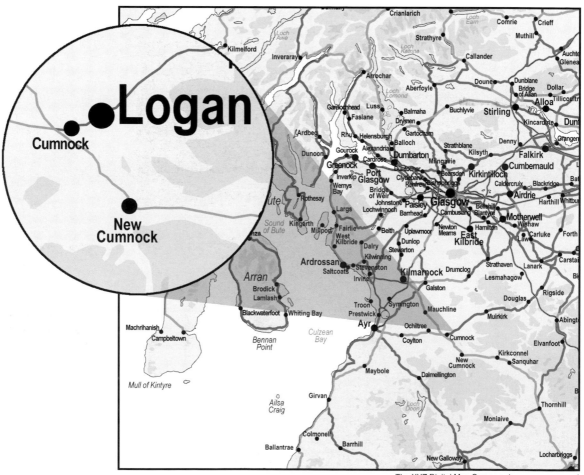

The XYZ Digital Map Company (www.xyzmaps.com)

Smoking chimneys of Lugar Rows and the furnaces

The Cronberry Rows

These 'Tarry Rows' were demolished in the mid-1920's

DUMBIEDYKES

The group, in this Edinburgh high and low-rise housing estate, began by recalling aspects of the city's Old Town district and the period when it had been cleared in the 1950's. As they progressed through the building of the Dumbiedykes estate in the 1960's to present day issues, several concerns surfaced. First was the worry about the housing stock transfer issue. Second was the impact of regeneration of the area, with the adjacent Scottish Parliament building and other new developments, while their estate, they felt, was neglected. Third was the feeling that there was something circular happening. Would the clearances of the slums of the Old Town be repeated with the threat of the run down of Dumbiedykes in the present? It was decided that a video encompassing these concerns, utilising their oral history testimonies, would be the best medium of expression. The resulting film, produced and edited in conjunction with Pilton

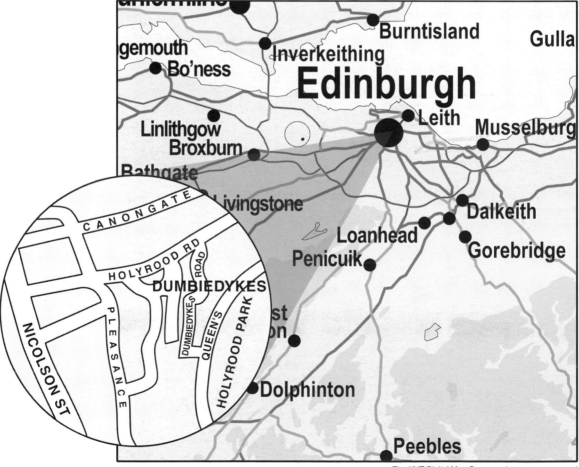

Video, is a fine example of how oral history can give a voice and platform to individuals and communities and address current issues in relation to the past.

The Workers' Educational Association, a national , democratic, voluntary organisation, seeks to encourage access to education throughout life, especially for those adults who have experienced barriers to learning as a result of economic circumstances, social isolation, limited confidence, low self esteem or lack of educational opportunity.

Publisher: WEA Scotland
Riddle's Court - 322 Lawnmarket - Edinburgh EH1 2PG - Tel: 0131 226 3456
WORKERS' EDUCATIONAL ASSOCIATION - Charity No. 314001